HALF-HOURS WITH ISAIAH

Felix M.T. Wong

HALF-HOURS WITH ISAIAH

BY THE REV.

JOSEPH PITTS WILES, M.A.

*Formerly Foundation Scholar
of Trinity College, Cambridge*

PREFACE BY

THE RIGHT REVEREND

H. C. G. MOULE, D.D.

BISHOP OF DURHAM

BAKER BOOK HOUSE
Grand Rapids, Michigan

Reprinted 1979 by
Baker Book House

ISBN: 0-8010-9614-6

PHOTOLITHOPRINTED BY CUSHING - MALLOY, INC.
ANN ARBOR, MICHIGAN, UNITED STATES OF AMERICA
1979

PREFACE

I HAVE been asked by my dear and honoured friend in Christ, the Author of this book, to prefix to it a few introductory words. It is a pleasure to meet his wish.

I have read the whole of the contents with large general agreement. The main lines of interpretation much commend themselves to my judgment. . And I think, as I weigh the Author's method and manner of treatment, in which worshipping reverence and open-eyed quest of the true meaning so closely meet together, that even readers who may advocate another type of interpretation and application in some respects, will find these pages full of suggestion. To all they will set an example of patient, humble, *attentive* investigation of the meaning of the words in which, through man, the Holy Spirit spake to the fathers, and speaks to us.

My deepest sympathy with this book is attracted by its calm, unreserved allegiance to the written Word as indeed " the Word of God, which liveth and abideth for ever." One of the saddest phenomena of religious thought within, say, the last thirty years in particular, is the common tendency to regard the Scriptures, and especially the Old Testament, as very much more " the best thinking " of men than as the Word to man, through men, of God, carrying nothing less (this is the crucial point) than *His authority*. To my friend the Expositor, in this volume, that latter view is the sure and certain truth. And he is most certainly of one mind, in this matter, with the Apostles of the Lord Jesus Christ and with their Master Himself.

God speed the message of these pages, to the benefit of His Church and the glory of His name.

H. DUNELM

Auckland Castle,
Bishop Auckland
Aug. 3, 1915

INTRODUCTION

M ANY readers of the Holy Bible are entirely unacquainted with the languages in which it was originally written, and are otherwise shut out from various sources of knowledge which are open to the theologian and the commentator. For such readers this book is intended; and its one object is to make plain to them the true and primary meaning of the Prophecies of Isaiah.

The Half-Hours were at first written for publication in a monthly magazine called *The Sower*, edited by my dear and valued friend Mr. M. J. Tryon, of Stamford. Each article was thoroughly weighed by me, and carefully criticised by the late Dr. Sinker, of Cambridge, before it was sent to *The Sower*. It has been possible, therefore, to republish them in this book without any material alteration. Some of my remarks seem strangely to anticipate the present war; but they were all written long before it began, and I confess that I had not the faintest suspicion that such trouble was in store for us.

The method followed by me in composing the Half-Hours is accurately described on page 155, except that I ought to have mentioned other languages beside English, French, and German. The Septuagint (Greek), the Vulgate (Latin), and other translations were from time to time consulted ; and my own slight acquaintance with Hebrew was amply supplemented by the help of my learned friend, Dr. Sinker.

An extract from one of his letters may well find a place here, as an acknowledgment of the debt which I owe, but can no longer pay, to him. The letter from which it is taken is dated April 4th, 1911 :—

"As to your MS., with the exposition [of Isaiah xxxiv., xxxv.] broadly viewed I was very pleased, and have no criticisms to offer. I send you a few verbal notes, which I thought perhaps might be not without interest. I don't know Jenour's book at all. It seems very good and just. What a glorious chapter Isaiah xxxv. is ! Each time I read it I feel it more and more."

This extract will give the reader some idea of the labour bestowed on the present unpretending volume, and of the careful criticism to which every Half-Hour except the last has been subjected. When the last reached my dear friend, he was too ill to read it ; and two or three days later his daughter returned it with the (to me) sad news that he had finished his course.

If the text of the Authorised Version had been printed in parallel columns with my paraphrase, the bulk and cost of the book would have been greatly increased, and I have therefore decided to omit it. The reader can remedy this defect by constant reference to his Bible.

The introductory remarks at the beginning of each Half-Hour are not written at random, but are carefully designed to lead insensibly to a correct understanding of the passage in question. For instance, Isaiah begins his message (i. 2) by calling heaven and earth to hear his words, and represents the Lord as complaining of the rebellion of His own children ; hence the First Half-Hour begins with a reference to similar appeals made by Moses, and with a quotation of his words, " Ye are the children of the Lord your God."

I here return sincere and affectionate thanks to my friend the Bishop of Durham for his kind preface. His closing statement, that in my reverence for the Old Testament Scriptures, I am " of one mind with the Apostles of the Lord Jesus Christ, and with their Master Himself," is a testimony which I receive with unfeigned humility ; and it has stirred up my heart to render thanks to Him who has taught me, from

my youth onwards, to revere and love His Holy
Oracles. To Him I can say with Hezekiah :—*

How shall I thank Thee for these words of grace,
    Or bless the hand that lays aside the rod ?
My rescued feet shall softly tread Thy ways ;
    My chastened soul shall humbly walk with God.

Thus dost Thou hold our souls in life, O Lord ;
    Thy frowns correct us, and Thy smiles revive ;
Diseases fly before Thy healing word ;
    Thy loving-kindness makes the dying live.

With bitterness Thine hand did fill my cup,
    But bitter woe hath brought me sweet delight :
Thy love from hell's dark gate hath raised me up,
    And cast my sins for ever from Thy sight.

The grave's still chambers ring not with Thy praise,
    No hope in Thy sure promise there is known ;
Thy living saints their living psalms shall raise,
    And sires to sons shall hand Thine honours down.

My Saviour, unto Thee my praise belongs
    Through all the added years Thy love has given ;
Thy temple-courts shall echo to my songs,
    And glad thanksgivings shall ascend to heaven.

* See pages 174, 175.

CONTENTS

HALF-HOURS WITH ISAIAH

FIRST HALF-HOUR

Chapter I.

WHEN Moses renewed God's covenant with the
children of Israel shortly before their entrance
into the promised land, he said, " Ye are the children of
the Lord your God : ye shall not cut yourselves, nor
make any baldness between your eyes for the dead.
For thou art a holy people unto the Lord thy God, and
the Lord hath chosen thee to be a peculiar people unto
Himself above all the nations that are upon the earth "
(Deut. xiv. 1, 2). He also called the heavens above and
the earth beneath to bear witness to the covenant
between them and the Father who had thus adopted
them : " When ye shall have remained long in the land,
and shall corrupt yourselves and make a graven image,
or the likeness of anything, and shall do evil in the sight
of the Lord thy God, to provoke Him to anger, I call
heaven and earth to witness against you this day, that
ye shall soon utterly perish from off the land whereunto
ye go over Jordan to possess it. . . . I call heaven
and earth to record this day against you, that I have
set before you life and death, blessing and cursing.
. . . Give ear, O ye heavens, and I will speak ;
and hear, O earth, the words of My mouth " (Deut. iv.
25, 26 ; xxx. 19 ; xxxii. 1). During seven centuries
earth and sky, which had been thus solemnly taken

to record, bore witness to the long-suffering goodness of God and the wickedness of His adopted family : throughout the whole of that long day He stretched forth His hands to a rebellious and gainsaying people (Rom. x. 21). We need not insert here even the outlines of the sad history, but may refer our readers to our first and fourth Half-Hours with the Minor Prophets.

Before avenging the breach of His covenant according to the tenor of Leviticus xxvi. and Deuteronomy xxviii., the Lord repeatedly chastened Israel, and summoned them to repentance, both by the voices of His prophets and by the dispensations of His providence. At length the time came to send them the last call to repentance, and the last promise to receive their submission and spare the land ; it was sent by Isaiah, the son of Amoz : "If ye be willing and obedient, ye shall eat the good of the land ; but if ye refuse and rebel, ye shall be devoured with the sword : for the mouth of the Lord hath spoken it." This, with the promise of the restoration of Zion after the destruction of transgressors, is the substance of Isaiah's first message, recorded in the first chapter of his prophecy.

We know that the writings of the prophets are not always arranged in the order in which they were delivered. For instance, the twenty-fourth chapter of Jeremiah contains a message delivered after Jeconiah had been carried captive to Babylon, and the twenty-fifth was written in the reign of his father Jehoiakim. It is not therefore certain that the first chapter of Isaiah belongs to the reign of Uzziah, when the prophet began his ministry. But if it does, then, since Uzziah's reign was strong and peaceful (see 2 Chron. xxvi.), the picture of desolation which Isaiah draws in verses 5-9 must either be a prediction of the troublous times of Ahaz and Hezekiah, or refer to the ravages committed by the Syrians in the earlier reign of Joash, when that king had murdered good Zechariah in the courts of the house of the Lord. (See 2 Chron. xxiv. 23, 24.) They may also refer to the events recorded in verse 13 of 2 Chron. xxv., and in verses 23 and 24 of that chapter. In any case the lesson taught is the same : if such chastisements bore no fruit, nothing remained but to root out the people from the land given to their fathers.

The prophet begins his message by an appeal to the same heavens and earth which Moses had called to bear witness to the covenant between God and His adopted children.

" The revelation of Isaiah the son of Amoz, which God gave unto him concerning Judah and Jerusalem, in the days when Uzziah, Jotham, Ahaz, and Hezekiah reigned over Judah.

" Bear witness, ye heavens, bear record, O earth, to the truth of the words which the Lord speaketh : The children whom I have fed and reared have rebelled against Me. The ox knoweth his owner, but Israel knoweth not his Father : the ass knoweth his master's crib, but My people consider not the kindness of their God. Ah, it is a nation of sinners, a people laden with iniquity, à generation of transgressors, who have corrupted their way before Me. Ye have forsaken the Lord, despised the Holy One that sanctifieth you ; ye are become aliens from the commonwealth of God, ye have back-slidden from His ways. What would it profit that I should chastise you further ? Ye will add rebellion to rebellion : your head is wholly sick with sin, your heart is wholly faint with evil. I have smitten you till the body is all unsound from head to foot, covered with wounds, bruises, and festering stripes, which have not been bound up, nor dressed, nor softened with oil. Your country is a desolation ; your cities are heaps of ashes ; ye have looked helplessly on while strangers have consumed the fruits of your land, and foreign foes have laid it in ruins. Jerusalem stands alone like a watchman's booth left in a deserted vineyard, or a keeper's lodge in a garden whence the gourds have been gathered—a besieged city. Had not the Lord of hosts preserved among us a small remnant of faithful sons and daughters, we had been overthrown as Sodom, destroyed as Gomorrah.

"Hear the word of the Lord, ye rulers of Zion who are in Mine eyes as princes of Sodom : give ear unto the voice of His law, ye people of Jerusalem who are in Mine eyes as citizens of Gomorrah : In vain do ye worship Me with your endless round of sacrifices. Enough of your burnt-offerings of rams ; enough of the fat of your fatted calves. I have no pleasure in the blood of bulls, and lambs, and goats. Ye come before My face, and with noisy feet ye trample My courts : but by whose command ? Bring your vain meal-offerings no more. I loathe the incense which I bade you burn, and the festivals which I bade you observe : I cannot away with them—iniquity and worship ! My soul abhorreth your ceremonies and your feasts : they are to Me a burden which I can no longer bear. Ye may spread forth your suppliant hands to Me, but I will not behold them ; ye may utter many prayers, but I will not hear them : for your hands are steeped in innocent blood. Cleanse your hands, ye sinners, and purify your hearts, ye double-minded ! Put away from before Mine eyes your wicked works. Abhor that which is evil : cleave to that which is good. Let your judgments be just : deliver the oppressed from the oppressor : uphold the cause of the orphan and the widow.

"Then come, I pray you, and debate your cause with Me, saith the Lord. Only acknowledge and forsake your iniquities ; and though your sins have been as scarlet, ye shall be made white as snow : though their stain upon you is crimson-red, I will make you white as wool.

If ye willingly submit to Me, ye shall still enjoy the land which I have given you ; but if ye refuse My call and rebel against My word, the sword of your enemies shall consume you : for the mouth of the Lord hath spoken it."

We know the issue of this last summons to repentance, this last holding forth of mercy's golden sceptre. It is recorded in the twenty-fifth chapter of the second book of Kings. But what is its bearing on our own beloved land, the land of righteousness and equity, of holy martyrs, of dear-bought freedom, of Bible truth ? Are there among us no sacrifices that the Lord hates ? Is there no incense that He loathes ? Is there no turning again to idolatry and superstition ? Let us hearken to the voice of the Lord, lest we be broken to pieces by His rod.

And now the prophet or the Lord (it is impossible to say which, for the prophet is the Lord's mouth) goes on to lament the corruption of Zion, and to foretell the furnace-blast which shall burn up the wicked as dross, and refine the righteous as gold and silver.

" O Zion, thou wast once the chaste spouse of thy God : but now, ah now, a shameless harlot ! Thou wast once a fountain of justice, a home of righteousness : but now, ah now, thou art the dwelling-place of mur-derers ! Thou wast precious as silver, but now art vile as dross ; thou wast as wine pure and strong, but now thy wine is become weak and worthless. Thy princes hate instruction, and cast My words behind them ; and when they see a thief they consent with him. They all love bribes, and pervert the law to obtain rewards ; they refuse justice to the orphan, and will not listen to the pleading of the widow.

" Therefore the King of righteousness, the Lord of hosts, the God of might who dwelleth in Israel, saith : Ah, I will rid Me of the burden of these My adversaries ;

I will avenge My injured justice on these My enemies.
O Zion, I will lay upon thee the hand of My power : I
will refine thy silver from its dross, and remove all its
base alloy.   I will give thee judges such as thou hadst
of old, and rulers such as ruled thee when thou wast yet
holiness unto the Lord.   (See Deut. i. 16, and Jer. ii.
2, 3.)   In the latter days thou shalt be called the City
of Righteousness, the Faithful City.   I will magnify
My justice in thy redemption, My righteousness in the
salvation of thy converts.   But they that transgress
My law and they that sin against My holiness shall be
destroyed together ; and they that turn from Me to
worship idols shall be consumed.   Ye shall reap shame
and disappointment from the oak-groves wherein ye
love to serve your idols ; and confusion shall be the
fruit of the gardens which have witnessed your unclean
rites : yea, ye yourselves shall be like unto them, oaks
whose leaf withereth, gardens which perish for want of
water.   Your mighty men shall be as tow, and the
idols which they have made shall be as sparks : both
shall burn together in a fire that shall not be quenched."

As we read these threatenings of righteous vengeance,
we think of the armies of Chaldea, and the bitter cry of
the Lamentations ; of the armies of Rome, and the
smoking ruins of city and temple ; of the lake that
burneth with fire and brimstone.   As we read the promise of restoration, we think of Ezra and Nehemiah ;
of Pentecost and the kingdom of God ; of those who
shall sit on thrones to judge the twelve tribes of God's
glorified Israel.   And as we read of pardon for scarlet
sins and crimson sinfulness, we think of the fountain
opened at Calvary, and humbly pray : Wash us, and we
shall be whiter than snow.

SECOND HALF-HOUR

Chapters II., III., IV.

THE second chapter of Isaiah opens with a prophecy of gospel days which Micah also was commissioned to utter. (See *Half-Hours with the Minor Prophets*, pp. 86–88.) Whatever relation this prediction may have to the future restoration of Israel, it is evident that it had a glorious fulfilment in the coming of Christ, the labours of His apostles, and the subsequent extension of the kingdom of God unto Judæa and Samaria, and the uttermost parts of the earth. Let us here state once for all our reasons for holding this view—a view which will influence the whole of our exposition of the prophetic writings so far as we may have opportunity and grace to continue it. For it will form no part of our plan to trace by the help of the prophecies the future history of the twelve tribes which are scattered abroad, a subject which seems to us to be beset with difficulties such as nothing but the course of God's providence can unravel.

Peter tells us expressly (Acts iii. 22–25) that all the prophets from Moses onwards foretold of " these days," the days when the Word should be made flesh. The same apostle speaks of Joel's prophecy as fulfilled at Pentecost (Acts ii. 16–21). And in like manner James, addressing the assembly of apostles and elders at Jerusalem (Acts xv. 15–17), refers to the prophecy of Amos concerning the rebuilding of David's fallen tabernacle and the calling of the Gentiles as one which was then in process of accomplishment. Other examples of such interpretations might easily be found in the New

Testament, but these will suffice to justify us in referring such passages to the days of Christ and His apostles. Many of the glories which the prophets foretold in figurative language, coloured by the dispensation under which they lived, were then abundantly realised. And what glories ! Must we not confess that it is far easier for us to underrate them than to appreciate their infinite greatness ? How could the mountain of the Lord's house be more truly exalted above all other mountains than it was by the fact that it became the scene of the labours of incarnate God, and the centre from which His gracious kingdom spread to all the nations of the earth ? This was that ministration of righteousness which exceeded in glory the ministration of condemnation ; this was that glory of Mount Zion which made the glory of Mount Sinai wax pale and pass away.

" The revelation which God gave to Isaiah, the son of Amoz, concerning Judah and Jerusalem.

" Furthermore, it shall come to pass in the fulness of time, saith the Lord, that the mountain of My house shall be established above all mountains, and My hill shall be exalted above all hills ; and unto it shall the gathering of the peoples be. And many nations shall assemble themselves and say, Come, let us go up to the temple of the Lord, to the dwelling-place of the God of Jacob : He will make known to us His will, and we will walk in His statutes. For the doctrine of the Lord shall go forth out of Zion, the word of His grace from Jerusalem. He shall establish righteousness among the peoples of the earth, and convince and convert many nations that are far off. Then they who have loved war shall learn to delight in peace, beating their swords into ploughshares, and their spears into pruning-hooks. Nation shall cease to rise up against nation, and the art of war shall be forgotten."

This picture of universal peace and love can only be

realised so far as the principles of Christ's Gospel rule in the hearts of men. To that extent it has been already realised in a wonderful way ; for such has been the fruit brought forth by the Gospel not only at Colossæ but in all the world (Col. i. 6).

Isaiah passes on to speak of the then present wickedness of the house of Jacob, and of the coming judgment of God. While his words refer in the first place to the overthrow of Jerusalem and Judah by Nebuchadnezzar's armies, they also foreshadow in magnificent language the day of judgment and perdition of ungodly men when the heavens shall pass away with a great noise, and the earth and the works that are therein shall be burnt up (2 Pet. iii. 7–10). We find the same two-fold significance in the prophecy of Christ recorded by Matthew (Matt. xxiv.).

" O house of Jacob, come ye, let us forsake our evil ways that we may walk in the light of the Lord's countenance : though He hath made the house of Jacob His peculiar people, yet have they forsaken Him, and He hath forsaken them. For they imitate eagerly the sorceries of the east, and the witchcraft of the Philistines ; they mingle with the heathen and learn their works. Their land is filled with endless stores of silver and gold, heaped up by their avarice ; with endless stores of horses and chariots, the arm of flesh in which they trust ; with endless stores of idols, the gods which they have made with their own hands that they may worship them. Prince and people alike bow down to the gods which their fingers have fashioned ; therefore, the Lord will not pass by their sin. In the caves of the rocks and in the holes of the earth shall they seek a hiding-place from the terrible glory of the Lord's majesty. Then shall the pride of man be brought low, and everyone that exalteth himself shall be abased : for in that day shall the Lord alone be exalted. For a

day cometh, the day of the Lord of hosts, when He shall
bring low every one that is proud, and haughty, and
lifted up, though he be tall as the cedars of Lebanon
and strong as the oaks of Bashan : and the Lord shall
bring down every mountain of power and every hill of
pride ; the lofty battlements of their strong forts, and
the thick walls of their fenced cities ; the merchant
ships which minister to their avarice, and the luxurious
wares which feed their pride. Then shall the proud
looks of man be brought low, every one that exalteth
himself shall be abased, and the Lord alone shall be
exalted. But the gods that have not made the earth
shall perish from it ; and they that worshipped them
shall call to the caves of the rocks and the holes of the
earth to hide them from the terrible glory of the Lord's
majesty, when He shall stretch forth His hand to shake
the foundations of the earth. Men shall cast the idols
of silver and gold which their hands have made and their
hearts have worshipped into the haunts of the moles
and the bats, that they may flee into the holes of the
rocks and the caves of the mountains from the terrible
glory of the Lord's majesty, when He stretcheth forth
His hand to shake the foundations of the earth. Trust
no longer in man, whose breath is in his nostrils ; for
what is he, that ye should lean on him ? "

It may seem a childish mistake, but we fear it is a
common one, to forget that Isaiah prophesied more than
a hundred years before the events took place which are
recorded in the closing chapters of the books of Kings
and Chronicles. The position of the prophets in our
English Bible tends to prevent the reader from seeing
that many of their predictions have been literally and
accurately fulfilled, and that the fulfilment is chronicled
in the chapters above referred to. We will here transcribe in full a portion of 2 Kings xxiv., and ask the
reader to remember that what is there related took place

about 160 years after Isaiah had uttered the prediction which we are now about to paraphrase. He will see as with fresh eyes how strikingly the prophet's threatenings were fulfilled in every detail.

" Jehoiachin was eighteen years old (see Isa. iii. 4 and 12) when he began to reign, and he reigned in Jerusalem three months. And his mother's name was Nehushta, the daughter of Elnathan of Jerusalem. And he did that which was evil in the sight of the Lord, according to all that his father had done.

" At that time the servants of Nebuchadnezzar, king of Babylon, came up against Jerusalem, and the city was besieged. And Nebuchadnezzar, king of Babylon, came against the city, and his servants did besiege it. And Jehoiachin, the king of Judah, went out to the king of Babylon, he, and his mother, and his servants, and his princes, and his officers : and the king of Babylon took him in the eighth year of his (Nebuchadnezzar's) reign. And he carried out thence all the treasures of the house of the Lord, and the treasures of the king's house, and cut in pieces all the vessels of gold which Solomon, king of Israel, had made in the temple of the Lord, as the Lord had said. And he carried away all Jerusalem, and all the princes, and all the mighty men of valour, even ten thousand captives, and all the craftsmen and smiths (see Isa. iii. 1-3) : none remained save the poorest sort of the people of the land. And he carried away Jehoiachin to Babylon, and the king's mother, and the king's wives, and his officers, and the mighty of the land, those carried he into captivity from Jerusalem to Babylon. And all the men of might, even seven thousand, and craftsmen and smiths a thousand, all that were strong and apt for war, even them the king of Babylon brought captive to Babylon " (2 Kings xxiv. 8-16).

The punishment of Judah is described with equal

precision by the historian who thus records it, and by
the prophet who predicts it 2160 years beforehand in the
following words :—

" For lo, the King whose name is the Lord of hosts,
shall wholly remove from Jerusalem the stay and the
staff of life : bread and water shall utterly fail. Hero
and warrior, magistrate and prophet, magician and elder,
captain, noble, and counsellor, skilled artisan and
cunning wizard—all shall be swept away. The princes
of the land shall be resourceless youths, and little
children shall rule over the people. They shall be
oppressed by the tyranny of rival factions ; children
shall rise up in proud rebellion against elders, and
dependents against superiors. And if a man shall plead
with his own brother, saying, ' Thou art wealthy ; take
thou the office of ruler, and guide the ruined state,' he
shall protest, saying, ' I will not undertake to heal the
breaches of the state : my wealth is gone ; how then
shall I bear office, or be a ruler of the people ? ' For
Jerusalem shall become a ruin, and the cities of Judah
shall become heaps ; because their words and their
deeds are stout against Me, saith the Lord, and provoke
the eyes of My glory. The fashion of their own countenance beareth witness against them ; they publish their
own shame, as did the men of Sodom, and hide it not.
Woe to their soul ! For they have treasured up wrath
against themselves.

" Say ye to the righteous that it shall be well with
him ; for he shall in no wise lose his reward : say ye to
the wicked that it shall go ill with him ; for God shall
render unto him according to his works.

" I have given up My people to the oppression of
childish rulers and the tyranny of women. (Compare
2 Kings xi. and xxi.) O my people, your leaders lead
you astray and make your paths crooked. Therefore,
the Lord will arise and plead His own cause ; He will

arise and execute judgment among His people.   He
will judge their elders and their princes ; for they
have eaten up the vineyard of the Lord of hosts, and
their palaces are filled with the pillage of the poor.
What mean ye, O ye princes, that ye crush My people ?
ye elders, that ye grind the poor ? saith the Lord of
hosts.

" Moreover, I will visit the pride of the women, saith
the Lord. The daughters of Zion are haughty : their
heads are erect with pride, and their eyes are full of
wantonness : they walk with mincing steps, and their
feet are adorned with tinkling ornaments : therefore
will I smite their haughty heads with loathsome disease,
and their bodies shall fall a prey to the lust of the troops
of the heathen. In that day I will remove the finery of
their tinkling ankle-rings, their nets, their crescents,
their pendants, their bracelets, their kerchiefs, their
head-tires, their chains, their sashes, their scent-caskets,
their amulets, their rings, their nose-jewels, their robes,
their mantles, their shawls, their satchels, their
mirrors, their gauze, their turbans, and their veils.
Sweet spices shall give place to putrid sores, the
girdle shall be replaced by the slave-driver's rope,
instead of well-set hair shall be baldness, instead of
a stomacher sackcloth, instead of beauty the scar of
the branding-iron.

" Zion's men shall fall by the sword, and her might
shall be consumed by war : her gates shall lament and
mourn ; and she, as a widow, shall sit solitary upon the
ground. Her men shall be few, so that one man shall
be sought by seven women, who shall say, We will not
burden thee with our maintenance, if thou wilt only let
us be called thy wives, to take away the reproach of our
widowhood and childlessness."

Is there no warning here for women who profess to be
Christians, and yet spend in dress and vanity money

that should be given to the poor ? Let such reflect that the Lord of hosts taketh an inventory of their wardrobes, and will one day mete out a reward to their sin if they repent not. Is there no warning here for men who trust in guns, and ships, and warlike prowess ? Let such remember that there is no real strength but the strength of righteousness, no real safety but under the protection of the Lord of hosts.

" And yet the day shall come when the Branch of the Lord shall grow up according to His promise, to be the beauty and the glory of His people ; and in His days the fruit of the earth shall be excellent and comely for the remnant of Israel. Then every one of Zion's remnant, every true citizen that shall be found in Jerusalem, shall be, and shall be called, a saint of the Most High, even all whose names shall be found in the book of life, in the holy registers of the city of God : and this shall come to pass when the Lord shall have put away the filth of the daughters of Zion, and shall have purged away the blood-guiltiness of Jerusalem by the breath of judgment and of burning. And then on every dwelling of Zion, and on all the assemblies of her citizens, the presence of the Lord shall rest, as of old it rested on the camp of Israel in a pillar of cloud by day and a pillar of fire by night : and the glory of the city shall be sheltered by the pavilion of His power, a shelter from the heat of the noonday sun, and a covert from the rain which shall descend and the winds which shall blow."

> " Glorious things of thee are spoken,
>   Zion, city of our God ;
> He whose word cannot be broken
>   Formed thee for His own abode.
> On the Rock of Ages founded,
>   What can shake thy sure repose ?
> With salvation's walls surrounded
>   Thou mayest smile at all thy foes.

" Round each habitation hovering,
    See the cloud and fire appear
For a glory and a covering,
    Showing that the Lord is near.
Thus deriving from their banner
    Light by night and shade by day,
Safe they feed upon the manna
    Which He gives them when they pray."

These lines of good John Newton are an eloquent commentary on the above prophecy of gospel days.

Third Half-Hour

Chapter V.

IN the eightieth Psalm the Israelitish nation is likened to a vine—owned, protected, and cared for by the Lord God of hosts. Brought out of Egypt, planted in Canaan, and cherished by the Lord's fostering goodness, the vine took deep root and filled the land. The mountains were covered with its shadow; its boughs were like the goodly cedars; it sent out its branches westward unto the Great Sea, and its shoots eastward unto the Euphrates.

In like manner the Lord Jesus said, when His days on earth were drawing to a close, " Hear another parable : There was a certain householder, which planted a vineyard, and hedged it round about, and digged a winepress in it, and built a tower, and let it out to husbandmen, and went into a far country ; and when the time of the fruit drew near, he sent his servants to the husbandmen, that they might receive the fruits of it." Then, having set forth in His parable the persecution meted out by the husbandmen to the prophets of God, and to God's own Son, the Lord concludes thus : " Therefore I say unto you, The kingdom of God shall be taken from you, and given to a nation bringing forth the fruits thereof."

These passages of Holy Scripture form a clear and effective comment on that part of Isaiah's prophecy which we wish to consider in our present Half-Hour. Whoso understands the eightieth Psalm, and the twenty-first of Matthew, cannot fail to grasp the general meaning of the fifth of Isaiah. We say the general meaning, because even enlightened and conscientious expositors differ in the interpretation of the various details of the parable. Perhaps it is not wise to say that the hedge means this, and the wine-vat means that, and the tower means the other. Some have said, for instance, that as the juice of grapes streams into the wine-vat, so the offerings and gifts of the people streamed to the altar of God ; and that we must therefore understand the wine-vat to mean the altar. Such refinements strike us as more ingenious than edifying. The substance of the whole symbolism is comprehended in the Lord's righteous complaint : " What could have been done more to My vineyard, that I have not done in it ? "

The prophet's opening words are somewhat mysterious and perplexing. On the whole, the most satisfactory solution seems to be this : the singer's " well-beloved " and " beloved " (the two words are very similar to each other in the Hebrew) are the same person, the Lord of hosts ; and the prophet uses this form of speech because he wishes to begin with a " dark saying upon the harp " (Psa. xlix. 4), and to reserve his explanation for the close of his parable (Isa. v. 7). We shall endeavour to word our paraphrase so as to give the English reader an idea of a striking and solemn " play upon words," which exists in the Hebrew of verse 7, where " judgment " and " oppression " (or rather " bloodshed ") differ by a single letter only, as do also " righteousness " and " cry."

" Let me sing a song for a friend whom I love, my beloved's own song touching his vineyard. My friend had a vineyard in a land flowing with milk and honey. He prepared the ground, cleared it of stones, planted it with noble vines, wholly a right seed (Jer. ii. 21), built therein a strong tower for its protection, and hewed out a vat to receive its wine : and lo, the crop that should have been grapes of Eshcol was grapes of Sodom. And now, ye that dwell in Jerusalem and Judah, I appeal to you, saith my friend, to judge between me and my vineyard. (Your own conscience shall acquit me of injustice.) For what more could have been done to make my vineyard fruitful ? Wherefore hath it yielded me grapes of Sodom instead of grapes of Eshcol ? Come now, therefore, and let me tell you what I will do to my vineyard : I will take away the hedge thereof, and the wild beast of the field shall devour it ; I will break down the fence thereof, and the boar out of the wood shall tread it down (Psa. lxxx. 13). I will make it a wilderness, neither pruned nor hoed, but overgrown with briers and thorns ; and my clouds shall let fall no rain upon it.

" My friend is the Lord of hosts : His vineyard is the house of Israel ; His cherished vines the men of Judah. He looked for right and behold might : He looked that the poor should have their wrongs redressed ; and, behold, they are oppressed."

Isaiah probably seemed unto his fellow-countrymen as one that mocked. Was not Uzziah the king strong and capable ? Had not God prospered him and helped him in his wars ? Had not the defences of Jerusalem and Judah been put in perfect order, and had not the king organised a well-disciplined army of more than a quarter of a million men, furnished with weapons of the newest and best type, and ready to take the field at any moment ? (2 Chron. xxvi. 1–15). Yes, all this was true ; but the cancer of departure from God was eating up the life of the nation ; or, to use the prophet's figure, grapes of Sodom were abundant on the vines of the vineyard of the Lord of hosts. Men of the world derided the prophet, relied upon the army, and perhaps dreamed of a navy with Elath on the Red Sea as its base (2 Kings xiv. 22) ; but the prophet of God saw further than men of the world : he saw and said that God was about to

punish the apostate nation ; and in due season the hand
of the Lord accomplished what the mouth of the Lord
had spoken.

It has never been the way of God's holy servants to
denounce general sin in general terms, and there to stop.
They descend to particulars, and bring their charges
home to individual consciences, saying : " This is the
sin : thou art the man ! " Such was the practice of
the Heir himself, when He came to claim the fruits of
His Father's vineyard. (See the woes uttered in Matt.
xxiii., and in other parts of the gospels.) Accordingly,
Isaiah now passes on to utter six woes against avarice,
riotous living, rebellion, perversion of equity, fleshly
wisdom, and injustice (verses 8–23) ; and then describes
the ruin which must follow :—

" Woe unto you, ye covetous landowners, who grasp
the houses and fields of My people that no heritage may
be left to them, and that ye may dwell alone in the land
that I gave them ! (See Levit. xxv. 23, 24, and 1 Kings
xxi. 1–3.) In the ears of My servant Isaiah have I
spoken, saith the Lord of hosts, saying : Verily, verily,
many a house shall be desolate, and many a mansion great
and fair shall be an empty ruin. Ten acres of your vineyards shall produce but one cask of wine ; and ten bushels
of seed-corn shall yield but one bushel to your sickle !
[The Bath, equal in capacity with the Ephah, was a
liquid measure which contained several gallons—some
say as many as eight ; but the statement given in
1 Kings vii, 23, 26, supposing the brazen sea to have
been hemispherical, seems to prove that the Bath was
equal to about four gallons. See also Ezek. xlv. 11.
The word Bath rhymes with Gath, and has no con-
nexion with our English word, " bath."]

" Woe unto you, ye winebibbers, that drink strong
drink from the dawn of day, and inflame yourselves
with wine till the night is far spent. Ye make merry at

your banquets with music and with wine ; but ye heed
not the government of your Creator, nor consider the
work of His hands. Therefore shall your God send you
into captivity, as those who refuse to know Him : your
nobles shall perish by famine, and your common people
shall languish for thirst. Therefore shall the grave
enlarge her maw, and open beyond measure the doors
of her mouth : she shall engulf your glory, your multitude, your carousings, and your carousers : small and
great shall descend together, and the haughty shall be
brought low : but the Lord of hosts shall vindicate His
justice, and the Holy One shall display the sanctity of
His name and law. Yet will He feed the poor of His
flock, though He give to the heathen the ruined lands of
the wealthy.

" Woe unto you, ye riotous livers, who draw the yoke
of lust as the ox draweth the plough, and drag your
loads of sin as the horse its waggon : ye that say to My
prophets, Why tarrieth your angry God so long ? Why
hasteneth He not, that we may see what He doeth ?
Let your Holy One execute His counsel now, that we
may know that He is God !

" Woe unto you, ye lovers of iniquity, who confound
evil with good and good with evil, darkness with light
and light with darkness, bitter with sweet and sweet
with bitter !

" Woe unto you, ye that trust in your own understanding, wise in your own eyes and prudent in your
own sight !

" Woe unto you, ye unjust judges, champions of
the wine-feast and heroes of the drinking-bout, who
acquit the wicked for a bribe, and condemn the
innocent notwithstanding his innocence ! Therefore
shall ye be as stubble before the fire, as dry grass
before the flame : your root shall rot and your blossom
shall perish : for ye have rejected My law, saith the

Lord : ye have despised My word, saith the Holy One of Israel.

" For these things hath Mine anger burned against My people, and I have stretched out My hand against them, saith the Lord. I have smitten them till the hills have trembled at My strokes, and in the streets of their towns their corpses have been strewn like dung. [But this people turneth not to Him that smiteth them ;] therefore, Mine anger is not yet turned away, and the rod in Mine hand is uplifted still. I will marshal the hosts of the heathen from afar ; I will summon them as bees from the ends of the earth (see Isaiah ix. 18) ; speedily and swiftly shall they come. Not one of them shall tire, nor stumble, nor slumber, nor sleep. Their loins shall be ever girded with strength, and their feet ever shod with swiftness. With sharpened arrows and bended bow shall they come : the hoofs of their horses shall be hard as flint ; the wheels of their chariots swift as the wind. Their voice shall be as the roaring of a lion, as the roaring of a young lion seeking its prey : yea, they shall roar, and seize, and carry away safely ; and there shall be no deliverer. They shall roar against you in that day as the sea roareth with its waves : and if ye look to the land ye shall find gloom and tribulation ; and the clouds shall darken the light of heaven."

So the Assyrian bee came (Isaiah vii. 18, and xxxvi. 1), the Chaldean lion seized his prey (Jer. xxxix. 1, and li. 34), and the Roman eagle flapped his wings in the sanctuary of God (Matt. xxiv. 15). The Lord of hosts was sanctified in the punishment of a nation of despisers, and the salvation of a remnant who trembled at His word. Our own land has been, and is, guilty of the same evils. While we write, the cry of the oppressed goes up from some parts of our empire where it is unheeded by man, but is heard by the God of heaven.

Wrongs lie at our door in China, India, and elsewhere. And with all this, in our own dear land, which has been and is the fountain of the world's Bibles, the most daring blasphemies are poured forth from press and pulpit. Meanwhile, from John Bradford's chariot of fire rings out the cry: "O England, repent, repent!" What will the end be, and when will it come?

FOURTH HALF-HOUR

Chapter VI.

"THESE things said Isaiah, when he saw His glory, and spake of Him" (John xii. 41). What things? The things contained in the sixth and fifty-third chapters of this book. Such a declaration, coming form holy John, is a clear and conclusive reply to two questions : 1. Did Isaiah write both of these chapters ? 2. Do they both refer to Jesus Christ ?

Some reader may say, Why should either of these questions be raised ? Do not all true Christians believe that Isaiah wrote the prophecy which bears his name, and that his predictions were fulfilled in the birth, life, and death of the Lord Jesus ? We quite agree with you, dear reader. So it is, or so it ought to be. But, alas ! in these latter days all the truths of Christianity are called in question by men who profess to be Christians. Infidelity has found such a footing in the professing Church of Christ as it never found before ; and in defence of the truth of God it is necessary for us to notice at least some of the errors which are thus spreading on all sides.

The simple principle on which all our exposition depends is this : the New Testament is the only trust-worthy expositor of the Old, and from its interpretation of the prophecies there is no appeal. We desire to share in the wisdom which was given to the apostles of Christ, and to let all other wisdom go, convinced that it is what Augustine once called it : learned ignorance. Applying this principle to the two questions referred to above, we find that Jesus Christ and His apostles regarded Isaiah as the author of the whole of the prophecy that bears his name, and taught their hearers that his prophetic utterances were fulfilled in the person and work of the Son of Man. We are not surprised to find that learned critics who, in spite of this evidence, are foolish enough to ascribe parts of the book of Isaiah to several unknown authors (as is the case, for instance, in the " Cambridge Bible for Schools and Colleges "), are also blind enough to be unable to see that its wonderful predictions were fulfilled in Christ.

It is enough for us to know that holy John said, concerning this sixth chapter, " These things said Isaiah when he saw Christ's glory and spake of Him." Advancing from this starting point, we expect to find in the portion of Scripture before us a revelation of the glory of Christ, and we find it there.

The words used are very simple, and scarcely need a paraphrase. But we have found it so useful to throw our explanations into a continuous and paraphrastic form that we are reluctant to abandon this method. Let our readers carefully remember that our one object is not to improve the words of God's inspired servants, but to throw light upon their meaning by the employment of other expressions, borrowed, if possible, from other parts of Holy Scripture. We feel sure that this method is more effective than a system of elaborate " notes," which few persons have time or inclination to consult.

Some have thought that the revelation which Isaiah here describes was his first call to the prophetic ministry, and therefore should properly stand at the beginning of the whole book. We have already pointed out that the writings of the prophets are not always arranged in the order in which their messages were delivered ; but in this case there seems to be no need of such an explanation. Judging by the statement contained in the first verse of the first chapter, we conclude that the first five chapters belong to the reign of Uzziah ; and we look upon the vision of the sixth chapter as a further revelation of the glory of God granted to the prophet at the time of that king's death. Isaiah needed such a revelation that he might deliver with boldness and authority the awful message of judgment which the chapter contains.

Competent spiritual judges have considered that the doctrine of the Trinity is plainly taught in this vision. The seraphim (" burning ones," see Psa. civ. 4) cry, " Holy, holy, holy " ; and the Lord Himself says, " Who will go for Us ? " The Father is holy, the Son is holy, the Spirit is holy. These holy Three are the One true God ; and from Them, from Him, cometh the message of the Holy Scriptures.

" In the year of the death of King Uzziah, I saw in vision the throne of God. Exalted high upon it sat the Lord, and the skirts of His robe of light filled the temple. Above Him stood the six-winged seraphim : with two of their wings they covered their faces (as unworthy or unable to look upon God) ; with two they covered their feet (as unworthy to be seen of Him) ; and with two they flew (to do His bidding). And they cried one to another, saying : Holy, holy, holy, is the Lord of hosts ; His glory fills the whole earth. The foundations of the doors were shaken by the thunder of their voices, and the temple was filled with the glory of the Lord. Then did I exceedingly fear and quake before Him, and said : Woe is me ! I perish. Sin hath defiled my lips, and the lips of the people among whom I dwell : and how can I see God and live ? Then one of the seraphim took in his hand the altar-tongs, and in them a burning coal from off the altar. He flew to me and touched my mouth with the coal, saying : Lo, this hath touched thy lips : sacrifice hath removed thine iniquity, and hath made atonement for thy sin. Then heard I the voice of the Lord, saying, Whom shall I send as My messenger, and who will go for Us ? Then said I, Here am I ; send me.''

Let us pause a moment to reflect that the true knowledge of God humbles a sinner in the dust ; that the blood of Jesus Christ cleanseth from all sin ; and that nothing but such cleansing can rightly embolden a man to act as the messenger of the Lord of hosts.

'' Then said the Lord unto me, Go, carry this message to the house of Israel : Ye shall hear, but not understand ; ye shall see, but not perceive. Your heart is waxed gross ; your ears are dull of hearing ; and your eyes have ye closed ; lest at any time ye should see with your eyes, and hear with your ears, and turn unto Me and be healed. Then said I, Lord, how long shall this people be thus given up to the hardness of their hearts ? And He said, Until the armies of the heathen have wasted their cities and cut off the people thereof, have left their houses without inhabitants, and have reduced the land to utter desolation : yea, until the Lord have sent them far off into captivity, and have caused the land to be forsaken of all them that dwell therein. Yet a small remnant shall be left in it ; but even this shall again pass through the fire. Nevertheless, as the stock of the teil-tree or the oak remaineth when the tree is cut down, so shall a holy seed remain, a remnant that shall revive and flourish.''

It must have seemed to godly people who saw the Chaldæan invasion, the Babylonian captivity, and the restoration under Zerubbabel, that the above prophecy of Isaiah had its complete fulfilment in those events. But it was not so. We know from the pages of the New Testament that a judicial blindness more terrible still fell upon the nation in the days when they heard the voice of Jesus, witnessed His miracles, rejected and murdered Him ; and that this was followed by a punishment more terrible than that which was inflicted by the agency of Nebuchadnezzar.   The Roman eagle was the predicted abomination of desolation ; and when it stood in the holy place, the teil-tree was cut down indeed.   But even then the Christian Church sprang up from its stock. Neither Chaldæan fires nor Roman flames could consume the indestructible life of the holy seed, the Israel of God.

Chapter VII.

AHAZ, king of Judah, walked in the ways of the kings of Israel, and made molten images for the worship of Baal. He also burned incense in the valley of the son of Hinnom, and burned his sons in the fire, after the abominations of the heathen whom the Lord had cast out before the children of Israel. As usual, sin brought trouble. The Edomites on the south, the Philistines on the west, and the two powerful kingdoms of Israel and Syria on the north, were by turns employed as instruments to punish Judah for these offences against its God. We are told that Syria smote Judah, and carried away a great multitude of them captives to Damascus ; and that Pekah, the son of Remaliah, king of Israel, slew in Judah 120,000 in one day, and carried away 200,000 captives to Samaria. The captives were, it is true, speedily released through the influence of Oded the prophet ; but these disasters must have brought Judah very low indeed. We can easily understand that when they afterwards heard that their two great enemies, Syria and Israel, had formed an alliance with the intention of setting a stranger on the throne of David, their hearts were moved as the trees of the wood are moved by the wind—trembled, as we say, like aspen leaves.

The seventh chapter of Isaiah deals with this crisis, and contains withal the wonderful promise, " Behold, the virgin shall conceive and bear a son, and shall call His name Immanuel." (It is worthy of note that Isaiah, and also Matthew, wrote " the virgin," not " a virgin.")

There are certain difficulties connected with this well-known passage which a faithful expositor must notice. The question has been often asked, How could a miraculous event, which was to take place some 700 years later, serve as a sign to Ahaz? Much has been written on this subject, and many arguments advanced, which we cannot stay to notice. The soundest of all conclusions seems to us to be that this great promise received a partial and typical fulfilment at the time then present, in the birth of an infant who was a sign of the approaching deliverance of Judah from Syria and Israel; but that its true and complete fulfilment came when a virgin of the house of David gave birth in the city of David to a Saviour which was Christ the Lord. This is quite in agreement with the method of Divine revelation. We find a similar instance, and a notable one, in the Divine promise to David concerning David's son: " I will be to him a Father, and He shall be to me a son," a promise partially fulfilled in God's love to Solomon; though, as we learn from Hebrews i. 5, it referred principally to Him who should rise to reign over the Gentiles, in whom the Gentiles should trust.

This view of the promise of Immanuel is so ably stated by Bishop Wordsworth in his annotated Bible, that we cannot do better than quote his words : " The question may be reverently asked, whether some glimpses and gleams of the future glorious fulfilment of Isaiah's prophecy in Christ were not given in the days of King Ahaz to be a present sign to that monarch, and a pledge and earnest of that future accomplishment which exhausted all its significance? It seems that Isaiah himself has answered this question. At the beginning of the next chapter he declares a consecutive message from Jehovah which reflects much light upon this prophecy. . . . I do not say that the prophecy was *fulfilled* in the birth of Maher-shalal-hash-baz, from Isaiah by the *prophetess*, who was probably a virgin when the present prophecy was uttered, (for she would otherwise have been called his wife; and the existence of another son of Isaiah, Shear-jashub, is no evidence to the contrary, for Shear-jashub was now old enough to be his father's companion, and his mother may have been dead.) It is not to be supposed that the birth of Maher-shalal-hash-baz was an accomplishment of the prophecy, ' Behold, the virgin shall conceive.' By no means. The prophecy of the birth of one who was to be called GOD WITH US could not, it is obvious, have been supposed to be fulfilled in all its depth and height by any mere child of man. But the birth of the child of the prophet and prophetess, and the routing of the two foes of Ahaz soon after that birth, was a pledge and an earnest of the future fulfilment and accomplishment in the birth of Immanuel."

It seems clear to us that the above view of this great promise is substantially correct, though the child who thus served as a type of Immanuel may not have been Maher-shalal-hash-baz, but some other, well known at the time. In any case, all who take the apostles of Christ for their teachers know for certain from the testimony of Matthew that the promise was fulfilled with an infinitely glorious fulfilment when Christ was born at Bethlehem.

This is not the place to discuss the meaning of the Hebrew word which is here translated virgin. We need only say that the oldest Jewish translators of the Scriptures give it this sense in their Greek version, known as the Septuagint, and that their testimony is confirmed by the inspired pen of Matthew.

The day that Ephraim departed from Judah—that is, the day when the ten tribes were formed into a separate kingdom under Jeroboam the son of Nebat—was an evil day for the children of Jacob. We have the authority of Isaiah for saying that no such calamity befel the house of David until it came under the oppression of Assyria in the reign of King Ahaz (Isaiah vii. 17). Then was the Assyrian power held as a hired razor in the Lord's hand, that its keen edge might pass over the whole nation from head to foot, and shave off its glory and its covering, even as a leper was shorn of all his hair, of his beard, and even of his eyebrows. (See Isaiah vii. 20, and Lev. xiv. 9.) The desolation caused by the ravages, first of the Assyrians, and then of the Chaldæans, who succeeded to their power and their work, is vividly set before us in the closing verses of this chapter ; instead of flocks and herds, a man should possess a cow and a couple of sheep, and the milk thus obtained, together with some honey, should be sufficient food for the scanty population left in the land. (See Jer. xxxix. 10.) Vineyards that had once been filled with valuable vines, and hill-sides that had been formerly tilled with mattock or with hoe, should become mere wildernesses covered with briars and thorns, or wild pasture-grounds for oxen and sheep. We hope that this brief survey may lead the reader on to a just understanding of this difficult chapter.

King Ahaz, disquieted by what he had heard of the alliance between Syria and Israel, had gone to the end of the conduit of the upper pool in the highway of the fuller's field, probably to secure to his city a supply of water during the expected siege ; and his son Hezekiah, then a lad of twelve years, may have been with him. If so, this was for Hezekiah a doubly memorable spot ; for there, some thirty years later, stood the general of the king of Assyria to deliver his master's blasphemous and insulting message in the ears of the people that were on the city wall. Isaiah was now sent thither to carry to King Ahaz a message of mercy and of judgment.

"In the year when I saw the Lord's throne in the

temple, Uzziah, king of Judah, died, and was succeeded
by his son Jotham ; Jotham was succeeded by his son
Ahaz. In his days Rezin king of Syria, and Pekah,
king of Israel, joined their forces to make war on
Judah, and laid siege to Jerusalem, but could not take it.
When Ahaz and his court heard that Syria had formed
an alliance with Israel for this intent, their hearts and
the hearts of the people trembled, as the leaves of the
forest tremble in the wind. Then came the word of the
Lord to Isaiah, saying : Take with thee thy son Remnant-
shall-return, and go forth to meet Ahaz : thou shalt
find him without the city in the highway of the fuller's
field at the upper end of the conduit which brings water
into the city to the upper pool. Say to him, Take heed
that thou be not disquieted. Let not thine heart be
discouraged because of these two smoking pieces of
firebrands ; fear not the fierce wrath of the kings of
Syria and Israel. They have devised an evil device
against thee, saying, Let us invade Judah, harass it,
storm its strong city, and set the son of Tabeal upon the
throne of David. Therefore thus saith the Lord
Jehovah : Their counsel shall not stand, nor their
purpose come to pass. For Rezin is king in Damascus,
and his power shall not extend beyond Syria ; and
within sixty-five years the kingdom of Israel shall be
scattered and destroyed. Meanwhile, the son of Remaliah shall be king in Samaria, and his power shall not
extend beyond the ten tribes. Moreover, if ye of the
house of David rely not on My *hand*, your kingdom shall
not *stand*."

It is thought that the sixty-five years referred to in
the above prophecy terminate at the time when the
Assyrians colonised Samaria with heathen settlers
(2 Kings xvii. 24, and Ezra iv. 9, 10). It is, perhaps,
impossible to reproduce in English the effective similarity of Isaiah's two words for " believe " and " be

established." We ask our readers to pardon our poor attempt at the impossible.

" Again the Lord bade me speak to Ahaz, saying : Ask the Lord thy God to give thee a sign that this message is from Him : ask for a miracle on earth, or in the heavens. But Ahaz said, I will not ask ; for it is written in the law that we may not tempt the Lord. (This, said he, not that he loved the law, but because he looked to Assyria for help.) Then said Isaiah : Hearken now, ye house of David : is it not enough for you to wear out the patience of the prophets, but ye must wear out the long-suffering of my God also ? Since ye will not ask, the Lord shall Himself give you a sign : Behold, the virgin shall be with child, and shall bring forth a son ; and his name shall be called Immanu El (With-us God). Curds and honey (infants' food) shall he eat till he shall have knowledge to discern between evil and good. And before he shall be able to discern between evil and good, the two countries whose kings thou fearest shall be reduced to desolation. (In a few short years the power of Syria and Israel shall be broken. For fulfilment see 2 Kings xvi. 9, and xvii. 6.) Moreover, the king of Assyria, on whom thou dost rely, shall be thy ruin : for by his hand the Lord shall bring upon thee, and upon Judah, and upon the house of David, such evil as hath not befallen them since the ten tribes revolted from Rehoboam.

" Then shall the Lord summon the hosts of Egypt, numerous as the gad-flies that haunt its marshes, and the squadrons of Assyria, countless as the bees that swarm in their land. They shall come and cover the face of the country, settling in its valleys and its rocky ravines, on its thorn hedges and all its meadow-land.

" In that day shall the Lord shave the country as one shaves from head to foot a man that is a leper. He shall hire His razor from the regions beyond the Euphrates, even the army of the king of Assyria.

" Then shall a husbandman rear a cow and a couple of sheep in place of his former herds and flocks ; and the milk that they shall give shall be more than enough to supply the few people that remain in the land. Every one of the scanty remnant shall live on curds and honey instead of corn and wine.

" In that day shall every one of the rich vineyards of the land become a wilderness of briars and thorns. There shall men hunt wild beasts, for the whole land shall be a wilderness. The hills whose fruitful sides were formerly tilled with the hoe shall be tangles of briars and thorns, wild pastures for oxen and sheep."

For the fulfilment of this prophecy of the desolation of Judæa, or at least a partial fulfilment of it, see Jer. xxxix. 9, 10. God is faithful both to His threatenings and to His promises. The hand that in the near future gave up Judæa to desolation, fulfilled in due season the mighty promise of the virgin birth. Our own Cowper has justly said :

> " Of all the crowns Jehovah wears,
>   Salvation is His dearest claim ;
> That gracious sound well pleased He hears
>   And owns Immanuel for His name."

Chapter VIII. 1–IX. 7.

IT was our intention to expound Isaiah vii., viii. and ix. 1–7 in one Half-hour, but the section was too long for our purpose. The whole of it is one continuous prophecy, and this latter part needs no separate introduction. Let the reader glance again at the introductory remarks already given, and then turn prayerfully with us to Isaiah viii. 1–8.

" The Lord also bade me take a large writing-tablet, and write on it in plain characters the inscription :

TO SPEEDYPLUNDER-SWIFTSPOIL.

The Lord also commanded that Uriah the priest, and Zechariah the son of Jeberechiah, two credible witnesses, should attest the publication of this prophecy. Moreover, the Lord gave me in those days a son by my wife, the prophetess, and bade me call him by the name which I had inscribed upon the tablet. Call thy son Speedy-plunder-swiftspoil, said the Lord : for before he shall be old enough to say father and mother, the king of Assyria shall plunder the riches of Damascus, and shall carry away the spoil of Samaria.

" Yet again the word of the Lord came unto me, saying, Since this people despiseth the gentle rill of Zion, and glorieth in an alliance with Syria, therefore, behold, I the Lord will bring against them the king of Assyria, with all the glory of his power, a flood strong and deep as the waters of his own Euphrates. The stream shall overflow its channels, burst its banks [and overwhelm Damascus and Samaria]. Moreover, it shall

47

rush onward into Judah, flooding the land and sweeping through it till Jerusalem herself shall stand chin-deep in the waters. As a vulture shall Assyria spread its wings over thy land, O Immanuel."

Accordingly, a king of Assyria went up against Damascus and took it, and carried its people captive to Kir, and slew Rezin, its king (2 Kings xvi. 9) ; another king of Assyria took Samaria, and carried Israel away into Assyria (2 Kings xvii. 6, and xviii. 9–12) ; and finally, a third king of Assyria came up against all the fenced cities of Judah and took them (2 Kings xviii. 13). But here the proud waves of the Euphrates were stayed. They reached to the neck of chastened Zion, and then subsided at the rebuke of her God. For it came to pass that the angel of the Lord went out and smote in the camp of the Assyrians a hundred and fourscore and five thousand (2 Kings xix. 35). The wings of the greedy vulture were clipped, and their dark shadow was removed from the land ; for, after all, it was the land of Immanuel !

The next paragraph bids defiance to the enemies of Jerusalem, with special reference to Syria and Israel : they shall never prevail against those who have a right to say, El immanu, God is with us ; let such fear their God, and they need fear none else ; but they who reject His counsels shall do so to their own ruin.

" Rage, ye peoples, against Zion, and your power shall be broken. Hearken, ye nations that come from far : gird yourselves to the battle, and ye shall be destroyed ; yea, gird yourselves to the battle, and ye shall be destroyed. Take counsel together against us, and it shall be brought to nought ; utter your purpose, and it shall not come to pass. For El immanu, God is with us. God hath spoken unto me by the might of His Spirit, and hath taught me not to do as my sinful countrymen do : He hath said, Ye that fear the Lord, join ye not in the party-cries of this people ; share not their fear, nor be afraid with their terror. Give glory to the Lord of hosts by reverencing His name ; yea, I say unto you, fear Him, and He shall be your refuge. But to the houses of Israel and Judah [who depart from Him] He shall be a stumbling-block and a rock of offence ; as a gin and a snare shall He be to the inhabitants of Jerusalem who believe not ; many shall stumble on this stumbling-stone, and shall be broken, snared and taken."

As then, so now ; to them that believe, Christ is a sure foundation ; but to the unbelieving and disobedient, a stone of stumbling. God's mercies and judgments are a great deep ; but He is righteous in all His ways, and holy in all His works. When His plain warnings have been despised by men, He speaks to them in parables, that seeing they may see and not perceive. This seems to be the meaning of what follows.

" The Lord hath bidden me keep His testimony secret, a sealed book for the use of those who are willing to learn of me. I will wait for Him, now that He hideth His face from the house of Jacob, and I will look for His appearing. Behold, I and the children, whom the Lord hath given me, are appointed to be signs and wonders unto Israel, setting forth the purposes of the Lord of hosts, whose dwelling is in Zion."

Isaiah's whole life must have been a sign and a portent to the guilty nation whose sins he reproved, and whose destinies he foretold ; and as to his sons, whenever they walked abroad their names reminded the people that a remnant of them should be saved, and that the enemies of God should speedily become a prey and a spoil. A deeper meaning of these words of the prophet is unfolded in Heb. ii. 13, where we learn that Isaiah and his sons were types of Christ and His redeemed.

Now follows a terrible picture of the darkness and distress that should come upon the apostate nation, to be removed later on by the light of the glorious Gospel of Christ, who is the image of God. [In verse 19, " to peep " means to chirp, or to speak with a ghostly voice.]

" When the sinners of My people shall say unto you that fear My name, ' Let us seek counsel from witches and wizards, with their familiar spirits, their sepulchral voices, and their mystical mutterings ' ; ye shall answer and say, ' Should not a nation go to its God for guidance ? Shall we seek to obtain from the dead instruction for the living ? Let us listen to Moses and the prophets !' If any man teach otherwise, surely his darkness shall never end in morning light. Such as depart from the Lord shall wander through the land in distress and hunger : despair shall consume them, and they shall curse their king who cannot, and their God who will not, deliver them. They shall look to heaven above and to earth beneath, and lo, they shall find nothing but distress and darkness, pain and gloom ; and into the blackness of darkness they shall be driven away."

Whatever the primary fulfilment of this prophecy may have been in Isaiah's time, or in the days that followed, it sets forth the terrible doom of all who forsake the Lord and give heed to doctrines of devils instead of hearing Moses and the prophets. Such men are wandering stars, to whom is reserved the mist of darkness for ever.

Yet the darkness of those days was to be succeeded by the rising of the Sun of Righteousness. Of this glorious dawn the prophet next speaks.

" But the land that was in anguish shall be delivered from darkness. In former times, thou land of Naphtali and Zebulon, the Lord brought thee low by the hand of Assyria (2 Kings xv. 29), but in the latter days He will honour thee. [The word here translated ' more grievously afflict ' may mean ' to honour.' But it is quite possible that our Authorised Version may be right in rendering it ' more grievously afflict.' If so, the prophet refers to the Assyrian invasion recorded in 2 Kings xvii. 5, 6.] The region by the sea, the region beyond Jordan, Galilee of the Gentiles, the people that walked in darkness, shall see a great light ; they have dwelt in the land of the shadow of death, but the light shall shine upon them. Thou, O Lord, shall multiply them and increase their joy. [We adopt here the reading which is translated in the margin of the Authorised Version.] They shall rejoice before the Lord as men rejoice over the produce of the harvest field, or over the spoils of victory. The yoke wherewith they have been burdened, the staff that has bruised their shoulders, the rod with which the oppressor has smitten them, shalt Thou destroy as Thou didst destroy the Midianites in the days of Gideon. Then shall the armour of war's shouting combatants, and the garments which they have dyed in the blood of the slain, be given as fuel to the fire ; for war shall cease. For in that day it shall be said, Unto us a child is born, unto us a son is given, [the seed of David and the Son of God]. Upon His shoulder shall rest universal empire. He shall be named Wonderful in Counsel, Mighty God, Everlasting Father, Prince of Peace. His government shall have no limit, and its prosperity no end. He shall sit on the throne and rule the kingdom of His father David, to establish and maintain it with judgment and with justice thenceforward for ever. With all my heart and with all my soul will I do this, saith the Lord of hosts."

It is done. Jesus hath preached in Galilee, and His light still shineth in the darkness of this world, though the darkness comprehendeth it not. He sitteth on the throne of His father David, and waiteth till all His enemies be made His footstool.

Chapters IX. 8—X. 4.

ISAIAH prophesied in the days of Uzziah, Jotham, Ahaz, and Hezekiah, kings of Judah ; and in the days of those kings events took place in the kingdom of Israel which the prophet foretells in the prophecy before us. It consists of four denunciations, each closing with the awful refrain, " For all this His anger is not turned away, but His hand is stretched out still." He predicts the punishment of the northern kingdom's pride (verses 8–12), the destruction of its impenitent rulers and lying prophets (13–17), the chastisement of wickedness by the scourge of civil war (18–21), and the overthrow of unrighteous lawgivers and judges by the strong hand of the Assyrian tyrant (x. 1–4).

Accordingly, we find in the fifteenth, sixteenth, and seventeenth chapters of the Second Book of Kings, that Tiglath Pileser, king of Assyria, overthrew the power of Syria, and slew its king Rezin, the ally of Pekah, king of Israel ; that the kingdom of Israel was deluged with blood by the strife of rival factions, who deposed and murdered one king after another ; and that the Assyrians under Shalmaneser afterwards turned their arms against Israel, sweeping away in one awful flood haughty rulers, lying prophets, wicked citizens, and unjust judges.

It is difficult to trace exactly the fulfilment of every detail of this sad prophecy of judgment ; but its broad lessons are obvious enough. It tells us as a nation that if we depart from God and walk in the ways of idolatry and oppression, we also shall find that the Lord's anger is not turned away, but that His hand is stretched out still. May it stir us up to pray for our own beloved land, that our rulers may legislate in righteousness, and that our present apostasy from the truth for which our fathers died may not go on till we reap the bitter harvest of the Lord's displeasure.   What Calvin observed in his day applies with equal, if not greater, force to our own times : ' Justly might the Lord address to us the same expostulation, and assuredly He addresses us by the mouth of Isaiah : neither ought we to look for another prophet to threaten new chastisements, seeing that our case is not different from that of the Israelites, and we are involved in the same blame with them.'

" The Lord sendeth forth this word against the house of Jacob, and it shall take effect upon the tribes of Israel.   They shall all know that He hath not spoken in vain ; the men of Ephraim shall know it, and the inhabitants of Samaria, who say in the pride of their stubborn hearts, ' Our foes have demolished our walls of brick, but we will build us walls of hewn stone ; they have cut down our lowly sycamore trees, but we will have stately cedars in their stead.'   Therefore the adversaries of your ally Rezin shall overthrow him (2 Kings xvi. 9), and the Lord shall bring them against you also, and shall stir up your foes.   But even so His anger shall not turn away from you : still shall His hand be stretched out to smite."

The same voice had spoken by Moses, saying : "If ye will not be reformed by Me by these things, but will walk contrary to Me, then will I also walk contrary to you, and will punish you seven times for all your sins" (Lev. xxvi. 23, 24).

" But Israel turneth not unto the God that smiteth him ; he seeketh not the Lord of hosts.   Therefore, the Lord will cut off from the nation head and tail, topmost branch and lowest rush, in one day : the head, the elders in high office ; the tail, the prophets who teach the people lies.   For they that lead you, lead you astray ; and they that follow fall into the ditch.   Therefore the Lord shall take no pleasure in the strength of your young men, and shall withdraw His pity even from your orphans and widows. [Even these objects of His special compassion must suffer in the general ruin.] For the land is filled with the wicked, who give their hands to evil deeds, and their tongues to the utterance of iniquity. Therefore His anger even so shall not turn away from you : still shall His hand be stretched out to smite.

"For your sin kindleth a fire in Mine anger which shall devour the briars and thorns that cumber the ground. Yea, the fire shall mount to the thick trees of your forest, and the clouds of their smoke shall rise up to heaven. By my wrath shall the land be consumed, saith the Lord ; the people thereof shall be fuel for the fire, and shall destroy one another without pity. They shall plunder on the right hand, and still be hungry : they shall eat spoil on the left hand, and still be un-satisfied. They shall devour their own flesh and blood, Manasseh Ephraim, and Ephraim Manasseh ; and these shall unite to fight against Judah. But even so His anger shall not turn away from you : still shall His hand be stretched out to smite.

"Woe to the throne of iniquity, to the legislators of Israel, who frame mischief by a law, that they may deprive the needy of justice, and rob My people of their rights, making widows their spoil and the fatherless their prey. What will ye do, saith the Lord, in the day when I shall visit your sins, and shall bring the Assyrian from far to destroy you ? Whither will ye flee for help, and what hiding-place will ye find for your honour or your wealth ? I will hide My face from you, and nothing shall be left to you but to go forth into captivity or to fall by the sword. And even so Mine anger shall not turn away from you : still shall Mine hand be stretched out to smite."

Verily, there is a God that judgeth in the earth !

Chapter X., 5–34.

WE might fill many pages in explaining and discussing rival interpretations of the prophecy which we are about to consider. But it will be more in accordance with our usual plan, and probably more profitable for our readers, if we set forth as simply as possible the conclusion at which we have ourselves arrived as to its true meaning.

First, the Lord issues a summons to the Assyrians to destroy Samaria (verses 5, 6), and to chastise Jerusalem (12) ; but points out that the Assyrian king, though his power is but the rod or the axe with which the Lord smites, has no aim but the advancement of his own interests and the gratification of his own lust of plunder (7–15). For this reason the Lord will punish his pride (12). Taught by their enemies' downfall, the remnant of Israel—that is, those of Judah who escape destruction—shall no longer lean upon Assyria, as did Ahaz (see 2 Chron. xxvii. 16, 20, 21), but shall trust in the Lord, who has ordained their chastisement (20–23). Meanwhile, the faithful few who are found in Judah, including good Hezekiah, are encouraged by the Lord not to fear the heathen power which He is using for their correction. Yet a little while, and His indignant chastisement of His own people shall be accomplished ; and then, because of His faithful love to the anointed line of David, He will destroy the yoke of the oppressor (24–27).

Then follows a prophetic description of the advance of Sennacherib's army against Jerusalem (28–32). We do not know the precise position of some of the places that are named ; but it seems clear that Aiath is the same as Ai, about nine miles north of Jerusalem, and that when the invader reaches Nob he will be near enough to the capital to shake his threatening hand at its walls. Migron and the other places named lie more or less in the line of march from Ai to Nob, and the " passage " mentioned in verse 29 is a mountain pass, at one end whereof Sennacherib's general will leave the baggage of his army while the troops file through on their way to Jerusalem.

But, behold, while he halts at Nob and shakes his hand at the daughter of Zion, the Lord of hosts shall lop the boughs of his forest and lay low his lofty cedars, that he may return with shame to Nineveh (33, 34).

It is true that the above interpretation is open to certain objections, but they are not insurmountable, and we believe that our readers may safely regard this as a correct explanation of the prophet's words.

" Ho, ho, come forth from thy land, Assyria, thou rod of Mine anger ; thou that holdest in thine hand the staff of Mine indignation ! I send thee against a nation of evildoers ; I charge thee to go up against a people that hath provoked My wrath, that thou mayest despoil them, plunder them, and trample them beneath thy feet as the mire of the streets. But the execution of My will is not thine aim, nor the thought of thine heart : thou thinkest to destroy many nations and to cut them off. Thou sayest, ' Are not all my nobles kings ? Have I not overthrown Calno, even as I overthrew Carchemish, Hamath as Arpad, and Samaria as Damascus ? Mine hand hath reached the kingdoms of gods whose images are better than those of Jerusalem and Samaria. I have conquered Samaria and her idols : shall I not prevail against Jerusalem and her idols ? '

" Therefore, thus saith the Lord : When I shall have accomplished all My will in chastising My people, I will punish the king of Assyria for the proud thoughts of his heart, and the lofty looks of his eyes. For he hath said, By the power of mine own hand I have done this, and by the wisdom of my own prudent counsels I have brought it to pass. I have changed the boundaries of nations ; I have despoiled them of their treasures ; and as a mighty man I have dethroned their kings. As one findeth a bird's nest, so have I found the riches of the nations ; as one gathereth the eggs that are left therein, so have I gathered the wealth of the whole earth : none dared to stir his wing, or open his mouth, or chirp.

" Shall the axe boast itself against the hewer ?   Shall the saw vaunt itself against the carpenter ?   Thou art as a rod that would shake him that shaketh it, as a staff that would lift up the hand that lifteth it, the hand that is more than wood.   [Literally, As a staff lifting up not-wood.]

" Therefore the Lord of hosts shall consume thy fat ones with leanness, and shall kindle beneath thy glory a flame like the flame of fire.   The Light of Israel shall be as a fire unto thee, and the Holy One of Israel as a flame : the fire shall burn and the flame shall consume thy briars and thy thorns in one day.   It shall consume thy mighty men body and soul, even those that are the glory of thy forest and of thy fruitful field ; and the courage of those that are left unto thee shall fail as when a standard-bearer fainteth : for they that are left of the trees of thy forest shall be so few in number that a child could count them.

" In that day the remnant of Judah, they that are escaped of the house of Jacob, shall no longer lean upon the arm of flesh that hath smitten them ; but shall stay themselves upon the Lord, the Holy One of Israel. Then [shall be fulfilled that which I have spoken, ' Shear jashub,'] a remnant shall return, the remnant

of Jacob, unto the mighty God. For though My people
Israel be as the sand which is by the sea-shore innumerable, a remnant only shall return to Me : I have
determined to consume them by the overflowing of My
righteous anger : yea, the Lord, the Lord of hosts, hath
decreed a consumption through the length and breadth
of the land.

"Therefore thus saith the Lord of hosts unto those
that fear His name in Zion : Fear not the Assyrian,
though he smite you with his rod, and bruise you with
his staff, as did your taskmasters in the land of Egypt.
For yet a very small moment, and My displeasure against
you shall be ended, and Mine anger against your foes
shall issue in their destruction. I will stir up a power
that shall scourge the Assyrian as Midian was scourged
at the rock of Oreb (Judges vii. 25). I will stretch
out Mine hand over your enemies as Moses stretched
out his rod over the sea for the destruction of Egypt.
Then shall the burden of the Assyrian be removed from
thy shoulder, and his yoke from off thy neck : I
will destroy the yoke, that the line of Mine anointed
may not fail.

"But meanwhile, behold he cometh ! He is at Ai :
he marcheth on to Migron : he leaveth his baggage at
Michmash : his troops file through the mountain pass,
and lodge for a night at Geba. Ramah trembleth at
his approach, and the men of Gibeah flee at his coming.
Cry aloud for fear, O Gallim ! Hearken Laish ! Let
Anathoth send up an answering wail ! Madmenah is
deserted, and they that dwell at Gebim gather their
treasures to flee. On this self-same day he halteth at
Nob, and shaketh his hand at the mount of Zion, at the
hill of Jerusalem !

"But behold, the Lord, the Lord of hosts, shall stay
his further progress, and lop the boughs of his forest
with terror. His haughty warriors shall be as high

trees that are cut down, as lofty cedars laid low. The destroyer shall hew down as with steel the thick trees of his forest, and the angel of My might shall fell the cedars of his Lebanon.''

So the Lord sent His angel, which cut off all the mighty men of valour, and the leaders and captains in the camp of the king of Assyria (2 Chron. xxxii. 21) ; but Hezekiah dwelt safely under the shelter of the anointing oil wherewith the Lord had anointed the line of David.

Chapters XI., XII.

GOD'S judgments are a great deep, and so is His Word. Knowing and feeling this, we often take up this work of exposition with much fear, and intersperse our labours with many cries for divine teaching and divine keeping. We consult, as far as we can, the works of godly and learned men who have gone before us, and then endeavour to form a modest but independent judgment of our own ; finally, we aim at laying this before our readers with all possible simplicity and brevity. When any passage remains a mystery to us after all our efforts, we leave it unexplained; for it is evidently better to express no opinion at all than to pervert and darken words which God has spoken.

In the present Half-Hour we have had to face unusual difficulties, as will appear from the following extracts. We give these extracts partly to show that others have felt the same difficulties as we feel ourselves, and partly to prove that our own exposition is not novel, but has the support of able students of God's Word.

Dr. Gill, writing on Isaiah xi. 6, says : " This, and the three following verses, describe the peaceableness of Messiah's kingdom. . . . The wild and tame creatures shall agree together, and the former shall become the latter ; which is not to be understood literally of the savage creatures, as if they should lose their nature and be restored, as it is said, to their paradisiacal estate, which is supposed to be the time of the restitution of all things ; but figuratively of men comparable to wild creatures who, through the power of Divine grace accompanying the Word preached, shall become tame, mild, meek, and humble."

Again : in the latter part of this eleventh chapter the prophet plainly predicts that the Lord will gather the scattered seed of Jacob " from the four corners of the earth." What is the real nature and manner of this restoration of Israel ?

Calvin says, with respect to Isaiah xi. 14 : " The Jews, who dream of an earthly kingdom of Christ, interpret all this in a carnal sense, and apply it to I know not what external power ; but they ought rather to judge it according to the nature of Christ's kingdom. Partly, no doubt, the accomplishment of this prediction was seen when the Jews returned from captivity, and God brought them into moderate prosperity, contrary to the wish and in spite of the opposition of all the neighbouring nations ; but believers were led to expect a more splendid victory, which they at length obtained through the preaching of the Gospel."

Dr. Gill, treating of the same question, says : " Those of His people among the ten tribes that were scattered about in various countries, when the Gospel was preached throughout the world by the apostles, were called by it and gathered into gospel churches among the Gentiles, of whom the first churches of Christ consisted ; and so will it be in the latter day, when all Israel shall be saved." Jenour took a similar view of the restoration of the Jews : " It is difficult to imagine any reason why the Jews should continue to remain a separate people after they have become Christians." But he adds, with prudent reserve and modest respect for the opinions of others : " This, however, is one of those questions upon which so much reasonable argument may be urged on both sides, that the event alone can determine it."

The Lord help us now to throw some real light on

the glorious promises which He has made, and grant unto us and our readers an increasing knowledge of that blessed Saviour in whom they all centre. With this we shall be content, without assuming that we have fully entered into the mind of the Spirit of God in the prophecy before us.

" But though the tree of David's line be cut down to the ground, and become lowly as in the days of Jesse, yet out of its stock shall come forth a shoot, and out of its roots shall grow up a fruitful branch. One shall arise who shall be anointed with the Spirit of the Lord. He shall be filled by that Spirit with wisdom and understanding, with counsel and might, with the knowledge and fear of God ; and the fear of God shall make Him of quick understanding. He shall not judge as man judgeth, by the outward appearance ; neither shall He found His reproofs on the witness of man. With righteousness shall He execute judgment for the poor, and with equity shall He plead the cause of the meek. He shall smite the ungodly with His word as with a rod, and shall slay the wicked with the utterance of His lips. He shall be girded with righteousness for the service of God, girded with faithfulness for the salvation of His people."

Thus far we have an accurate description of the birth of Christ, and of His ministry on earth in the days of His flesh. Matthew, Mark, Luke, and John are the best commentators on the above prophecy, which nevertheless in some respects awaits a further fulfilment at the Redeemer's second appearing. (See 2 Thess. ii. 8.) And now follows what we believe to be in the first place an allegorical description of the blessed fruits of Christ's gospel ; though we judge by what Paul has said about the conversion of Israel to Christ that the day will come when it shall be fulfilled on a grander scale than hitherto.

"Wolf and lamb shall dwell together; leopard and kid shall lie down side by side; calf, young lion, and fatling shall be companions, and a little child shall lead them; cow and bear shall walk with one another in peace, and their young shall lie down together; the lion shall eat straw like the ox. (See Acts ix. 19–22, and 26–29.) The infant shall play with the asp, and the little child with the adder, unharmed. (Compare Mark xvi. 18.) Nothing shall in any wise hurt or destroy the citizens of My holy mountain: for the knowledge of the Lord shall fill the earth as the waters fill the ocean-bed. And He that shall rise from the lowly stock of Jesse shall be exalted as an ensign in the presence of all peoples, and all nations shall be gathered unto His name: the place of His feet shall be glorious.

"And in that day the Lord shall a second time stretch forth His hand to deliver the remnant of His people that shall be left; He shall recover them from Assyria, from Egypt, from Pathros, from Ethiopia, from Elam, from Babylon, from Syria, and from the lands beyond the sea. He shall set up a standard to gather the Gentiles, and shall bring together the seed of Jacob from all places whither they have been driven. The envy of Israel shall depart, and the wrath of Judah shall end. (See 2 Sam. xix. 40–43.) Israel shall no more envy Judah, nor Judah be wroth with Israel. They shall make common cause; they shall conquer their enemies on the west and on the east, and shall reduce them to obedience. (See Rom. xv. 18–21.) And the Lord shall utterly destroy the arm of the Egyptian sea, and shall dry up the Euphrates with the wind of His power, dividing it into seven streams so that men may cross it dryshod. Thus there shall be a highway from Assyria for the remnant of His people that shall be left, even as there was through the Red

Sea for the children of Israel when they came up out of Egypt."

Of the restoration of Israel here foretold we will not now venture to say more than has been said in the introduction to our present Half-Hour. But this is abundantly clear, that the true glory of that nation must consist in happy subjection to Him whom they have rejected and crucified ; and that in due season all obstacles will be removed by the power of their promise-performing God. And when through the mercy now shown to us Gentiles they also shall obtain mercy, then will they join with us in the song of triumph which we, by the grace of God, are already learning to sing, the song of Moses and the Lamb ; the song whose echoes reach us from the shore of the Red Sea (Ex. xv. 2), and in louder tones from the glassy sea like unto crystal that is before the throne (Rev. iv. 6 ; xv. 2–4).

" And in the day of My power My people shall say : ' I will praise Thee, O Lord, for Thou wast justly angry with me ; but Thine anger is past, and Thou comfortest me. Behold, God is my salvation ; I will not fear : for what can harm me ? The Lord is my strength ; I will make melody in my heart unto Him : for my spirit hath rejoiced in God my Saviour.'

" Thus shall ye draw water with joy out of the well-springs of salvation. And in that day ye shall say : ' Praise the Lord ; call upon His name : publish His salvation among the nations, and make known unto them the name that is above every name. Sing praises unto the Lord, for He hath triumphed gloriously : tell the glad tidings to every creature. Cry aloud, O Zion ; lift up thy voice, O Jerusalem ; for great is the Holy One of Israel, who is come to dwell in the midst of thee.' "

This prophecy doubtlessly points onward to times that are yet future, and is in part explained by the words

of Paul in Rom. xi.   But the glory of its past and present
fulfilment is exceeding great, as is shown by the pages
of the New Testament.   The Son of God is come, and
has brought life and immortality to light by His Gospel.
The glory of the law has been eclipsed by the glory that
excelleth.   Oh, reader, may God teach us to draw water
with joy, while it is called to-day, out of the wellsprings
of salvation !

TENTH HALF-HOUR

Introduction to Chapters XIII., XIV.

"IS not this great Babylon, that I have built for my royal capital, by the might of my power, and for the honour of my majesty?" So spake King Nebuchadnezzar as he walked on the roof of his lofty palace (Daniel iv. 29, *margin*), and surveyed the golden city which lay outstretched beneath him. More than a century had passed away since Isaiah had foretold its swiftly-approaching downfall and utter desolation, and meanwhile its wealth and power had been rapidly increasing. Probably the king had never seen or heard the prophet's prediction; but if he had, the words must have seemed to him like idle tales. How could he have credited them while beneath and around him he saw the world's proud capital, the imperial city which his own energy had so enlarged and beautified that he looked upon the whole as the work of his hands?

And what a work! Just as we can scan from the top of St. Paul's the boundless panorama of our own great London, so could the king contemplate from the dizzy height of his palace roof the walls, the gates, the quays, the streets, and the buildings, the luxurious parks, and the crowded markets of that city which was the pride of the Chaldeans, the wonder and terror of the world.

At a distance of seven miles, more or less, to north, south, east, and west, his eye could trace the long double line of walls which none could scale or overthrow. Like cliffs they rose above the surrounding country to the height of the ball upon St. Paul's Cathedral; their top was a broad road half as wide again as London Bridge ; and one side of the square which they formed would have stretched from that bridge far beyond the town of Croydon, the entire circuit being fifty-six miles. Two hundred and fifty strong towers rose at intervals from these battlements, and a hundred gates of massive brass pierced the walls below to give ingress or egress to busy merchant caravans, or victorious infantry and cavalry. Similar walls skirted the Euphrates, which rolled its waves through the midst of the city, and similar gates opened on the quays which ran along both sides of the river. Within the vast area thus enclosed stood palaces and temples whose bricks were stamped with the great king's name, and whose sculptured slabs told of his achievements. One inscription, found at Babylon about fifty years ago, has been thus translated : " I, Nebuchadnezzar, King of Babylon, the mighty Lord, the elect of Merodach, the Supreme Ruler, the adorer of Nebo, the Vicar-King, who judges without injustice, the Minister of the Gods, the eldest son of Nabopolassar. He has created me, the God who begat me ; He has entrusted to me the dominion over the legions of men. I have changed inaccessible heights into roads for chariots. I have amassed to my city of Babylon silver, and gold, and precious stones, and timber of all kinds, the minerals of the hills, and the jewels of the seas, an infinite treasure ; and I have brought thither the greatest trees from the summits of Lebanon. I have covered with pure gold the beams of high cypresses for the carpenter's work of the sanctuary of the temples, and I have constructed the tower of Borsippa with gold, silver, and other metals, and stones, and glazed bricks, and lentisk, and cedar."

Let us again stand by the king on his tower of observation. His eye can trace the lines of broad streets which cross the city and intersect one another at right angles, can observe the motley throng of men from various nations hurrying along to the crowded markets, and can rest with satisfaction on legions of disciplined soldiers gathered from all parts of his vast empire to defend his capital or to extend his dominions. Who can compare with him for royal majesty and absolute power ? What hand can resist his will ? What arm can reach him to smite or to control ? Well may the thought arise in his heart, and find utterance at his mouth : " Is not this great Babylon that I have built ? "

But lo ! God, according to His word by Isaiah, raises up the Medes against the devoted city, the Medes who regard not silver nor delight in gold. Their bows dash the young men to pieces, and their eye spares not the children. And Babylon, the glory of kingdoms, the beauty of the Chaldees' excellency, becomes as when God overthrew Sodom and Gomorrah. It lies without inhabitant from generation to generation. There the Arab pitcheth not his tent, the shepherds make not their fold. The wild beasts of the desert lie there, night-owls screech on the shattered walls, and jackals prowl in the ruined palaces.

So complete was the destruction of this accursed city that for ages its very site was uncertain. Only in the nineteenth century were its ruins unearthed, and its exact position determined. Bricks have been found inscribed with the name of Nebuchadnezzar, sad memorials of his vain dream of universal sovereignty.

We will conclude this brief sketch of Babylon's glory and destruction with two quotations from " The Treasury of Bible Knowledge," a useful little book written by the Rev. John Ayre, M.A., and published in 1866 :—

" On the fall of Nineveh, Babylon became the great Asiatic power, the head of the countries over which Assyria had reigned. In this period of prosperity

Babylon was proud and luxurious ; but at length the Persian invasion came, and then the great city began to sink into the ruin from which she never emerged. The defences, after Cyrus's conquest, were dilapidated and neglected. It is true that Babylon was still one of the capitals of the new monarchy, and the Persians made it a place of royal residence. But it revolted, and was subdued again and again. Each conquest lowered it, and the process of decay went on till, when Alexander the Great desired to restore it to splendour, the task was found almost hopeless. All such plans, however, were frustrated by Alexander's death, and it ceased to be a metropolis. The Seleucidæ (the Syrian kings who succeeded to this part of Alexander's dominions) made Antioch their capital. Moreover, a new city, Seleucia, was founded near Babylon ; and for it, and for various other towns from time to time rising in its vicinity, Babylon furnished materials, till its inhabitants perished from it, and its most magnificent structures became unsightly heaps."

" On the banks of the Euphrates, about forty miles south-west of Baghdad, lies the town of Hillah. This town is in almost all directions surrounded by immense ruins, appearing the work of nature rather than of men, shapeless heaps of rubbish, lofty banks of ancient canals, fragments of glass, marble, pottery, and bricks, mingled with a nitrous soil which impedes all vegetation, and renders the neighbourhood a naked and hideous waste, re-echoing only the dismal sounds of the owl and the jackal, of the hyæna and the lawless robber. These piles mark the area once occupied by the mistress of the world."

If our readers now turn to Isaiah xiii. and xiv., we believe they will find that this little sketch throws much light on the prophet's words, and that they will await with interest the exposition which we shall endeavour to give in our next Half-Hour.

Chapters XIII. 1—XIV. 27.

THE best preventive of error is the knowledge of truth. Being convinced of this, we make it our constant aim in these expositions to give our readers, in as few words as possible, the literal and primary sense of Scripture. While we would carefully shun a false literalism which extracts error out of figurative statements, we would shun with equal care all spiritualization, however ingenious, which robs the Word of God of its true force and beauty. There is danger on both sides, and we can only hope to avoid it by using the best sources of information which the Lord puts within our reach, and relying continually on the guidance and keeping of the Holy Spirit.

The present Half-Hour needs no further introduction than that which was given in the last; but we advise all who wish to understand this portion of Isaiah to read that introduction again very attentively, in order that they may have some clear knowledge of the greatness of the city which God used as a rod to chasten His own people, and of the greatness of the ruin into which He righteously plunged it when that purpose had been accomplished.

" The judgment of Babylon, a prophecy revealed to Isaiah the son of Amoz.

" Set up a standard on the bare mountains of yonder land [Media] ; summon its hosts with loud voice, beckon them with the hand, that they may march into the gates of the tyrant city. I the Lord have bidden them as the appointed servants of My will ; yea, I have called

them as My warriors to execute Mine anger, and they
shall do My pleasure with gladness and pride. Hearken!
A sound upon the mountains as of the armies of a great
nation ; a tumultuous sound as of the kingdoms of the
heathen gathering together! The host prepareth for
battle, and the Lord of hosts is He that mustereth it.
They come, the Lord and the weapons of His wrath,
from a far country, from beneath the end of heaven,
to destroy the wide world of the land of Shinar. Howl,
all ye that dwell therein : for the day of the Lord's
judgment is near ; it shall come upon you as a destruction from Shaddai, a destruction from Him who is able
to destroy. He Himself shall cause that every man's
hands shall fail, and every man's heart faint. They
shall be filled with fear ; for anguish and sorrow shall
come upon them as travail upon a woman with child.
They shall look one at another with amazement, and
their faces shall flush with the flame of terror. Behold,
the day of the Lord's judgment upon Babel cometh, a
day terrible with wrath and with fierce anger ; it shall
make the land a desolation, and shall destroy the wicked
from off the face of it. The stars of heaven shall be
hidden, and the constellations shall withhold their light ;
neither the sun by day nor the moon by night shall shine
upon the land of the Chaldeans ; [all shall be gloom
and confusion there]. And I the Lord will punish their
world-wide empire for its evil, and the wicked who dwell
therein for their iniquity. I will put an end to the
arrogance of the proud, and will lay low the haughtiness of the terrible. I will cause that mortal men
shall be more rare in the land than fine gold, and the
sons of men more scarce than the gold of Ophir ; [for
I will cut them off and make them few]. The heavens
shall tremble at My rebuke, and the earth shall be
shaken as by an earthquake ; because the wrath of the
Lord of hosts is poured out, and the day of His anger

is come. And it shall be that their hired armies shall return, every man to his own people, and shall flee, every man to his own land, as a chased roe or a lost sheep. Every one that is found in the city shall be thrust through, and all that are joined unto them shall fall by the sword. Their fierce conquerors shall dash their babes in pieces before their eyes, plunder their houses, and violate their wives. Behold, I the Lord will stir up the Medes against them, an enemy whose cruel hand will accept no bribe of silver nor ransom of gold. With their bows they shall murder the young men ; they shall have no pity for the pregnant, no compassion for the children.

" And Babylon, the glory of kingdoms and the pride of Chaldea, shall become as Sodom and Gomorrah which God overthrew. It shall never more be inhabited, neither shall any man dwell therein from generation to generation. There the Arab shall not pitch his tent, nor the shepherd fold his flock. The wild beast of the desert shall lie there, and their houses shall be filled with doleful creatures ; there shall the ostrich dwell and the he-goat dance. The wolf shall howl in their desolate castles, and the jackal in their palaces of pleasure.

" The time of Babel's end cometh quickly, and her days shall not be prolonged, for the Lord will judge her that He may have mercy on captive Jacob, may again own Israel as the people of ·His choice, and may restore them to their own land. (For fulfilment, see Ezra i. 1–5.) Strangers also shall go with the house of Jacob, and shall cleave to them. Yea, the heathen shall take them, and shall bring them to their place, and shall serve them as servants and handmaids in the land which the Lord hath given them ; for Israel shall take their captors captive, and shall rule over their oppressors."

This promise was so clearly and remarkably fulfilled in the days of Cyrus, Ezra, and Nehemiah, that we do not feel at liberty to draw from it any certain conclusions as to God's future dealings with His ancient people.   Time will unfold His purposes with regard to them, and explain the true meaning of those parts of prophecy which really remain unfulfilled in their history.

We now come to a song of triumph which was to be sung by Israel after the overthrow of the Babylonian oppressor.   The forests of the earth rejoice that the great hewer of wood is fallen ; the shades of departed kings mock him as he joins their ranks ; passers-by marvel to see his unburied carcase lying in the open field ; his children are given to the sword ; his city is swept with the besom of destruction.

" And it shall come to pass, when the Lord shall have given thee rest, O Israel, delivering thee from thy sorrow, thy fear, and the hard bondage of thy slavery, that thou shalt take up thy parable against the king of Babylon and mock him, saying, How art thou fallen, O tyrant ! How art thou fallen, O city of gold !   The Lord hath broken your staff, ye wicked ; hath broken your sceptre, ye rulers ; the staff that smote the peoples in wrath with blows that ceased not ; the sceptre that ruled the nations in anger with an oppression that none checked. But now the whole earth rests and is quiet ; its inhabitants break forth into singing.   The fir trees and the cedars of Lebanon rejoice at thy fall, and say, Now that thou art brought low none cometh to hew us down. The chambers of the grave are moved at the sound of thy coming, and they that dwell therein rise up to meet thee.   The departed chiefs of earth are stirred up, and the kings of the nations rise from their ghostly thrones ; they all greet thee, saying, ' Art thou also become weak as we ?   Art thou become like unto us ? '

" Thy pomp sinketh into the grave, and the music of

thy stringed instruments ceaseth. Corruption is thy couch, the worms thy coverlet. How art thou fallen from heaven, bright son of the dawn! How art thou cut down to the ground, who didst crush the nations! Thou saidst in thine heart, I will mount up to heaven; I will raise my throne above the stars of God. I will sit above the mount of the congregation that is in the uttermost regions of the north. [This may refer to a superstition of the Babylonians as to the abode of their gods.] I will be higher than the clouds; I will be like unto the Most High. Yet thou shalt be brought down to the grave, to the depths of the pit. They that pass by shall look carefully upon thee, shall consider thee, and shall say, Is this the man that made the earth to tremble and shook its kingdoms? that made the world a wilderness and overthrew its cities? that held his prisoners fast, so that they returned not to their homes? The kings of the nations have honourable burial; they rest, all of them, each in his own tomb; but thou art cast out far from thy sepulchre as a branch that is abhorred; thou art girt about with a heap of slain that are thrust through and cast into a pit of stones; thou art as a carcase trodden under foot. Thou shalt not have a king's burial, for thy violence hath destroyed thy land and slain thy people. Thy seed is a seed of evildoers, and the name thereof shall perish for ever. Let slaughter be prepared for thy children because of the iniquity of their fathers [which they inherit and perpetuate]; let them not rise up to possess the earth and to fill the face of the world with cities. Yea, I will rise up against them, saith the Lord of hosts, and will cut off from Babel name and remnant, son and grandson. I the Lord will give it for a possession to the bittern, and will make it a watery marsh. I will sweep it with the besom of destruction, saith the Lord of hosts."

When Isaiah uttered the above prophecy, Babylon had not yet overthrown the Assyrian empire, on the ruins of which she was to rise to greatness until her own turn came to be destroyed. The prophet, therefore, turns next to Assyria (verses 24–27), whose power was felt and feared in his own days, and foretells a crushing blow to be inflicted upon its armies in the land of the Lord, upon the mountains of Israel. This was speedily fulfilled in the overthrow of Sennacherib's power by the destroying angel. The fulfilment must have served as a seal on the certainty of the sentence of destruction already passed upon Babylon, though the execution of this was delayed for a hundred years or more. Let us remember in our day that past fulfilments of God's threats and promises are pledges of His future faithfulness. He who said that Babylon and Nineveh should fall has said that He will one day judge the world in righteousness by that Man whom He hath ordained : and He who promised deliverance to Israel, has promised rest to the weary who come unto Him.

"I have sworn, saith the Lord of hosts, that the thoughts of My heart shall come to pass, and that the purpose of My will shall be accomplished. The Assyrian invadeth My land ; there will I break his power : he ascendeth My mountains ; there will I tread him down. Then shall his yoke be removed from the neck of My people, and his burden from their shoulder. I have purposed to destroy My foes from off the whole earth ; I have stretched out My hand against them among all nations. And when the Lord of hosts hath purposed, who shall bring it to nought ? When His hand is stretched out, who shall turn it back ? "

The fate of Babylon, written by the finger of God in the days of her prosperity, has since been written by the pen of history. The two records are one, for their Author is one.

Chapter XIV. 28–32.

ISAIAH was commissioned, as we have seen (xiv. 26, 27), to reveal the purpose that was purposed by the Lord of hosts concerning the whole earth, and the stretching out of His almighty hand upon all the nations, the purpose that none could disannul, the hand that none could turn back. Accordingly he foretells first the desolation of the golden city, the exactress of gold (Isa. xiv. 4, *margin*), which he knew as Babel, and which we have learned from the Greeks to call Babylon ; and then the previous destruction of the rival city Nineveh, the centre and strength of the Assyrian empire. He next proceeds to speak of the judgments which are to be poured out on other enemies of God, and of His people : Palestina (that is, Philistia), Moab, Syria, Ethiopia, Egypt, Arabia, Tyre, and Edom must each and all, after having served the divine purpose in the government of the world, be brought low and pass away into obscurity or utter destruction. Truly God set His servants the prophets over the nations and over the kingdoms, to root out, and to pull down, to destroy, and to throw down, to build, and to plant ! (Jer. i. 10).

From the days of Shamgar, the son of Anath (Judges iii. 31), the judge " which slew of the Philistines six hundred men with an ox goad," Philistia was a scourge to Israel. Samson was raised up to fight against them at a time when they had dominion over Israel (Judges xiv. 4), and after many a bloody struggle with them slew more of them at his death than in his life. Saul was continually at war with them, and often with little success; for we read that at one period during his reign, "there was no smith found throughout all the land of Israel; for the Philistines said, Lest the Hebrews make them swords or spears; but all the Israelites went down to the Philistines, to sharpen every man his share, and his coulter, and his axe, and his mattock. . . . So it came to pass in the day of battle, that there was neither sword nor spear found in the hand of any of the people that were with Saul and Jonathan." When David became king over all Israel, the Philistines twice came up against him, and twice were subdued before him, by the guidance and favour of God (2 Sam. v. 17–25). Further victories were gained over them by Jehoshaphat and Uzziah; but in the days of Ahaz they were again used by the Lord to scourge Judah for iniquity. We read in 2 Chron. xxviii. 18, 19: "The Philistines also had invaded the cities of the low country, and of the south of Judah, and had taken Beth-shemesh," and other towns and villages, and dwelt there; "for the Lord brought Judah low because of Ahaz, king of Israel; for he made Judah naked, and transgressed against the Lord."

In the year when this king died, Isaiah delivered the prophecy which we are now to consider, wherein he threatens the Philistines with greater reverses than they had yet endured. Shortly afterwards Hezekiah, the son and successor of Ahaz, gained a decisive victory over them: "He smote the Philistines, even unto Gaza, and the borders thereof, from the tower of the watchmen to the fenced city." Some commentators have concluded from this that Uzziah is the "serpent" referred to in verse 29, and his great-grandson Hezekiah the "cockatrice," the "fiery flying serpent," that was to carry on the work of destruction. For our own part, we shrink from the thought that so good a man as Hezekiah is spoken of under the figure of a poisonous reptile ; and we lean to the opinion that the power of Assyria is here intended. Perhaps the death of the Assyrian monarch, Tiglath Pileser, had caused rejoicing in " whole Palestina "—that is, throughout the land of the Philistines ; and Isaiah checks it by telling them that his successors, Sargon and Sennacherib, will be more hurtful still, as an adder or a viper is more hurtful than an ordinary serpent.

" The word of the Lord against Philistia, a prophecy uttered in the year in which King Ahaz died.

" Thou art wholly given up to rejoicing, O Philistia, because the rod that smote thee is broken. Rejoice not : for out of the serpent that hath bitten thee shall spring one that shall smite thee as with the fangs of an adder, and slay thee as with the poison of a viper. Then the heirs of poverty [whom thou hast oppressed] shall feed undisturbed in the pastures of Judah, and the needy shall lie down therein in safety ; [for thou shalt distress them no more]. I will destroy thy power by famine, and slay the remnant of thy people with the sword. Let the gates of thy fortresses lament, and let thy cities cry out for fear ; for thou shalt be wholly given to destruction, O Philistia. Lo, the smoking flame of war cometh from the north, an army of warriors, of whom none faileth to appear at the appointed time.

" What tidings shall we then send to the nations ? That our enemies are fallen because the Lord hath established Zion on the foundation of His covenant, and ordained her to be a refuge for the afflicted of His people."

We have no historic record of the fulfilment of this prophecy ; but it was probably very soon fulfilled in part, though we learn from Jeremiah xlvii. that a similar judgment was still hanging over Philistia in his day. All oppressors of God's people are haters of God, and must needs perish in the end.

THIRTEENTH HALF-HOUR

Chapters XV., XVI.

THE general drift of this prophecy against Moab is perfectly clear to us, and we hope that we shall make it equally clear to our readers. But the details of the prophecy suggest many questions which it is impossible for us to answer with certainty. For instance, is Bajith (or rather Bayith, *i.e.*, House) a Moabitish city, or simply the temple of Chemosh? Is the "heifer of three years old" (xv. 5) an animal whose furious bellowing is taken as an image of the despairing howls of smitten Moab, or is it to be translated "Third-Heifer," and taken as the name of a town that lay in the path of the fugitives? Is Dimon (ver. 9) the name of a city not elsewhere mentioned, or is it the name of Dibon, altered to suggest the thought of blood as "dama" does in Aceldama? Again, in chap. xvi., is Sela (Rock) the rocky capital of Edom to which the Moabite exiles have fled, or is it some rocky fastness in the land of Moab? To whom is addressed the exhortation, "Take counsel, execute judgment," in ver. 3, and who are the outcasts that are to be received and sheltered? Are they Israelites fleeing from Sennacherib's army to find safety in the land of Moab, or Moabites fleeing from that army to find protection in Judah? We might extend this list of difficulties, but not profitably for our readers. We have frankly stated so many of them to arouse interest, and to show the real nature of our task of exposition. It is probable that most of these questions would be easily answered if we were as well acquainted as Isaiah was with the land of Moab and the circumstances of the times.

A few words about Moab. The origin of the nation was evil (Gen. xix. 36, 37), and the whole course of its history was marked with wickedness. Its hostility to Israel was almost unceasing. The vain attempt of Balak to lay a curse upon the chosen people, and his more successful efforts to lead them into sin; and Eglon's iron-handed oppression, brought to a close by the left hand of Ehud after a period of eighteen years: these are but two chapters in the history of this undying feud. Moab was among the enemies whom Saul subdued (1 Sam. xiv. 47, 48). David also prevailed against them, and brought them under tribute (2 Sam. viii. 2); and we find them still paying tribute to Ahab, king of Israel, but refusing it to his son Jehoram (2 Kings iii. 4, 5).

We need not trace the history of Moab further; but we will quote at full length the passage last referred to, that we may remind our readers of the singular confirmation it has received in our own days: "And Mesha, king of Moab, was a sheep-master, and rendered unto the king of Israel an hundred thousand lambs, and an hundred thousand rams, with the wool. But it came to pass, when Ahab was dead, that the king of Moab rebelled against the king of Israel." For many centuries this was the only known record of Mesha's name. But in the year 1868 there was found at Dibon, in the land of Moab, a stone which was a monument, or formed part of a monument, erected by this king to his god Chemosh, and which is now raised from the grave of twenty-seven centuries to bear witness to the historic truth of God's Word. A full account of this "Moabite Stone" cannot be given here. Before us, as we write, lies a photograph of it, with its ancient inscription written in language easily translated by one acquainted with Biblical Hebrew. A few of its boastful words shall close this introduction to the inspired prophecy of Moab's overthrow.

" I, Mesha, am son of Chemosh-Gad, king of Moab, the Dibonite. My father reigned over Moab thirty years, and I reigned after my father. And I raised this stone to Chemosh, at Korcha, as a monument of deliverance. For he delivered me from all invaders, and let me see my desire upon all my enemies."

Nay, King Mesha! The salvation of Chemosh is a vain thing. He and his people must perish together ; for the mouth of Jehovah hath spoken it.

" The word of the Lord against Moab. Verily in the night shall the town of Ar be ravaged and destroyed ; verily in the night shall the town of Kir be ravaged and destroyed. Moab shall go up to his temple, and they of Dibon to their high places, that they may weep before their god. The men of Moab shall wail at Nebo and at Medeba ; they shall mourn with shaven heads and shorn beards, shall gird themselves with sackcloth in the streets of their cities, shall lament with streaming tears on their housetops and in their squares. The men of Heshbon and of Elealeh shall wail, and the sound of their cry shall be heard afar, even unto Jahaz. Yea, the warriors shall cry out for fear, and the soul of Moab shall tremble within him. My heart also is pained for Moab, for his fugitives flee far away to Zoar and to Third-Heifer ; they ascend the hill of Luhith, weeping as they go ; they flee with cries of terror along the road to Horonaim. Nimrim, with its well-watered fields, shall be smitten with drought, its grass shall wither, and its herbage shall fail ; every green thing shall disappear. Its inhabitants shall flee with the wealth that they have gotten, and the treasures that they have stored up, that they may hide them from the spoiler among the willows of the valley. For the cry of fear shall fill the land of Moab, and shall extend from Eglaim even unto Beer-elim. Dibon shall be Dimon [it shall be an Akel-Dama], its rivers shall be red with the blood of the slain. For I will bring upon it trouble after trouble ; lions shall destroy the fugitives of Moab, even all that are left in the land.

" Send your tribute of lambs, O Moab, to the king of Judah, as in the days of old ; yea, send them through the wilderness from your rocky fastness to the city of Zion. [Ye will need the help of Judah], for your exiled daughters shall flock to the fords of Arnon on your frontier as frightened birds, as fledgelings driven from their nests. And do thou, O Judah, deal prudently and justly with thy ruined foes. Hide them as in midnight shade from the light of day ; shelter the exiles and betray them not. Let the outcasts of Moab find a refuge with thee, and deliver them from their spoilers ; for I have destroyed thine oppressors ; I have caused their violence to cease ; I have consumed them out of thy land (see 2 Kings xix. 35, 36). The throne of David shall be established in mercy, and in his tabernacle a king shall reign in truth, a judge who shall be diligent to do justice and swift to execute righteousness. [Hezekiah ? or Christ ? Both.]

" We have heard of Moab's pride ; he is exceeding proud. We have heard of his arrogance, his pride, his wrathfulness, and his vain boastings. Therefore shall destruction come upon him, and the whole land shall be filled with wailing. Over the ruined vineyards of Kir-hareseth ye shall mourn in utter despair. For lo, the fields of Heshbon and the vineyards of Sibmah languish. The princes of the enemy have broken down the choice vines thereof, whose branches stretched even unto Jazer, strayed into the wilderness, spread themselves abroad, and reached beyond the sea. (The vines of Sibmah seem to be used here as a figure of the prosperity of Moab. Compare Psa. lxxx. 8–16.) There-fore, as I wept for Jazer, so will I weep for the vine of Sibmah ; my tears shall flow as a fountain for Heshbon and Elealeh ; for the shout of the spoiler falls upon vintage and harvest. Gladness is perished from the land, and joy from its fruitful fields. In the vineyards the grape-gatherers sing not, nor rejoice ; in the wine-presses are no treaders to tread out the wine ; the Lord hath caused their vintage-cry to cease. Therefore my heart-strings sound for Moab as the strings of a mourner's harp, and my bowels for Kir-hareseth. For it shall be, when Moab shall appear before Chemosh, and shall weary himself with visits to the temple of his god, and shall go thither to pray continually, that his prayer shall avail him nothing.

" Thus hath the Lord spoken concerning Moab long ago. But now, thus saith the Lord : Within three measured years the pride of Moab shall be brought low, with all the multitude of his people ; and the remnant of them shall be few and small."

We know not how this prophecy was accomplished, but it is probable that the armies of Assyria were the agents employed by Jehovah to execute justice on the people of Chemosh.

Chapters XVII., XVIII.

WE shall better understand the seventeenth chapter of Isaiah if we recall the events referred to in the seventh chapter. We are there told that in the days of Ahaz, king of Judah, two enemies went up against Jerusalem to make war upon it, namely, Rezin, king of Syria, and Pekah, king of Israel. Their intention was to put an end to the dynasty of the house of David, and to set a stranger on the throne of Judah. To allay the terror caused by this invasion, Isaiah then foretold that it would come to nothing, and that in a short time both the confederate kings would be cut off by the armies of Assyria.

To the same purport is the prophecy now before us. Damascus, the capital of Syria, is to be made a ruinous heap, and Israel is to be brought so low that only a remnant shall survive the harvest of destruction, a remnant small and few, like the gleanings of an olive orchard. This remnant, taught in the school of affliction, shall learn to trust only in their Maker, their idols lying around them in heaps of destruction in the day of grief and desperate sorrow.

This chastisement shall be wrought by Assyria; yet woe to the rushing hosts of that mighty empire! For the time shall quickly come when the Lord shall drive them away as chaff before the wind, as thistledown before the whirlwind. Sennacherib's host shall perish in a night, and Judah shall say in the morning:

" The might of the Gentile, unsmote by the sword,
Hath melted like snow in the glance of the Lord."

We write for the unlearned, even for such as can scarcely

distinguish between Syria and Assyria. Let us point out to them that the two are quite distinct from one another, though their English names are similar. Syria, known to the Hebrews as Aram, lay immediately to the north of the kingdom of the ten tribes, and had Damascus for its capital, as Isaiah tells us (Isa. vii. 8). Assyria (Asshur) was far away to the north-east, beyond the great river Euphrates, and had for its capital "the bloody city" of Nineveh (Nahum iii. 1).

"A prophecy of judgment on Syria.

"Behold, Damascus shall cease to be a city; it shall become a heap of ruins. The cities of Aroer [perhaps a district of Syria] shall be abandoned; they shall become a wilderness where flocks shall lie undisturbed. Moreover, the fortresses of Israel shall be destroyed, and the kingdom of Damascus shall perish. The remnant of Syria and the pride of Israel shall alike pass away, saith the Lord of hosts. In that day the pride of Israel shall be consumed, and his flesh shall waste away. They shall be cut down by the sword like the standing corn which the reaper gathereth with his arm and cutteth with his sickle; yea, they shall be cut down in the land of Israel as the crops are cut down in the fruitful valleys of Judah. Yet a remnant shall be left unto Israel, a gleaning, even as, when an olive tree has been shaken, two or three berries are left in the topmost boughs, four or five at the ends of the fruitful branches, saith the Lord God of Israel. Then shall they no longer look to the altars of their own invention, to the gods which their own fingers have fashioned, their idols of wood and their images of the sun-god. In that day the strong cities of Israel shall be deserted, even as the strongholds in the forests and mountains of Canaan were abandoned before Joshua and the armies of Israel; the land shall again be a desolation. For thou hast forgotten, O Israel, the God of thy salvation, and hast not remembered the rock of thy strength ; therefore thou hast planted thy land with the pleasant plants of idolatry, and hast set it with the strange slips of false gods. In the day when thou plantedst them thou didst hedge them in with care, and thou wast diligent to make thy seed to grow ; but the harvest shall be a heap of ruin in the day of grief and of desperate sorrow."

These threatenings against Syria and Israel were fulfilled in the invasion of those countries by Assyria (see 2 Kings xvi. 9 ; xvii. 4, 5, 6). But when Assyria under Sennacherib should dare to attempt the destruction of Zion, her armies were to perish at the rebuke of Zion's God. Of this the prophet next speaks.

"Ah, I hear the noise of many peoples, which roar as the sea roareth ; the rushing of many nations, which rush as the rushing of mighty waters. Yea, the nations shall rush against Jerusalem as the rushing of mighty waters ; but God shall rebuke them, and they shall flee away. The breath of His wrath shall chase them as the wind chaseth the chaff upon the mountains, as the blast of the storm chaseth the thistledown. At eventide their might shall be terrible ; but before the morning breaks they shall be no more. Such is the portion of them that would make us their prey, the lot of them that seek to plunder us."

The next chapter (xviii.) is much more difficult to explain. When a great interpreter like Calvin says plainly, " I cannot determine what is the nation of which Isaiah speaks," we may be sure that we have no easy passage before us. Our own view is that the land which is said to lie " beyond the rivers of Ethiopia " is Ethiopia itself, which is referred to in this way because it stretched far southwards beyond the regions watered by the Nile and its tributaries. Then we have to face the question what nation is intended in verses 2 and 7, " scattered, and peeled, and terrible from its beginning."

Calvin considers that it is the Israelitish nation, so often overrun and plundered by hostile armies that its very history was a terror to men, according to that word of Moses (Deut. xxviii. 37), " And thou shalt become an astonishment, a proverb, and a byword among all nations whither the Lord shall lead thee." On the other hand, Dr. Gill and other able expositors consider that the nation referred to in these verses is the same as that mentioned in verse 1, namely, Ethiopia. These interpreters substitute " drawn out and polished "—that is, tall and comely—instead of " scattered and peeled," and take the words as an allusion to the height and stateliness of the Ethiopian warriors : and we have come to the conclusion that this is, on the whole, the simplest and best explanation, though the other has the support of Calvin's great name.

It may not be out of place to insert here a tribute to his honour which comes to us across the Atlantic. A learned American expositor, Professor Alexander, of New Jersey, writing some sixty years ago, said : "Calvin still towers above all interpreters in large commanding views of revelation, with extraordinary insight into the logical relations of a passage, even where its individual expressions were not fully understood. This quality, together with his fixed belief of fundamental doctrines, his eminent soundness of judgment, and his freedom from all tendency to paradox, pedantic affectation, or fanciful conceit, place him more completely on a level with the very best interpreters of our day than almost any intervening writer."

" Hearken, O land that spreadest out thy rustling wings [thy noisy armies], O land of Ethiopia that stretchest out beyond thy rivers ; thou that sendest thy ambassadors by the Nile, navigating its waters in vessels of papyrus [pliant boats able to shoot the cataracts]. Go, ye swift messengers [who are come

even unto Judah], return to your own land, to your
nation of warriors tall and stately, a people terrible in
war from their rise until now, a nation that measureth
out the land of its foes and treadeth it down, a nation
whose territory is traversed by mighty rivers. [Tell
your countrymen what the Lord hath done for Zion.]
Yea, all ye inhabitants of the world, all that dwell on
earth, behold the ensign of deliverance that is lifted up
upon our mountains, and hearken to the trumpet of
victory that is blown there. [For the standard of the
Lord is lifted up against the Assyrians, and His voice as
a trumpet heralds their overthrow.] For thus hath the
Lord said unto me : I will be still [while Assyria plans
her conquest] ; I will look on from My dwelling-place
[while she prepares for her vintage of triumph]. Her
plans shall seem to thrive as herbs in the heat of the
summer sun, as the grape harvest beneath the dewy
cloud in the hot days before the vintage. But before
the harvest of her vines, when the blossom of her
schemes is past, and the flower thereof is become a
ripening grape, the sprigs shall be cut off with pruning
hooks, and the branches shall be lopped. [For fulfilment see 2 Kings xix. 35.] And the lopped boughs [the
corpses of Sennacherib's army] shall be left together
unto the carrrion birds and the beasts of prey ; the
carrion birds shall feast on them through the summer,
and the beasts of prey through the winter. Then shall
the people of Ethiopia bring presents unto the Lord of
hosts, to the place where His name is known, to Mount
Zion."

Ethiopia soon stretched out her hands unto God
(Psa. lxviii. 31), and many brought gifts unto the Lord
of hosts to Jerusalem, and presents to Hezekiah, king
of Judah (2 Chron. xxxii. 23) ; and in the latter days of
the gospel there was found in her land of mighty rivers
a living church of Christ (Acts viii. 27 and 39).

Chapters XIX., XX.

IN the days when Isaiah lived and preached there were some who, like the good King Hezekiah, looked to the God of Israel for deliverance from the conquering armies of Assyria. But in those days, as in the days of Paul, and as in our own times, that saying was true, " All men have not faith." Unbelief, fostered by idolatry, was ever leading the men of Judah to look to Egypt for help, instead of looking to the Lord. To check this sin and folly, Isaiah now tells his countrymen that God is about to visit Egypt with His just judgments. The great Judge who maketh the clouds His chariot is about to come into that dark land, to overthrow its idols, to afflict it with civil war, to bring to nought its boasted wisdom, and to give it up to the oppressive tyranny of cruel lords and fierce kings. Yet, after all this desolation and destruction, the mercy of God was to be shown even to Egypt. The Egyptians were to cry unto the Lord for deliverance, and to obtain it. They were to come to the knowledge of the living God, and to worship Him in spirit and in truth. They were to meet their old enemy, Assyria, on the highway of the gospel (compare Isaiah xix. 23 and xxxv. 8), linked together in love by the instrumentality of that Israel whom they formerly oppressed ; and these three nations were to be a blessing to the whole earth.

Some of the prophet's language is highly figurative ; and, as we have more than once pointed out, it is of the utmost importance that we should not put a literal construction on such sayings. For instance, when we

read that the Lord shall come into Egypt riding on a
swift cloud, we must not, of course, suppose that God
would be seen in bodily form seated on a cloud, and
coming into the land to destroy its idols. We must take
this saying in the same sense in which we take the
psalmist's words when he tells us that God maketh the
clouds His chariot, and walketh upon the wings of the
wind (Psa. civ. 3). We are quite aware of the evil of a
false and fanciful " spiritualization " of the Word of
God, but we see also that errors of judgment and
delusive expectations arise from the opposite evil of
taking literally language which was intended to be
figurative. Our own judgment in these questions is but
feeble, and we are prone to err. It is therefore a relief
to us to refer our readers once again to the acute and
enlightened judgment of Calvin. It is our conviction
that some, who contend in our day for the literal interpretation of certain expressions of Scripture, are quite
wrong in their assumption that they have more light than
the reformers. Would to God that they had as much !

Calvin says, with respect to the altar that was to be
set up in Egypt (xix. 19) : " The prophet employs the
word *altar* to denote as a sign the worship of God, for
sacrifices and offerings were the outward acts of piety.
. . . Josephus relates that Onias [a Jewish high priest
who fled into Egypt and built a temple there, about
160 years before Christ] brought forward this passage,
alleging that what the prophet had foretold ought to be
accomplished. This wicked and ambitious priest persuaded the king of Egypt to do this, though it was
openly opposed by the Jews. . . . But Isaiah simply
describes the pure worship of God under the figure of
signs which were then in use ; for he had his eye upon
his own age, and the men with whom he had to do. . . .
We ought carefully to observe such forms of expression,
which are frequently employed by the prophets."

Again, with respect to the sacrifice and oblation mentioned in verse 21, Calvin justly says : " This passage must be explained in the same manner as the former, in which he mentioned an altar. What would have been the use of sacrifices after the manifestation of Christ ? He therefore describes metaphorically that confession of faith and calling upon God which followed the preaching of the gospel. . . . We must attend to the difference between the Old and New Testaments, and under the shadows of ceremonies we must understand to be meant the reasonable worship of which Paul speaks."

" The burden of the word of the Lord against Egypt.

" Behold, the Lord rideth upon the storm, and cometh into Egypt. The idols of Egypt shall fall before Him, and the heart of the nation shall quail for fear. Thus saith the Lord, I will send civil discord into the land ; brother shall fight against brother, friend against friend, city against city, province against province. [Egypt was afterwards divided into twelve rival kingdoms.] The understanding of Egypt shall fail, and its counsel shall come to nought. In their perplexity they shall seek direction from their idols, their sorcerers, their spirit-consulters, and their wizards ; [but they shall seek unto them in vain.] For I will give them over into the hands of cruel tyrants, and fierce kings shall oppress them. [Assyrian, Persian, Greek, Roman, Turk.] The waters of the Nile shall fail, and its stream shall sink and become dry. [An expressive symbol of utter ruin, in a land which depended on the Nile for its harvests.] The meadows by the Nile, the reeds that line its banks, and all that is sown round about it, shall be dried up, driven away, and destroyed. The fishers shall mourn the ruin of their source of wealth, they that angle in the river shall lament, and they that net fish in its waters shall languish. Moreover, the workers in finely combed flax and the weavers of white stuffs shall

be confounded [at the destruction of their trade]. The
pillars of the land [its nobles] shall be broken, and they
that work for hire shall be seized with despair. [If we
follow the Authorised Version here (verse 10) the sense
is substantially the same, "trade shall be ruined."]
The princes of Pharaoh's ancient capital (see Numbers
xiii. 22) shall be blinded with folly, and his wisest statesmen shall be but brutish counsellors. Wherefore do
they flatter him, bidding him say, ' I am the son of wise
rulers, the heir of ancient kings ? ' Where is the wisdom
of thy wise men, O Pharaoh ? Let them tell thee now
what is about to come upon thee ; let them discover the
purpose of the Lord of hosts concerning Egypt. The
princes of thy capital are blinded with folly, the princes
of Memphis are deceived ; they that have been as a
corner-stone unto Egypt lead her into ruin. The Lord
hath given them a cup mingled with the spirit of per-
verseness, and their perverse counsels have caused the
land to stumble in its policy as a drunkard stumbleth in
his vomit ; Egypt can find no work for high or low, rich
or poor. Then shall the men of Egypt be weak as
women ; they shall shake and fear under the hand
which the Lord of hosts stretcheth out to smite them.
And the land of Judah [the source of this prophecy of
of evil] shall be a terror to Egypt ; all that hear its
name shall fear ; for it proclaimeth the purpose of
the Lord of hosts, which He hath purposed against
Egypt."

These judgments were to serve in the end as fatherly
chastisements, and to prepare Egypt to receive the
knowledge of the true God, and to obey the gospel of
His Son. Of this the prophet now proceeds to speak.
His opening words (verse 18) are difficult to explain.
Some interpreters understand them to mean that the
mercy shown to Egypt would be so great that out of
every six cities five would be saved, and only one given

to destruction. Others suppose that the word five is used indefinitely to denote a small number, just as in 1 Cor. xiv. 19, where Paul says: " I had rather speak five words with my understanding . . . than ten thousand in an unknown tongue." Again, the words translated, " the city of destruction," become in Hebrew, with the very slightest change in shape and sound, " the city of the Sun," and are so written in some manuscripts. Perhaps the prophet, according to his manner on occasion (for instance, in verse 7), makes a kind of play upon the name of the idolatrous town, and says, It shall no longer be Heliopolis (City of the Sun), but Deletopolis (City of Destruction). We are not, however, convinced that anyone has fully grasped his meaning.

" In that day many cities in Egypt shall speak the language of the land of the Lord of hosts, and shall swear allegiance unto Him, but some shall be given up to destruction. In that day the worship of the true God shall be set up in the midst of Egypt, and shall extend unto its frontiers. And this shall serve as a sign and testimony unto the Lord of hosts throughout the land; they shall cry unto the Lord against their oppressors, and He shall send them a Saviour and an Advocate, who shall deliver them. [Alexander was to deliver them from the yoke of Persia, Christ from the yoke of Satan.] And the Lord shall reveal Himself to Egypt, and the Egyptians shall know Him in that day; yea, they shall worship Him with offerings of praise and sacrifices of thanksgiving, shall make their vows in His name, and shall perform them. For the Lord shall smite Egypt as a father smites his son; He shall smite, and He shall heal. Then shall they repent and turn to God, and He shall hear their cry and save them.

" In that day shall the highway of holy love (xxxv. 8) unite Egypt and Assyria; they shall hold free intercourse as brethren, and shall unite to serve God. Israel also

shall be one with them, and the three together shall be
a blessing to all lands, because the Lord of hosts hath
blessed them, saying, Blessed be Egypt My people,
and Assyria the work of My hands, and Israel Mine
inheritance."

It is no flight of fancy to see this prophecy fulfilled in
the gospel of that glorious Saviour in whom Jew and
Gentile are one. Time will show whether a second
fulfilment awaits it.

From this sweet picture of "good things to come"
in gospel days, the prophet returns to the prediction
of Assyria's victories over Egypt and its Ethiopian
allies. Until recently, nothing was known of King
Sargon, whose name occurs only here in the Bible, and
was not to be found elsewhere; but monuments have
been discovered which tell us that he reigned over
Assyria for eighteen years, and was succeeded by his
son Sennacherib. Tartan is an official title rather than
a name, and denotes the commander-in-chief of the
Assyrian armies. Ashdod (Azotus) was a Philistine
city which was afterwards besieged by a king of Egypt
for twenty-nine years. We may hence judge of its
strategic importance in a struggle between Assyria and
Egypt.

"In the year when Sargon, king of Assyria, sent his
commander-in-chief against Ashdod, and that city was
besieged and captured, the word of the Lord came to
Isaiah, the son of Amoz, saying, Go, lay aside thy garment of sackcloth, and put off thy shoes from thy feet;
and he did so, laying aside his upper garment and walk-
ing barefoot. Then said the Lord, As My servant
Isaiah has laid aside his garment of sackcloth and has
walked barefoot for three years, that he may be a sign
and a portent against Egypt and Ethiopia, so shall the
king of Assyria lead the Egyptians into captivity, and
the Ethiopians into exile, naked, barefoot, and exposed

to shame. And they who have relied on the help of
Ethiopia, and boasted of the power of Egypt, shall be
terrified and confounded. Yea, the inhabitants of
Judæa shall say, Behold, such is the lot of those to
whom we looked for help against Assyria ; how then
shall we escape ? "

We can make no better comment on the above chapter
than that which is supplied by the words of Jeremiah :
" Cursed is the man that trusteth in man, and maketh
flesh his arm, and whose heart departeth from the
Lord."

Chapter XXI.

THIS chapter contains three prophecies: the first (verses 1–10) is a woe against the desert of the sea, the second (verses 11, 12) a woe against Dumah, the third (verses 13–17) a woe against Arabia.

It is clear from verse 9 that the desert of the sea is Babylon; but why is it so called? The simplest answer seems to be that which is supplied by the words of a later prophet, who addresses Babylon thus: "O thou that dwellest upon many waters, abundant in treasures, thine end is come" (Jer. li. 13). The Euphrates ran through the midst of the city, and when its waters overflowed they formed a huge sea, which turned the surrounding plain into a wilderness of water. It is, moreover, worthy of notice that an Assyrian inscription has been discovered in which Merodach Baladan, the king of Babylon, is styled the king of the sea. The title " desert " is doubly appropriate, because Babylon was to be made a desolation. (See Isa. xiii. 19–22.)

The word Dumah occurs in 1 Chron. i. 30 as the name of one of the twelves sons of Ishmael; but it seems to be used here as a mystical or poetical name for the land of Edom, afterwards known to the Greeks and Romans as Idumæa. The prophet hears a voice calling to him from Mount Seir, the dwelling-place of the children of Esau, and gives it a short and mysterious answer. Dumah means silence, and may have been used to indicate that Idumæa must sink into the silence of desolation. (See Malachi i. 3.)

Let us now endeavour to explain the three prophecies in order.

The first of them soon received a first and partial fulfilment in the capture of Babylon by Sargon, king of Assyria ; but it is also a wonderfully accurate prediction of the overthrow of that city by the Medes and Persians, which was to take place after the lapse of a century and a half. It was uttered for the instruction and comfort of the Jewish remnant who should then be lying as God's wheat on the threshing-floor of a Babylonian captivity ; it tells them that Cyrus with his Medo-Persian army will come to smite the oppressor and to let God's captives go. (See Isa. xlv. 1-4, and 13.)

The Greek historian Xenophon, who lived about 250 years later than Isaiah, describes the capture of Babylon in terms which show the accuracy of this prediction, and help us to understand its details. He tells us that Cyrus, seeing that the walls were impregnable, formed the plan of draining off the water of the Euphrates, and using its bed as a roadway into the heart of the city. He hoped that the gates in the walls along its banks might be left open, or insufficiently guarded ; and the issue showed that his expectations were well founded. He set his troops to dig large trenches in the neighbouring plain in such a way that when all was ready the waters of the river could be made to flow into them. Meanwhile the Babylonians laughed at him, thinking that he was vainly throwing up earthworks against their colossal walls. What cared they for a siege ? Had they not in their city stores of provisions for twenty years ? Xenophon then continues :

" After the trenches had been dug by his army, Cyrus, having heard that a festival was to be celebrated during which the Babylonians spent all the night in drinking and revelry (compare Daniel v.), took a large body of his men and opened the mouths of the trenches which

communicated with the river, and in the night the waters
flowed into the trenches, and thus a way practicable for
his men was opened into the city. . . . He then summoned the chief captains of his infantry and cavalry,
and said unto them : ' My friends, the river has retired
and supplied us with a road into the city. Let us enter
with good courage, remembering that they against
whom we are going are the men whom we conquered
when they were awake and sober ; but now many of
them are asleep, many are drunken, and all are in
disorder. And do ye, Gadatas and Gobryas [two traitors
to the Babylonians], guide us as soon as ye can to the
palace.' ' Yes,' replied Gobryas, ' and it would be no
wonder if the gates of the palace were open, for all the
city seems to be in a revel on this night. However, we
shall find a watch before the gates of the palace, for a
watch is always set there.' ' We must attend to it,'
replied Cyrus, ' and go and take them as much by
surprise as possible.'

" Thus having spoken, they advanced. Of those who
met them, some were put to the sword, others fled back
into the city, shouting. But Gobryas and his men
joined in the outcry, as if they also were revellers, and
making all possible haste soon reached the palace.
They found the palace gates locked ; but those who had
been told off to attack the guards fell upon them while
they were drinking round a great fire, and began to cut
them down. The shouting and the din being heard
within the palace, the king gave orders to see what was
the matter, and some of his attendants opened the gates
and ran out. When Gadatas and his men saw the
gates open, they pursued and attacked those who had
been sent out, and who now hastily retired. They
found the king already on his feet, with his drawn
scimitar in his hand. He was overpowered and slain
by the troops of Gadatas and Gobryas, and his atten-

dants also were put to death, some endeavouring to shelter themselves, others running away, and others resisting as best they could."

Such is the account given by Xenophon of the scene briefly referred to in Daniel v. 30. Let the reader add to it the statements of another Greek writer (Herodotus) that Cyrus had many camels in his army, and that the Persians once gained a victory by means of a great number of asses which they had with them, and he will understand some points in this prophecy of Isaiah which would otherwise be obscure.

" The word of the Lord against the city of the wilderness of waters (Jer. li. 13).

" As the whirlwinds come from the stormy south, so cometh thy destruction from the wilderness, from the land of thy terrible foes ; a grievous vision thereof is revealed to me.

" Thou art ever dealing treacherously, thou treacherous city ; thou art a spoiler that is ever gathering spoil. [Therefore thus saith the Lord:] Go up against her, O Elam ; besiege her, O Media ! For I will put an end to all her oppression, and will cause the sighing of her captives to cease. The Lord hath shown me thy ruin, and at the sight thereof my loins are filled with the anguish that will overtake thee ; thy pangs have taken hold of me as the pangs of a woman in travail. I am too troubled to hear, too terrified to see : my heart panteth, and horror hath overwhelmed me. My night of pleasure is become a night of fear. [I tremble as if I were Belshazzar.] Ye prepare your banqueting-table, ye careless revellers ; ye set a watch about the palace, that ye may eat and drink in security. . . . [But hark ! The foe is come !] Arise, oil your shields for the battle, and fight for your lives ! For the Lord hath said unto me, Let a watchman stand on the walls of Babylon, and declare what he seeth ; he shall see an army with its horsemen in double file, with its beasts of burden carrying baggage and implements of war ; he shall listen intently, and give good heed.   Then heard I a watchman cry as with the voice of a lion, ' My lord, I have watched from my tower day by day and night by night; [for the siege is long].   And now, behold, I see advancing a troop of men and a double line of horse.'   The watchman spake further and said, ' Fallen, fallen is Babylon ; her idols are overthrown, and her gods lie broken to shivers on the ground.'

" O remnant of my people, captives in Babylon, passing under the flail of tribulation as corn upon God's threshing-floor, I have declared unto you for your comfort the words which I have received from the Lord of hosts, the God of Israel."

For one who has faith in God, it is not difficult to believe that Isaiah looked forward through a century and a half, beheld captive Judah lying on God's threshing-floor in Babylon, and saw the army of Cyrus entering the city by the river-bed to set the captives free.

" The word of the Lord against Edom.

" The night of trouble cometh upon Mount Seir, and the men of Edom cry to me saying, Prophet of Judah, how long shall this night of our trouble last ?   Watchman, what is the hour of the night ?   My answer is : The morning breaketh, but to you it will be a midnight morning.   [The darkness of your trouble will deepen into destruction.]   Nevertheless, if ye will learn of me, learn of me.   Repent ye, and seek mercy."

For further threatenings against Edom see Jer. xlix. 7–22, and the short prophecy of Obadiah.

" The word of the Lord against Arabia.

" [Arabia shall be ravaged by the enemy, so that] the caravans of Dedanites that pass along its highways shall be driven into the woods.   They shall be thirsty and

beg for water, and their friends the Temanites shall
meet them in their flight to give them bread. Their
enemies shall chase them with the sword, and they shall
flee from the drawn sword, the bended bow, and the
raging of the battle. The Lord hath revealed this to
me, saying, Within a measured year all the power of
Arabia shall be brought low : nought shall be left
of her troops of archers and hosts of warriors but a
small and feeble remnant. The Lord God of Israel hath
spoken it."

Babylon and Edom, companions in hatred of the
people of God (see Psa. cxxxvii.), were to be companions
in ruin. Babel and Dumah must drink of the cup
which they had put to the lips of Judah (Lam. iv. 21,
22) ; and godless Arabia must drink also. Assyria,
Chaldæa and Persia were in turn used by the Lord to
fulfil these denunciations.

Chapter XXII.

THERE is no reason to doubt that the Valley of Vision spoken against in this prophecy is Jerusalem. The term valley may have been used because the mountains were round about the city (Psa. cxxv. 2) ; and it is fitly called the valley of vision, because it was the chosen sanctuary where the Lord revealed His will by vision and prophecy. The Lord said to Abraham, " Take now thy son, thine only son Isaac, whom thou lovest, and get thee into the land of Moriah ; and offer him there for a burnt-offering upon one of the mountains which I will tell thee of." On the sacred spot thus chosen by God in the land of Moriah—that is, the land of the Vision of Jehovah—Abraham heard the angel's voice from heaven bidding him spare his son, and telling him that in his seed all the nations of the earth should be blessed. Here in later days the Lord appeared to David ; and here was built Solomon's temple (2 Chron. iii. 1), the house which, as soon as it was built, was filled with the glory of God's presence. Jerusalem was indeed a Valley of Vision.

And yet it has been called the city of sixty sieges ! Again and again it was compassed about with armies, sacked and demolished by cruel foes. We cannot say with certainty to which of these sieges the prophet here refers ; but some of his words seem to point to the days when Hezekiah built up all the wall that was broken, that he might resist Sennacherib (see 2 Chron. xxxii. 5). If the prophet speaks of some other siege, it must be one of the three mentioned in 2 Chron. xxxiii. 11,

2 Kings xxiv. 11, and 2 Kings xxv. 1, when Manasseh, Jehoiachin, and Zedekiah respectively were taken prisoners.

If we were better acquainted with the details of these four sieges, we might be able to say with certainty which of them Isaiah here describes. He sees some of the people of Jerusalem rushing from its streets to find safety from their enemies upon the flat tops of the houses; he sees others fetching out stores of weapons from the armoury built by King Solomon (1 Kings vii. 2; x. 17); others repairing the fortifications and making sure the water supply; others relying on the success of these efforts instead of looking to the Lord, and crying in blind and presumptuous revelry, Let us eat and drink, for to-morrow we die.

"The word of the Lord against the place of His sanctuary.

"What aileth thee now, O Jerusalem? Wherefore have thy people sought refuge upon the housetops? Where is the wonted shouting of thy multitude, the roaring of thy crowded streets, and the joy of thy revellers? [Famine consumeth thee, and] thy warriors are slain, but not by the sword; they are fallen, but not in battle. Thy leaders have all turned to flee, but the archers have overtaken and bound them; all that are within thee have been made prisoners, even those who have fled to thee from afar to find a refuge within thy walls. I have said therefore to all that would console me, Turn from me that I may weep in the bitterness of my soul; seek not to comfort me for the ruin of my nation. For this is a day of vexation, destruction, and despair; the Lord, the Lord of hosts, hath brought it upon the place of His sanctuary. The walls thereof are battered, and the cries of the terrified citizens echo among the mountains. The troops of Elam's archers gird on their quivers and advance with chariots and cavalry ; the heavy-armed soldiers of Kir march to the attack with uncovered shields. [Shields stripped of the cases which covered them in time of peace.] And it is come to pass that thy fruitful valleys are filled with hostile chariots, and squadrons of cavalry are drawn up before thy gates. The fortified cities of Judah are fallen. Jerusalem hath drawn forth the weapons of its ancient armoury, surveyed the many breaches in its walls, gathered within it the waters of its pools. Ye have counted the houses that ye may break down a portion of them to repair your walls, and ye have digged within your city a reservoir for your gathered waters. Unto these things ye look, and not unto Him who hath brought this evil upon you ; ye have not respect unto Him who hath purposed it from of old. In this day of visitation the Lord calleth you to weep, to mourn, to repent in dust and ashes ; and, behold, joy and gladness, feasting and revelry. If to-morrow we die, let us eat, drink, and be merry to-day ! Therefore the Lord of hosts hath revealed this judgment in mine ears, Their sin shall not be purged ; to-morrow they shall die, saith the Lord, the Lord of hosts."

The remainder of this chapter is a prophecy against one Shebna, the treasurer over the palace, the king's chief adviser or prime minister. This man was making for himself a magnificent tomb hewn in the rock, when the prophet was sent to him to foretell his downfall, and his miserable death as a captive in a foreign land. His office was to be given to a better than he, a successor who may be looked upon as a type of Christ. (Compare ver. 22 and Rev. iii. 7.) As to Shebna's sepulchre built on high, we will quote an illustration from Cobbin's Bible : " Sir R. K. Porter was drawn up by ropes to one hewn in the rock, sixty feet from the ground, and others were yet above him."

We learn from 2 Kings xviii. 18 that Eliakim was the

chief of Hezekiah's household, and that Shebna held the subordinate office of scribe or secretary. It has been conjectured by those who assign this prophecy to the reign of Manasseh that when that king succeeded to the throne he removed Eliakim from his office, and put Shebna in his place as a man more willing to walk in wicked ways; that the threatenings here uttered against Shebna were fulfilled when Esarhaddon took Manasseh to Babylon (2 Chron. xxxiii. 11); and that Manasseh, after his repentance and restoration, raised Eliakim again to his former high office, and thus fulfilled the remainder of the prophecy.

" Thus saith the Lord, the Lord of hosts: Go to this Shebna, the treasurer, the ruler of the king's palace, and say unto him, What doest thou here, building thyself a tomb? Whom hast thou to bury therein, that thou hewest out thy tomb on high, digging in the rock a resting-place for thy bones? Behold, the Lord will hurl thee with violence from thy place, thou mighty man; yea, He will bind thee up as a ball and cast thee far away into the open field. There shalt thou die, and there shalt thou leave the chariots of thy pride, thou shame of thy master's house! I the Lord will thrust thee out of thine office, and thou shalt be deposed from thy high station. And when I shall have removed thee, I will call My servant Eliakim, the son of Hilkiah, clothe him with thy robes, and gird him with thy girdle. I will make him governor in thy stead, and he shall rule as a father over the men of Jerusalem and the house of Judah. I will lay upon his shoulder the government of the house of David, so that when he openeth none shall shut, and when he shutteth none shall open. I will fix him in his place as a nail is fixed in the wall, and his princedom shall be the glory of his father's house. All the glory of his father's house shall be upheld by him, the children and the grandchildren; yea, every member small and great shall find support in him. But Shebna shall fall, saith the Lord of hosts ; the nail that was fixed firmly in the wall shall give way, shall be broken down, shall fall ; and all that depended thereon shall perish, for the Lord hath spoken it."

As we reach the end of this message of judgment and mercy, we remember another of like import : " And all the trees of the field shall know that I the Lord have brought down the high tree, have exalted the low tree, have dried up the green tree, and have made the dry tree to flourish ; I the Lord have spoken, and have done it " (Ezek. xvii. 24). We think also of the words of the Judge of mankind : " Every one that exalteth himself shall be abased, and he that abaseth himself shall be exalted." And we pray, " Lord, grant that we may be clothed with humility."

Chapter XXIII.

TYRE! Where is it now? It is not; but where it once stood, fishers find a place to spread their nets. Long before its final fall its doom was thus written: "It shall be a place for the spreading of nets in the midst of the sea, for I have spoken it, saith the Lord God. . . . And I will make thee like the top of a rock; thou shalt be a place to spread nets upon, thou shalt be built no more; for I the Lord have spoken it, saith the Lord God" (Ezek. xxvi. 5, 14). A modern traveller tells us that in passing along the shore where the city once stood, he "came suddenly upon five or six fishermen sitting on some prostrate columns, with their nets spread on the sand at a short distance before them."

But what was Tyre when the prophets of God foretold its overthrow? If we can give a brief but correct answer to this question, we shall shed some light on the difficult chapter which we now undertake to expound.

It seems clear that the ancient city which was known in the days of Joshua as great Zidon, gave birth to the neighbouring town of Tyre (Joshua xix. 28, 29). If so, it is probable that the "daughter of Zidon," referred to in ver. 12 of this chapter, is not Zidon itself, according to the general sense of such an expression in the prophets, but the daughter-city Tyre. Both cities stood on the coast of Phœnicia, at the eastern end of the Mediterranean. The younger city consisted of two parts—one built on the mainland and known as Old

Tyre, and the other built on a rocky island, at some distance from the coast. This island was turned into an impregnable fortress, guarded not only by the surrounding waves, but by walls lofty, thick, and surmounted with strong towers. The ruins of the place show that it was a city of palaces, temples, and colonnades, a home of wealth and luxury. It sent out its merchant-ships to the ends of the earth, and " its own feet carried it far off to sojourn " (Isa. xxiii. 7), *i.e.*, its citizens went forth to colonise distant lands—Cyprus (Chittim), Carthage, and Tartessus (Tarshish) on the south-west coast of Spain. From Egypt they brought across the great waters of the Mediterranean the grain that grew on the banks of the Nile (Shihor), and from every district of the then known world rich produce of various kinds. Nor were they content to visit lands already known. They pushed on into unknown seas ; they came to Britain for tin ; and it is well nigh certain that Tyrian sailors circumnavigated Africa long ages before we moderns re-discovered the Cape of Good Hope.

Now, praiseworthy as all this industrious enterprise was, and even necessary for the well-being of Phœnicia, a small country hemmed in by the sea on the west, and by high mountains on the east, yet the ungodliness connected therewith made it in the eyes of the Lord as the indiscriminate commerce of a harlot with all comers. For Tyre knew not the maker of heaven and earth, nor glorified Him as God. She polluted herself continually with the cruel worship of Baal and the unclean orgies of Ashtoreth or Astarte. Moreover, when Jerusalem was taken by the armies of Chaldea, Tyre exulted at the prospect of an increase of her own trade through the fall of a rival city, saying, " Aha, she is broken that was the gate of the peoples ; she is turned unto me ; I shall be replenished now that she is laid waste." Then was the doom of Tyre revealed afresh by Him who is jealous for His land. (See Ezek. xxvi.)

Let us now turn to Isaiah's prediction of this great city's downfall, and of its subsequent reception of the gospel before its final desolation. We think that the prophet refers primarily to the siege of Tyre by Nebuchadnezzar, and not to that undertaken 250 years later by Alexander the Great. It would carry us too far from our plan and purpose if we attempted to discuss the many difficulties of interpretation which the chapter presents. We can only give results, and sometimes with much diffidence. Still, we hope to make the general meaning quite plain. There will be no need for us " to point the moral or adorn the tale " ; its voice to England is clear and loud. If she departs from God, her downfall is as sure as was that of Tyre.

" The word of the Lord against Tyre. Lament, ye ships that come from Tarshish, for Tyre is laid waste. No harbours remain to shelter or receive you there ; at Cyprus, on your homeward journey, ye shall hear of it. Be silent in despair, ye that dwell in the island-city, the city which the seafaring traders of Zidon have enriched. Over the Great Sea her ships have come bringing the grain of Shihor [the Black River, *i.e.*, the Nile], the harvests of the river of Egypt, to increase her wealth. She hath been the market of the nations. Blush for thy fallen daughter, great Zidon ; for a voice cometh from the sea, from the stronghold in the midst thereof, saying, I am childless and desolate, as if I had never travailed nor brought forth, nor nourished sons, nor reared daughters. The report shall reach Egypt, and she shall be sore troubled to hear of the fall of Tyre.

" Flee away over the sea and seek refuge at Tarshish, ye that dwell in the island-city. Is this your joyous town, that boasteth of her ancient origin and sendeth out her colonies to distant lands ?

"But who hath purposed the overthrow of Tyre, the city that bestoweth crowns on kings, the city whose merchants are princes, and whose traffickers are honoured throughout the world? The Lord of hosts hath purposed it, to stain the pride of the glory of man, and to pour contempt upon them that are honoured throughout the world.

"Ye shall be scattered over your land, ye men of Tarshish, as the waters of Nile spread over the land of Egypt, for your girdle is gone. [Tyre, who was your strength, is no more.] The Lord hath stretched out His hand over the city of the seas, and by her fall He hath shaken the kingdoms of the world. He hath commanded that the strongholds of the merchants of Phœnicia be destroyed. He hath said unto Tyre, Thou shalt no more rejoice; with violence shalt thou be put to shame, thou virgin city sprung from Zidon. Arise and flee over the sea to Cyprus; even there shalt thou seek rest in vain. Behold, Chaldea sendeth out its armies, and Tyre is no more; the hosts of Assyria [*i.e.*, the armies of Nebuchadnezzar] destroy it, and make it a haunt for wild beasts; they rear against it their besieging-towers, overthrow its palaces, and make it a ruin. Lament, ye ships that come from Tarshish, for Tyre is laid waste.

"Now it shall come to pass, when this shall be accomplished, that Tyre shall be a forgotten ruin for seventy years, the length of the reign of a king, and his son, and his son's son. (See Jer. xxvii. 3, 7.) And at the end of those seventy years it shall be with Tyre as with the harlot to whom the song saith:

> ' Forgotten harlot, take thine harp,
>   And ply thy trade again;
> Fill every street with sweetest song,
>   And win thee back thy men.'

For when seventy years shall be accomplished, the Lord

will restore Tyre, and she will resume her trade, and
renew her polluted commerce with all the kingdoms of
the world upon the face of the earth. But she shall
give of her goods and of her gains to the holy service
of God. She shall not hoard them up in her treasuries
as of old time, but shall give them unto the servants of
the Lord to buy food and clothing withal."

Two quotations may explain the concluding words of
this prophecy :

(1) " We landed at Tyre. . . And finding disciples
we tarried there seven days : who said unto Paul
through the Spirit that he should not go up to Jerusalem. And when we had accomplished those days,
we departed and went our way ; and they brought us
on our way with wives and children, till we were out of
the city ; and we kneeled down on the shore and prayed.
And when we had taken our leave one of another we
took ship, and they returned home again "—to Tyre !

(2) Nearly three centuries after Christ Eusebius
wrote : " This prophecy is fulfilled in our times. For
now that the Church of God is established at Tyre, as
in other nations, a large portion of her merchandise is
consecrated to the Lord and to His Church . . . according to the precept of the Lord, that they who preach the
gospel should live of the gospel."

As we look back at Isaiah's prophecies against various
nations, from chap. xiii. to chap. xxiii., we see more
distinctly than ever who it is that governs this lower
world ; and we feel to be in hearty agreement with an
ancient writer (Tertullian), who said, " What can more
clearly prove the truth of prophecy than the daily
auditing of the accounts of this world's history, in which
the disposal of kingdoms, the fall of cities, the end of
nations, the state of times, corresponds to what was
announced some thousands of years ago ? "

Chapter XXIV.

THIS and the three following chapters (xxiv.–xxvii.) seem to form one continuous prophecy. The prophet foretells grievous calamities to be followed by a marvellous deliverance, which shall bring great joy to all nations and a great revenue of praise to the God of Israel. There has been much variety of opinion as to the meaning of the oracle : some refer it to times yet future, others consider that it was fulfilled, at least in its primary sense, in the overthrow of Jerusalem by Nebuchadnezzar, the restoration of the Jews by Cyrus in the days of Ezra, and the subsequent going forth of the Gospel from Judæa to the ends of the earth (Acts i. 8).

It has occurred to us that a safe guide to the interpretation of this part of God's Word is furnished by the prophet Zephaniah, who some sixty years later opened his message with the following words : " I will utterly consume all things from off the land, saith the Lord." Zephaniah tells us distinctly that the land thus threatened with desolation is the land of Judah (Zeph. i. 4), and he closes his short prophecy with a prediction of the glories of gospel days. Comparing his language with that of Isaiah in this place, " The Lord maketh the land empty," we are struck with the similarity of expression, and are led to the conclusion that the two prophets are predicting the same events, namely : the overthrow of Judah by the Chaldeans, the Babylonian captivity and deliverance therefrom, and the coming of

Christ to accomplish the work of redemption, and thus to make a feast of fat things for all nations.

The above is our own independent view of the matter, and we think our readers will see that it rests on solid grounds. We are glad to be able to add that, with certain small differences, it agrees with Calvin's interpretation, though it differs very considerably from that of Dr. Gill. A wise note in the Annotated Paragraph Bible suggests that this prophecy "does not refer exclusively to any one period or event, but is rather intended to show the extreme measures to which God would resort in order to purify His people." This is possible ; but we are inclined to think that the four chapters are correctly summed up by Dr. Louis Segond, in his French version of the Bible : " The land of Judah laid waste, Babylon destroyed, and Jerusalem restored." The fact that Isaiah speaks of " the earth " is no objection to the above view ; for the same Hebrew word is translated " the land " in Zeph. i. 18, and often has that limited meaning. We conclude these introductory remarks with a quotation from Calvin : " Others suppose that he means the whole world, but think that he refers to the last day, which I consider to be an exceedingly forced interpretation ; for after having threatened the Jews and other nations, the prophet adds a consolation, that the Lord will one day raise up His Church and make her more flourishing, which certainly cannot apply to the last judgment." This is surely a very forcible argument ; for no small remnant like unto the gleanings of an olive tree (Isa. xxiv. 13) will escape when the earth and the works that are therein shall be burned up (2 Peter iii. 10).

" Behold, the day cometh when the Lord shall give up the land of Judah to desolation, and shall make it a wilderness ; yea, He shall turn it upside down, and scatter its inhabitants among the heathen. One common ruin shall overtake priest and people, master and servant, mistress and maid, seller and buyer, lender and borrower, creditor and debtor. The land shall be wholly given up to devastation and pillage : for the mouth of the Lord hath spoken it. The land shall mourn and wither ; the people thereof shall faint and wither, and their haughty nobles shall faint with them. (See 2 Kings xxiv. 14.) For the land hath been defiled by the sins of the people ; they have transgressed the laws of their God, changed His ordinances, and broken the covenant which He had made with them and with their children unto all generations. (See Ex. xxxi. 16, and Deut. xxix. 14, 15.) For this cause the curse uttered by Moses (Lev. xxvi. ; Deut. xxviii.) shall devour the land, and they that dwell therein shall be punished for their guilt ; they shall be consumed by the flame of war, till but few of them are left. The new wine shall be but a mournful drink, the vine shall wither, all they that were merry-hearted revellers shall sigh. The joyous timbrels shall be silent, the mirth of banqueters shall end, the sound of the harp shall cease. There shall be no wine-feasts enlivened with song ; strong drink shall give no pleasure to them that drink it. The city shall be a desolate ruin ; the houses shall be closed, and no man shall enter into them. Men shall wail in the streets for the wine that is no more ; all joy shall give place to gloom, and all mirth shall depart from the land. In the city shall be nought but desolation, and the gates that defended it shall be destroyed. A small remnant shall be left in the midst of the land among the surrounding peoples, like the olives on a tree which has been shaken, or the grapes left on a vine after the vintage.

" Yet, after those days, the remnant of Israel shall lift up the voice in songs of gladness, and shall praise the majesty of the Lord from distant lands beyond the sea. Let them glorify the Lord from the rising of the sun [the 'fires,' or rather 'lights,' here mentioned are probably the sunrise—that is, the east], and praise the name of the Lord God of Israel from the lands of the far west. Their songs shall be heard from the ends of the earth giving glory to the righteous God."

Was not this prophecy of praise after desolation fulfilled, at least in part, when the Jewish synagogues that were scattered over the Roman empire heard the gospel from the apostles of Christ and received it with joy and thanksgiving?

The prophet now returns to the sad days of desolation which were nearer to his own times.

" But I said, Destruction cometh upon me, destruction cometh upon me! Woe is me! The spoilers spoil the land, the spoilers utterly spoil the land. The inhabitants thereof are driven in terror, as hunted beasts are driven to the pitfall or the snare. He that fleeth from the sound of terror falleth into the pit, and he that escapeth from the pit falleth into the snare. [There is no escape from destruction in one form or another. See Amos v. 19.] For the heavens pour down a deluge of ruin, and the foundations of the earth are shaken. The land is utterly broken down, the land is torn to pieces, the land is moved as by an earthquake. The land reels to and fro like a drunkard; it is shaken like a tottering hut; its own transgression lieth heavy upon it; it falleth, and cannot rise again. For at that time the Lord shall punish the lofty in their high places, and the kings of the earth upon the earth. [Some think that these 'high ones' are wicked spirits; but perhaps the fulfilment is found in 2 Kings xxiv. 11–15; xxv. 18–21.] They shall be gathered together as prisoners are gathered in a dungeon, and shall be carried into captivity. Their punishment shall surely come, though it tarry many days. Yet the Lord of hosts shall reign

in Zion and in Jerusalem, and before the brightness of
His presence the moon shall blush and the sun shall be
ashamed ; for He shall show His glory to the elders of
His people."

Nothing is so bright as the glory of God revealed in
the face of Jesus Christ. Saul of Tarsus found it to be
above the brightness of the mid-day sun (Acts xxvi. 13).
The glory of God is manifested in every deliverance of
His people ; but it will be seen in all its lovely and awful
splendour when " the Lord Jesus shall be revealed from
heaven with His holy angels, in flaming fire taking
vengeance on them that know not God, and that obey
not the gospel of our Lord Jesus Christ ; who shall be
punished with everlasting destruction from the presence
of the Lord, and from the glory of His power ; when
He shall come to be glorified in His saints, and to be
admired in all them that believe " (2 Thess. i. 7–10).

Parts of the above exposition may appear to some of
our readers vague and unsatisfactory. We bring it
before them as the best that we can give, and conclude
with an extract from the preface to the Annotated
Paragraph Bible, an excellent book to which we have
already referred : " It must not be supposed that
everything in the Bible can be fully comprehended.
It is probable that the Divine Being intended that
revelation should have its difficulties, in order to further
our moral discipline, to make trial whether we would
submit our reason to His will, to exercise our faith and
diligence, to make us willing to wait till the light of
eternity shall disclose all ; perhaps also to afford us
evidence that the book is divine ; for when we find
difficulties surrounding us in our search into all the
other works of God, was it to be expected that this one
alone should be free from them ? "

Chapters XXV. 1—XXVI. 6.

THE apostle Paul, after unfolding God's mysterious counsels as to the gathering in of the Gentiles through the gospel which the Jews rejected, and the subsequent conversion of the Jews through the gospel which the Gentiles had received, cried out in holy wonder : " Oh, the depth of the riches both of the wisdom and knowledge of God ! How unsearchable are His judgments, and His ways past finding out ! For who hath known the mind of the Lord ? Or who hath been His counsellor ? Or who hath given to Him, and it shall be recompensed unto Him again ? For of Him, and through Him, and to Him, are all things ; to whom be glory for ever. Amen." In like manner the prophet Isaiah, when God revealed to him divine decrees relating to the overthrow of Babylon, the preservation of Judah, and the glories of that gospel which was to spread from Jerusalem to the ends of the earth, cried out in holy wonder : " O Lord, Thou art my God ; I will exalt Thee, I will praise Thy name ; for Thou hast done wonderful things ; Thy counsels of old are faithfulness and truth." He saw the destruction of Babylon as clearly with the eye of his mind as if he had lived to behold it with the eyes of his body, and said to his God : " Thou has made of a city a heap ; of a defenced city a ruin."

Such, in our opinion, is the real and primary sense of the prophet's words in this place. Some have thought that he is celebrating the deliverance granted to Hezekiah by the miraculous destruction of Sennacherib's army; and it is true that the Lord was then "a strength to the poor, a strength to the needy in his distress." We read that, "Isaiah, the son of Amoz, sent to Hezekiah, saying, Thus saith the Lord, the God of Israel, Whereas thou hast prayed to Me against Sennacherib, king of Assyria, I have heard thee." And we know that the hand of God brought down the heat of Assyria's wrath as quickly and as easily as a thick cloud stays the heat of the scorching sun of the desert. Yet the whole of the language of this prophecy seems to us, as we said in our last article, to refer more exactly and definitely to the downfall of Babylon and the subsequent deliverance of Judah. And why was Judah thus preserved, the mountain of Jerusalem thus delivered? Because in days which were then future Jerusalem was to be the scene of Christ's great work of redemption, and the centre from which His gospel should be carried to the ends of the earth by messengers endued with power from on high (Luke xxiv. 46–49).

May the Lord help us to cast at least some light upon His Word by our feeble attempt to paraphrase it.

"Jehovah, Thou art my God. I will extol Thee, and will praise Thy name; for Thou hast done wonderful things. Thine ancient counsels Thou hast faithfully and truly accomplished. Thou hast made the city of Thy foes a heap, its battlements a ruin; Thou hast destroyed the fortress of the heathen, and it shall never be rebuilt. Thou hast gotten to Thyself a name by the overthrow of the mighty (compare carefully Isa. xxv. 3 and Rom. ix. 17); the cities of warlike nations shall see it and fear Thee. Thou hast been a tower of strength to him that was weak, a tower of strength to him that was needy and afflicted: Thou hast been his refuge from the storm of war, his shelter from the heat of wrath, when the onset of the terrible was as the blast of the storm against a wall. As a cloud subdues the power of the desert sun, so hast Thou subdued the tumult of the heathen : as the shadow of a cloud cuts off the heat, so hast Thou ended the triumph of the terrible."

Isaiah had seen the might of Assyria checked by the work of the destroying angel, and had seen Sennacherib's host retire in shame and confusion. But though the language of this prophecy applies very fitly to that interposition of God's power, yet it is an evident prediction of further disaster for the enemies of Judah, and probably refers expressly to the destruction of Babylon. But why must the house of Jacob be thus preserved through every danger and brought back from every exile—an indestructible nation ? Because salvation was to be of the Jews ; because from them, according to the flesh, Christ was to come ; because the great feast for all nations was to be made by the Lord at Jerusalem. Of this feast of divine love the prophet next speaks, likening the provisions of Christ's gospel to dainty meats and choice wines.

" [Yea, Thou wilt deliver the mountain of Thine house,] O Lord of hosts ; for there wilt Thou make in days to come a feast for all nations—a feast of fat things, a feast of old wine, a feast of the richest of fat things, of the choicest of old wine. And by the light of the Sun of Righteousness, which shall shine forth from Jerusalem (see Acts i. 8), wilt Thou drive away the thick darkness that covereth all the peoples of the earth, and destroy the veil of ignorance that blindeth all the nations ; Thou wilt abolish death, and bring to light life and immortality ; Thou wilt comfort Thy redeemed with eternal consolation, and wilt exalt them to honour in the eyes of all the world : for Thy mouth, O Lord, hath spoken it. And in the day when men shall behold the Messenger of Thy covenant they shall say, Lo, this is our God ; we have waited for His coming (Luke ii.

38), and He is come to save us : this is the Lord ; we
have waited for Him, and we will be glad and rejoice in
the salvation which He bringeth. For the hand of the
Lord's love shall ever protect Zion ; but her enemies
shall be trodden down where they stand, as straw is
trodden down upon a dunghill. They may stretch forth
their hands to struggle with disaster as a swimmer
struggles with the waters ; but God will lay low their
pride, and bring to nothing the devices of their hands.
The battlements of their lofty walls shall He bring down
and lay low : He shall level them with the ground, and
bury them in the dust.

"And then shall this song be sung in Judah : We have
a strong city ; its walls and its bulwarks are the salvation which God hath appointed for it. Let its gates be
open day and night, that the righteous and the faithful
may enter in. Their mind shall be stayed upon God,
and He will keep them in peace that is peace indeed,
because they trust in Him. Ye citizens of the city of
God, trust ye in the Lord for ever ; for the Lord, the
Lord God, is the Rock of Ages. It is He that hath
brought down the foes that dwell on high, whose city
was walled up to heaven : He hath laid it low, He hath
levelled it with the ground, He hath buried it in the
dust. The foot of those who were oppressed by it
shall tread it down, the feet of the poor and the steps
of the needy."

In the above explanation we have taken the figure of
a swimmer (xxv. 11) as designed to represent the helpless struggles of Moab, or other enemies of God's people,
amid the waves of God's overwhelming judgments ;
but there is another view which ought not to pass
unmentioned. Some consider that the strong arms of
a swimmer sweeping the waters from his path, so to
speak, are an image of the resistless strokes of God's
hand when He stretches it out to subdue His foes. Let

the reader choose between these two expositions of a difficult passage : we prefer the former.

The apparent vagueness of this and other prophecies is not accidental; neither is it a defect. The word of God is not like the word of man. He utters one marvellous prediction, and it has a whole cycle of fulfilments. The progress of time and the progress of eternity will alone unveil fully the thoughts of His heart.

Chapters XXVI. 7–XXVII. 1.

WE know that the utterances of the prophets were often called forth by the events of their own times, and often had a primary reference to those events and to their immediate consequences. When we have a record of the events we find that much light is thereby thrown upon the prophecies; but this record has not in every case been preserved to us. Since such has been the Lord's good pleasure, we may conclude that it is not necessary for us to be acquainted with those circumstances. Indeed, those who believe that God spake in time past by the prophets have no difficulty in believing that His words have a deeper meaning than at first appeared, and were intended to be useful to His people in all generations. The prophecy contained in Isa. xxiv.–xxvii. is one to which the above remarks apply, and we can only say, as we have said in a previous Half-Hour, that it seems to us to refer primarily to the troubles which were to culminate in the Babylonian captivity, to the temporal deliverance which was to follow, and to the subsequent coming of Christ into the world to accomplish the work of redemption, and set up His gospel kingdom among men.

We have felt considerable difficulty in dealing with the word " my," as used in xxvi. 9 and 19. The prophets do not frequently speak in their own person; they speak rather in the name of the Lord, so that their " I " is God's " I," and their " my " is His " My." We see Paul's history and experience much more distinctly in his writings than we see those of Isaiah in his.

Yet occasionally the prophet gives utterance to his own personal feelings, and we are inclined to think that this is the case in both of these passages. Verse 19 is particularly difficult. Many good commentators take it as an utterance of Christ, and consider that He says here: " My dead body shall rise again, and by virtue of My resurrection My people shall rise also." While we recognise the importance of this truth, we do not think that this passage is designed to teach it; but fearing to seem presumptuous in rejecting a widely-received interpretation, we think it best to quote Calvin here at some length; not that his authority necessarily overrides that of other expositors, but because our judgment in this, as in most other matters, coincides with his. He says : " This word is inserted for the express purpose that the prophet may join himself with the whole church, and thus may reckon himself in the number of ' God's dead men ' in the hope of the resurrection. As to his mentioning himself in particular, he did so for the sake of more fully confirming this doctrine; for thus he testifies his sincerity, and shows that his confession is the result of faith, according to that saying, ' I believed, and therefore have I spoken.' . . . In this manner he testifies that he does not speak of things unknown, but of those things which he has learned by actual experience, and shows that his confidence is so great that he willingly ranks himself in the number of those dead bodies which he firmly believes will be restored to life. . . . This gives greater force to his doctrine, and he contrasts it with the statement which he formerly made (ver. 14) about wicked men, ' they shall not live '; for the hope of rising again is taken from them. If it is objected that the resurrection will be common to believers and to the reprobate, the answer is easy; for Isaiah does not speak merely of the resurrection, but of the happiness which believers will enjoy. Wicked men will indeed rise again, but it will be to eternal destruction ; and, therefore, the resurrection will bring ruin to them, while it will bring salvation and glory to believers."

One other quotation from the same author will be of service to us and to our readers ; it refers to the well-known words, " Thou hast wrought all our works in us." Calvin says : " By works he means all the blessings which the Lord bestows on those who believe in Him, as if he had said, ' transactions, business, actions,' and everything included in the French phrase *nos affaires*—our affairs. Accordingly, those who have quoted this passage for the purpose of overturning free-will have not understood the prophet's meaning. It is undoubtedly true that God alone does what is good in us, and that all the good actions which men perform are from His Spirit. But here the prophet merely shows that we have obtained from the hand of God all the good things which we enjoy ; and hence he infers that His kindness will not cease till we have obtained perfect happiness. . . . There is no reason why we should bring forth this passage [in support of free grace] against the Papists ; for they might easily evade it, and we have a great number of other passages exceedingly conclusive."

This integrity of interpretation is most instructive. The advocate of free grace must not wrest the Scriptures in order to oppose free-will. Sound doctrines have no need of unsound support. The passage in question should be translated, " Thou hast wrought all our works for us," and we believe that it is correctly explained in the above quotation. Now let us hear Isaiah.

" He that is just walketh in uprightness ; Thou, O God, who art upright, makest his path plain before him. Yea, we submit to Thy righteous judgments, O Lord, and in the midst of them we wait for Thee ; our soul longeth to know the virtue of Thy name, that name which is Thy memorial unto all generations. (See Ex. iii. 15.) With all my heart do I long after Thee in the night season, and when the morning cometh I seek Thee with all my understanding ; for Thy judgments, [dreadful though they be, are needful to] teach the inhabitants of the world righteousness. For even if, in Thy long-suffering goodness, Thou sparest the wicked, yet will he not learn righteousness ; in a land where Thy righteous word is known he will deal unrighteously, and will neither perceive nor reverence Thy majesty. Thou doest Thy lofty works of judgment and mercy, yet the wicked see not Thine hand. But they shall see it ; they shall see Thy zeal for Thy people, and shall be put to shame ; yea, the fire of Thine anger shall consume Thine enemies. Thou, Lord, wilt bring us into the peace which Thou hast ordained for us ; for hitherto Thou hast performed all things for us (Psa. lvii. 2). O Lord our God [Thou hast fulfilled Thy word (Deut. xxviii. 47, 48), and because we would not serve Thee], Thou hast caused other lords to have dominion over us ; but now, delivered by Thee from their oppression, we will swear by Thy name alone. Our oppressors are dead, and shall not live again ; they are deceased, and shall not rise again ; Thou hast visited them with Thy judgments, destroyed them, and blotted out their name for ever. But Thine own nation, O Lord, Thou hast increased ; yea, Thou hast increased Thy nation, and that to the glory of Thy name ; Thou hast extended wide the borders of their land."

The prophet here speaks of certain events as accomplished and past, though they were yet future when he spoke. We do not pretend to define them completely ; but we see a distinct fulfilment of his words in the restoration of the Jews after the captivity at Babylon, and a fulfilment equally distinct, but infinitely more glorious, in the extension of God's kingdom under the gospel dispensation. From this sweet foreview he returns to the troubles which lay nearer to his own days.

" Lord, when Thou hast afflicted us, we have sought Thee ; we have poured out sighs and prayers (Heb., a whisper) beneath Thy chastening hand. Our pangs and cries in Thy sight have been like unto those of a woman in travail ; but our labour and pain have resulted in wind and disappointment. Our own arm has wrought no deliverance, and our enemies have not been overthrown by it. [But Thou shalt restore us.] Thy dead shall live, and among them I shall live also. They that dwell as dry bones in the dust shall awake from the sleep of captivity and death, and shall sing Thy praise ; for the dew of Thy favour is as the dew that revives the herbs of the field, and at Thy word the earth shall give up her dead."

The prophet here teaches the same lesson as his fellow-servant Ezekiel learned from the vision of dry bones : the restoration of God's Israel from the grave of exile, and, at least by implication, the resurrection of the dead. Then again he returns to speak words of comfort to support Israel under the trials which were at that time approaching.

" [Thus saith the Lord :] Come, My people, enter into the pavilion of My presence, and shelter behind the doors of My protection ; hide there for a little moment until the storm of My wrath be past. For, behold, I will arise to punish the inhabitants of the earth for their iniquity ; the earth shall disclose the blood which she hath opened her mouth to receive (Gen. iv. 10, 11), and shall no longer cover her slain. For then the Lord shall with the sword of His justice, a sword sore, and great, and strong, punish leviathan, the serpent keen and crooked, and shall slay the dragon whose abode is in many waters."

What is here meant by leviathan, the monster of the deep, the dragon of the seas? Is it a figure of the Babylonian power, of some other tyrannical empire, or of the old serpent that deceiveth the nations? Perhaps it is impossible for us to say with certainty; but this we may safely say: the power of Babylon, the power of Rome, the power of Satan, yea, all powers hostile to Israel, must fall sooner or later before the two-edged sword that proceedeth out of the mouth of the Son of God.

Chapter XXVII. 2–13.

" WHAT did the Lord mean by these words ? " is a more important question than "What ingenious interpretation can I give to these words ?" An understanding of the true sense of the Scriptures is always more profitable in the end than fanciful interpretations of them, even when the latter seem to yield spiritual results. This principle is constantly before our eyes in writing these Half-Hours, and if to some of our readers the interpretations which we give seem dry and uninteresting in comparison with more experimental writings, we dare not attempt to gratify their tastes, and so defeat our own cherished purpose, which is to give a short and trustworthy explanation of the words which God has spoken by His prophets. Good seed is dry, but it grows when sown in good ground.

A humble distrust of our own judgment makes us glad of the support of other expositors ; but if any commentator seems to us to lean to his own understanding, and to indulge in unwarrantable speculations, we wish to be bold enough to differ from him, or at least to omit his ideas from our pages. Calvin and Jenour are the most sober exponents of Isaiah that we have met with ; and on the present occasion quotations from them will relieve us of the necessity of saying more by way of introduction to our paraphrase.

On Isaiah xxvii. 6 Calvin writes : " What he now says, that the world shall be filled with the fruit of those roots, was accomplished at the coming of Christ, who collected and multiplied the people of God by the gospel ;

and Israel was united with the Gentiles in one body, so that the distinction which formerly existed between them was removed (Eph. ii. 14). Now we know that the gospel and all the fruit that sprang from it proceeded from the Jews (Isa. ii. 3 ; John iv. 22)."

Dear reader, take the trouble to look at the passages to which the good man here refers you.

Jenour, writing on verses 12 and 13, makes some valuable remarks, which we will quote. We must point out, however, that the River of Egypt, or rather the Brook of Egypt, is not the Nile, as Jenour supposes, but a stream which runs into the Mediterranean at a point some fifty or sixty miles south-west of Gaza, and is referred to in Num. xxxiv. 5 and elsewhere as the southwest limit of the promised land.

Jenour says : " The gathering of the Jews from the countries whither they were to be dispersed is here predicted by two different metaphors ; the first taken from the method of gathering fruit, and the second from the manner of assembling an army. As olives are gathered by beating and shaking the trees, so Jehovah would gather His people that were dispersed between the Euphrates (the river) and the Nile [rather, the Wady el Arish], by violently shaking with war the countries in which they were retained captives ; and would bring them together to worship Him at Jerusalem, as armies are assembled by the sound of the trumpet. . . . Such clearly appears to be the right interpretation of the last four verses of this chapter, which shows that the prophecy relates, at least primarily, to the state of the Jewish church previous to the coming of Christ into the world. . . . Nor is this method of explaining the prophecy less profitable than what may appear a more spiritual one. For the same general inferences may be deduced, and the same practical use made of it, whichever way it be understood. With regard to the yet future restoration of the Jews to Palestine, whether the prediction in the twelfth and thirteenth verses has or has not reference to that event, I will not pretend to determine. But the particular mention of Egypt and the country bordering on the Euphrates makes it probable that their return from those parts upon the proclamation of Cyrus is all that was intended in this instance."

With these judicious words we quite agree; but we think they need to be supplemented with another short quotation from Calvin: "This was indeed accomplished under Darius, but the prophet undoubtedly intended to extend this prophecy further; for that restoration was a kind of dark foreshadowing of the deliverance which they obtained through Christ, at whose coming the sound of the spiritual trumpet—that is, of the gospel—was heard not only in Assyria or Egypt, but in the most distant parts of the world. Then were the people of God gathered to flow together to Mount Zion—that is, to the church. We know that this mode of expression is frequently employed by the prophets when they intend to denote the true worship of God, and harmony in religion and godliness; for they accommodated themselves to the usages of the people, that they might be better understood."

We come now to the Lord's own words.

"In the day [when I shall have overthrown the enemies of My people] men shall acknowledge with the voice of joy and praise that Israel is My pleasant vineyard, saith the Lord. I Myself do keep it; I will water it continually, and will keep it night and day, that it may be safe from all harm. I will not be angry with My vineyard. Let the briars and thorns that cumber it [apostate Israelites, or the foes of Israel] come before Me that I may contend with them, march against them, and consume them all by the fire of My wrath; or let them submit to Me, trust Me, and make peace with Me ; yea, let them make peace with Me [and let My foes become My friends]. The days are coming when Jacob shall again take root, flourish, bud, and bear fruit which shall fill the whole world.

"Have I smitten Israel as I have smitten his smiters ? Have I slain Jacob as I have slain his slaughtered foes ? [And Isaiah answered, No, Lord.] When Thou sendest into exile the daughter of my people, Thou dost correct her in measure, though Thou removest her as with a tempest in the day of the stormy wind from the east. Thy chastisements shall purge away the iniquity of Jacob, and the whole fruit of them shall be the removal of his sin. The stones of the altars which he has built to his idols shall be ground to pieces like crushed chalk-stones, and he shall never again rear images for the worship of Asherah or the sun.

"Meanwhile, My chastening hand, saith the Lord, will make his fenced cities a solitude, a desolate and forsaken dwelling-place, where the calf can feed uninterrupted, lie down in quiet, and browse undisturbed upon the branches of the shrubs. My people shall be as withered boughs which are broken off, gathered by women, and used to kindle a fire ; for it is a people that do err in their heart, and they have not known My ways (Psa. xcv. 10) ; therefore I who have made them will not pity them ; I who have formed them will show them no favour.

"But in the day when I shall restore them, I will gather them, as a man gathers the gleanings of his olive trees, from all places whither they have been driven, between the Euphrates and the border of Egypt ; I will gather you one by one, ye children of Israel. Yea, it shall come to pass in that day that I will gather you as with the sound of a great trumpet ; and ye shall return from the land of Assyria, where ye were ready to perish, and from the land of Egypt, whither ye had fled; and ye shall worship Me in My holy mount at Jerusalem."

When the people had actually fled into Egypt for fear of the Chaldeans, the Lord said again, by the mouth of Jeremiah (xliv. 28): "Yet a small number that escape the sword shall return out of the land of Egypt into the land of Judah; and all the remnant of Judah that are gone into the land of Egypt to sojourn there, shall know whose word shall stand, Mine or theirs."

Let us now turn to the book of Ezra: "Now in the first year of Cyrus, king of Persia, that the word of the Lord by the mouth of Jeremiah might be fulfilled, the Lord stirred up the spirit of Cyrus king of Persia, that he made a proclamation throughout all his kingdom, and put it also in writing, saying, Thus saith Cyrus king of Persia. . . . Who is there among you of all His people? his God be with him, and let him go up to Jerusalem" (Ezra i. 1–3). This was indeed a trumpet-call to the ready-to-perish in Assyria and the outcasts in Egypt, and the decree was without doubt proclaimed with many a flourish of trumpets. Thus God has fulfilled to the letter the word spoken by Isaiah.

Since Jesus Christ came in the flesh, the notes of a greater trumpet have been heard among the nations; and blessed are they who are gathered out of the Assyrias and Egypts of this evil world by the trumpet-call of the everlasting gospel.

Chapter XXVIII.

HOSHEA, the last king of Israel, had been reigning in Samaria three years when Hezekiah became king of Judah in Jerusalem. The two kingdoms and their capitals differed widely in some respects, though heavy judgments awaited both. Samaria was under the government of the last of a series of godless kings, and was filled with a godless population, briefly described by Isaiah as "the drunkards of Ephraim." Six more years were allotted to the city by the Lord's long-suffering, and then its foundations were to be laid bare (Micah i. 6); its stones were to be poured down into the valley, the fat and fertile valley which encircled the hill on which it stood; and the miserable inhabitants were to be carried captive into Assyria. (See 2 Kings xviii. 10, 11.) On the other hand, Judah was to have a further respite of nearly a century and a half, and two of its kings were to be righteous rulers, who should sit in the throne of judgment under the guidance of the spirit of judgment, and whose armies should be strengthened to drive back their foe to the gates of his own city (Isa. xxviii. 6). It was at this juncture that Isaiah was commissioned to utter the prophecy which we have now to explain.

Some commentators consider "the crown of pride," mentioned in verses 1 and 3, to be the city of Samaria, whereas we take it to be rather the arrogance of its inhabitants, with a reference, perhaps, to the garlands of flowers which they wore at their riotous wine-feasts. Verses 9–13 have received explanations which are in harmony with spiritual truth, but do not seem to us to give the real sense of the prophet's language. It is true that there commonly comes to believers, when their first enjoyments wane and their youthful zeal droops, á weaning-time during which they are taught the value of sound doctrine, and learn, often very slowly, to walk by faith and not by sight. But we consider, after much reflection, that this is not the meaning of this passage.

We need say nothing more by way of introduction, if we can only give a clear and suggestive paraphrase of the chapter.

"Woe to the haughty garlands of the drunkards of Samaria! Woe to the withering wreaths with which they proudly adorn themselves! Woe to them that dwell above the rich valleys, where sottish winebibbers plant their vineyards! Behold, the Lord hath in readiness a servant, mighty and strong. As a tempest of hail-stones breaketh the vines, as a hurricane destroyeth all things, as rushing floods of waters ravage the land, so shall the Assyrian destroyer overthrow with his hand the power of Israel. The haughty garlands of the drunkards of Samaria shall be trodden under foot, and the withering wreaths with which they proudly adorn themselves on the mountain above the rich valleys shall be as the early fig that ripens first: it is found, it is plucked, it is devoured. [So shall the Assyrian swallow up Samaria.]

"But in that day the presence of the Lord of hosts shall crown Jerusalem with glory, and His favour shall be as a diadem of beauty unto the residue of His people. He will give righteous discernment unto the king of Judah, and will so strengthen his army that it shall drive back his foes to the gate of their own city. [This was fulfilled in Hezekiah's reign.] But in later days Judah too shall fall; for they also err through wine, and are gone out of the way by reason of strong drink. Priest and prophet alike have erred through strong drink, are drowned in wine, and are gone astray through drunkenness. The visions of the prophets are visions of error ; the judgments delivered by the priests are false. (See Lev. x. 8–11.) Their banqueting tables are wholly defiled by the filthy vomitings of drunken men. Who is there among them to whom one can teach the knowledge of God's will, or whom one can cause to understand the message that He sendeth ? Are they not all babes in understanding, like children weaned but yesterday from their mother's breast ? One must teach them as a child is taught ; rule after rule, rule after rule ; line after line, line after line ; a little to-day, a little to-morrow.

" [And even so they refuse to learn.] Therefore, saith the Lord, I will speak to this people by men of strange lips, by a nation whose tongue they cannot understand. (See Deut. xxviii. 49.) For I have sent unto them by My prophets, saying : In My ways shall ye find rest for yourselves and for the weary in Judah ; in My ways shall ye find refreshment : but they would not hear Me. Therefore will I give them up to their ignorance, and they shall still find My word to be as a vain repetition of rule after rule, rule after rule ; line after line, line after line ; a little to-day, a little to-morrow ; it shall not profit them. They shall seek to go forward, and shall be driven backward, broken by their oppressors, snared and taken captive by their enemies.

" Hear ye therefore the word of the Lord, ye scorners in high place at Jerusalem. Ye have said in your hearts, Death will not overtake us, the grave will not open for us ; for we have made a covenant of peace with death and the grave. If affliction shall pass through the land like a flood, it will not reach us : we shall find a refuge in the wisdom of our lies, a hiding-place in the astuteness of our falsehood. Therefore thus saith the

Lord God : [There is but one refuge.]   Behold, Messiah is the one foundation that I have laid for Zion to rest upon, a stone, a tried stone, a precious corner-stone, which is a sure foundation.   Whoso believeth in this stone and buildeth thereon shall never flee before his foes nor be put to shame ; for I will make judgment My measuring-line in measuring this stone, and righteousness My plummet in laying it.   But the hail of My wrath shall sweep away every lying refuge, and the flood of destruction shall overflow every hiding-place of falsehood.   The compact which ye have made with death shall be made void, and your agreement with the grave shall not stand.   [Neither death nor the grave shall spare you when I judge Jerusalem.]   When affliction shall pass like a flood through the land, ye shall be crushed by it.   Whensoever it cometh it shall reach you :   morning after morning shall it come ; it shall come by day and by night.   Then shall ye perceive the meaning of My warnings, and shall be filled with terror. The bed of hope on which ye have rested shall be found too short, and the coverlet of your falsehood shall be found too narrow.   For the Lord Himself will arise against you, as He arose against the Philistines at Baalperazim ; He will be wrath with you as He was wrath with them at Gibeon.   (See 1 Chron. xiv. 11 and 16.)   He will arise to do His work, His wondrous work, to accomplish His act, His wondrous act.   Therefore, mock not at His warnings, lest there be no deliverance for you.   For the Lord, the Lord of hosts, hath shown me that He hath determined to execute judgment on the whole land.

" [And now I will take up a parable, and justify my God by a dark saying.]   Give ear, therefore, and hear my voice ; hearken unto me, and hear my speech.   Is the ploughman always ploughing, and never sowing ? Is he always opening furrows in his field, and breaking up his clods with the harrow ?   When he hath prepared the face of the ground, doth he not sow his vetches and his cummin, and put in the wheat, the barley, and the spelt in the right way and in the right place ?   His God giveth him wisdom to do this, and teacheth him how to till his fields.   [And shall not God have His times for warning, for chastisement, for judgment, and for mercy ? Are not His people His husbandry ?]

" The husbandman doth not thresh the tender vetches with the heavy threshing-wain which he drags over the wheat, nor is that wain drawn over the frail cummin ; a staff is heavy enough for the vetches, and a rod is heavy enough for the cummin. And even the stronger wheat— do men thresh it till they have crushed it ? Nay, they will not thresh it continually, nor drive a threshing-wain and horses over it till it is ground to powder. Even so is it with the dispensations of the Lord of hosts, who is wonderful in counsel and excellent in wisdom."

God doth not afflict willingly, nor grieve the children of men without a cause ; and we know that all things work together for good to them that love Him, to them who are the called according to His purpose.

Chapter XXIX.

WE have already had occasion to notice that certain prophecies have more than one fulfilment. This is the case with the twenty-ninth chapter of Isaiah, an oracle which foretells heavy judgments for Jerusalem, and subsequent blessing upon a remnant of the house of Jacob. If we read the first four verses of this chapter, and then turn to the first chapter of the Lamentations, we can scarcely fail to see that Isaiah's words of woe had a terrible fulfilment in the days of Jeremiah. But if we afterwards turn to Luke xix. 41–44, we see that the woe was to have another fulfilment in the overthrow of Jerusalem by the Romans, some forty years after the crucifixion of Christ. In like manner we may find more than one fulfilment of the promise, " Lebanon shall be turned into a fruitful field," a promise wonderfully fulfilled in the calling of the Gentiles, but probably covering a wider range. Some writers refer much of this chapter to times yet future ; but we feel that it would be unwise and unsafe for us to speculate on such questions, and therefore prefer to leave them for the most part untouched. Our business is to make plain the meaning of the prophet's words, and to show how far they have been fulfilled ; and if we find that this fulfilment has been apparently complete, we come to the conclusion that it is impossible for us to say what the Lord yet intends to do of a similar nature.

The word Ariel is found in Ezekiel xliii. 15 (consult the margin at that place), and is there translated altar (R.V., altar hearth). It is made up of two Hebrew words, and may mean either "hearth of God," or "lion of God"; but the former meaning seems on the whole more appropriate both in this chapter of Isaiah and in the passage in Ezekiel above referred to. The glory of Jerusalem was its temple, and the centre-piece, so to speak, of the temple was the altar, where sin was confessed and put away. Jerusalem therefore might, in the mystical language of prophecy, be fitly spoken of as Ariel, "The city of sacrifices." It was soon to be a city of sacrifices in another sense than this; for the guilty inhabitants were to be the victims, and the soldiers of Nebuchadnezzar the sacrificers. (See Lam. 1. 13–16.)

We incline to the opinion of Calvin that the strangers and terrible ones mentioned in verse 5 are not the besiegers of Jerusalem, but mercenary troops hired by the Jews, and destined to be scattered as dust and chaff by the armies of Chaldea. We also adopt his view that the hungry dreamers of verses 7 and 8 are the unhappy men of Judah who dreamed of safety, but awoke from their dream to find the city surrounded by "all the families of the kingdoms of the north" (Jer. i. 14).

If our readers will carefully consider these introductory remarks, and will take the trouble to consult the passages of Scripture to which we have referred them, we think they will be better able to understand the following prophecy; may they and we be greatly profited by the lessons which it teaches.

"Woe unto thee, thou Altar of God, thou Altar of God, thou city wherein David pitched his camp! Pass ye on from year to year filling up your round of feasts! The time cometh when I will destroy thee, thou Altar-city, and will fill thee with moaning and moans. [The prophet uses here two words almost exactly alike.] Thou shalt serve as an altar for the sacrifice demanded by My justice. I will pitch My camp against thee round about, will bring against thee My besieging towers, and surround thee with My forts. Then shalt thou be brought low ; thy voice shall come from the ground, and thy feeble speech from the dust ; yea, thy voice shall be as the voice that answers a wizard out of the ground, and thy speech as a ghostly whisper out of the dust. [Thy sighs shall be many and thine heart faint, Lam. i. 22.] And the multitude of thy hired soldiers shall be driven away as the dust, the multitude of thy warriors as the chaff before the wind ; suddenly and instantly shall it be. The Lord of hosts will visit thee in vengeance with the thunder and earthquake-shock of war, with its uproar, its whirlwind, its tempest, and its devouring flames. (See 2 Chron. xxxvi. 19.) The multitude of the heathen that shall besiege thee, O Altar-city, the hosts that shall besiege thee and assault thy stronghold and fill thee with distress, shall be as the numberless phantoms of a dream or a night vision. As a hungry man dreameth that he is eating, but awaketh and is hungry still ; as a thirsty man dreameth that he is drinking, but awaketh and is faint and thirsty still—so shalt thou awake from thy dream of safety to find the hosts of the heathen encamped about Mount Zion."

Most commentators give a different interpretation to this similitude of a dream. That which we have given is Calvin's. His words are : " When the Jews through false hope shall promise to themselves deliverance, as if their enemies would be driven far away, they shall quickly feel that they have been deceived ; in the same manner as a person whom hunger leads to dream that he is feasting luxuriously, as soon as he awakes feels that his hunger is keener than before." It seems to us that this interpretation agrees better with the rest of the pro-phecy than that which is generally given—namely, that the prophet here foretells the defeat and disappointment of Zion's enemies. The great reformer's view of the passage is at least worthy of the reader's consideration. We pass on.

"[Do you refuse to believe My words?] Then gaze at Me and wonder; shut your eyes, if ye will, and blind yourselves. Ye are drunken, but not with wine; ye stagger, but not under strong drink; [ye are drunken with sin, and besotted with unbelief.] The Lord in judgment hath plunged you into deep sleep; your prophets should have been eyes to you, but God hath closed those eyes; your seers should have been heads to you, but He hath blinded them. And all the revelation that He has given by His own prophets is become as a sealed book to you. They that know how to read say, We cannot read it, for it is sealed; and the illiterate say, We cannot read it, for we know not how to read. [From the highest of you to the lowest, ye are blind to the meaning of God's word.]

"Moreover the Lord saith: Forasmuch as this people honour Me with mouth and lip, but not with the heart, and offer Me a worship taught by the traditions of men, therefore, behold, I will proceed to execute upon them judgments marvellous and miraculous; the wisdom of their wise men shall come to nought, and the understanding of their counsellors shall fail. Woe unto them! For they seek to bury their plans in depths which the Lord shall not fathom, and to do their works in darkness which He shall not penetrate; saying, Who can see us? who knoweth what we do? They turn things upside down, and look upon the potter as if he were the clay. Shall the vessel say of the potter, he made me not? Shall that which is formed say of him that formed it, he hath no understanding? Therefore, in a very little while the dry land shall be turned into watersprings; but the fruitful land shall be turned into barrenness, for the wickedness of them that dwell therein (Psa. cvii. 33-37). [The kingdom of God shall be taken from you, and given to a nation bringing forth the fruits thereof, Matt. xxi. 43.]

"Then shall the ears of the deaf be unstopped, that they may hear the word of God; and the blind eyes that have dwelt in obscurity and darkness shall be opened to see His glory. The joy of the Lord shall abound unto the meek, and the poorest of men shall rejoice in the favour of the Holy One of Israel. For they that oppress My people shall be brought to nought, and they that devise iniquity in the night-season shall be cut off; they shall no longer subvert a man in his cause, lay snares for righteous counsellors, and turn aside the right of a man with falsehood. Therefore thus saith the Lord, the Friend of Abraham, concerning the house of Jacob, They shall no longer be put to shame by their foes, neither shall their faces wax pale with fear. They shall see in the midst of them their children, whom My hands shall create (Eph. ii. 10), and shall fear Me and glorify My name; yea, they shall fear the Holy One of Jacob, and shall revere the God of Israel. Even those that erred in spirit shall understand My ways, and they that murmured against Me shall learn the knowledge of My will."

How much of this gracious word of promise is meant for the Jew, and how much for the Gentile? In Christ Jesus neither circumcision availeth anything, nor uncircumcision, but a new creature. And as many as walk according to this rule, peace shall be on them and mercy, and upon the Israel of God. Brethren, the grace of our Lord Jesus Christ be with your spirit. Amen.

Chapter XXX.

THIS chapter appears to contain three prophecies. In the first five verses the statesmen of Judah are rebuked for seeking help against Assyria from their old enemy Egypt. In so doing they were committing a double offence against God. First, they were trusting in an arm of flesh, instead of trusting in the Lord (Jer. xvii. 5); secondly, they were rebelling against a distinct command of the God who had brought them forth out of Egypt, and had said, "Ye shall henceforth return no more that way." (See Deut. xvii. 16, and xxviii. 68.)

In the next twenty-one verses the same subject is handled at greater length. The occasion of this prophecy seems to have been the departure of a caravan of asses and camels laden with presents for the Egyptians, to purchase their help against Assyria. The prophet is instructed by the Lord to engrave upon a tablet, and write in a book, an enduring record of the wickedness of this policy, and the hopeless ruin to which it should lead. Yet not hopeless; for the Lord, after a season of suspense, during which He would show His displeasure and magnify His justice (ver. 18), would turn again in mercy toward the remnant of His people, would dry up their tears, give them wholesome instruction through faithful prophets and teachers, cause them to turn with disgust from their former idols, fill their land with fruitfulness, and make the sun to shine upon it with seven-fold glory.

The remainder of the chapter (verses 27–33) predicts

the destruction of Sennacherib's host by the burning breath of God's righteous vengeance.

We by no means wish to imply that these prophecies have no deeper meaning than that which we have sketched above. The sunlike brightness of the moon, and the seven-fold glory of the sun, may well refer to the splendour of that heavenly city which shall need neither sun nor moon, because the Lamb is the light thereof ; and the flame which was to consume the Assyrians in the valley of Hinnom (Ge-Hinnom, Gehenna) may foreshadow the everlasting punishment of the wicked in the Tophet where their worm dieth not, and their fire is not quenched. But we wish to keep to our task of explaining the direct and primary meaning of the words of the prophet.

" My children rebel against Me (Isa. i. 2) ; woe unto them, saith the Lord. For they trust in their own wisdom, not in Mine ; they form an alliance which My Spirit sanctioneth not ; they add sin to sin ; they go forth to seek help from Egypt, but have not sought My counsel—they rely on the power of Pharaoh, and trust in the protection of Egypt. Therefore your reliance on Pharaoh shall prove your shame, and your trust in the protection of Egypt your confusion. Your embassy of princes has reached Pharaoh's court at Zoan, and has entered his palace at Tahapanes (Jer. ii. 16). But your princes and yourselves shall be ashamed of a useless alliance with a people that can neither help nor profit you, whose friendship shall put you to shame, and shall fill the mouths of your enemies with reproaches. [See the words of Rabshakeh in Isa. xxxvi. 6.]

" The prophecy concerning the caravan that hath been despatched to Egypt.

" Through the great and terrible wilderness, the home of the lion and the lioness, of the viper and the swift and deadly serpent, the ambassadors of Judah carry rich gifts upon asses, and treasures upon camels, to buy the friendship of a people that shall not profit them. For the help of Egypt is vain and useless, therefore have I called her Haughtyland the idle. [That is, a country which boasts, but does nothing. The word here trans lated ' strength ' is Rahab, *i.e.*, Arrogance, a name given to Egypt in Isa. li. 9, and elsewhere. The trans- lation of this passage given in the Authorised Version, though it expresses a great spiritual truth, can hardly be defended as correct.] Go therefore, said the Lord unto me, engrave on a tablet before the men of Judah this protest against their sin, and write it in a book, that in time to come it may be a witness against them for ever. For they are a people of rebellion, children of falsehood, children that will not give ear to the word of the Lord. They say to the seers, See no more visions ; to the prophets, Prophesy no more of justice and judg- ment : give us smooth words and prophecies of peace, though they be false ; leave your way, forsake your path, and let us hear no more of the Holy One of Israel. Therefore thus saith the Holy One of Israel, Because ye despise My word, and trust in wickedness and per- versity, and make them your refuge, therefore your wickedness shall be like unto a swelling in a high wall, bulging and ready to burst, which breaketh suddenly in a moment, even as a potter's vessel is broken when one breaketh it utterly in pieces, so that no fragment is left large enough to take a few embers from the hearth or a little water from the well. For the Lord God, the Holy One of Israel, hath said, By returning unto Me, and relying on My power, ye shall find deliverance ; by quietly putting your trust in Me ye shall become strong. But ye would none of His counsel. Ye said, Nay ; for we will flee from our foes on horses ; therefore ye shall flee from them : we will ride upon swift steeds ; there- fore shall your pursuers be swift. The battle-shout of

one of your foes shall put to flight a thousand of you ;
the shout of five of them shall put to flight your army.
And ye shall be left few in number, like beacons on a
mountain-top, or signals on a hill.   Therefore will the
Lord defer His grace for a season ; yet will He be
gracious to your remnant ; He will magnify His
justice, yet will He show you mercy.   For the Lord
is a God of justice ; blessed are all they that wait for
His mercy.

" For My people shall still dwell in Zion at Jerusalem.
[The Assyrian shall not carry them away captive, as he
did the men of Samaria.]   Their weeping shall be ended.
Their God will surely be gracious to them when they
cry to Him ; He will hear and answer.   And though He
feed you with adversity, and make you drink the water
of affliction, He will give you the consolation of His word.
Your prophets shall no longer be driven from among
you [by the wickedness of your kings], but your eyes
shall see them.   [Daniel, Ezekiel, Haggai, Zechariah,
Malachi.]   Their word shall be in your ears, following
your footsteps, and saying, This is the way, walk ye in
it, in all the turnings and windings of your pathway.
Then shall ye dishonour your silver-plated idols and your
gilded images ; ye shall cast them forth as an unclean
thing, saying, Away with them !   And God shall send
rain to water the seed that thou sowest, the produce of
thy ground shall give thee bread in abundance, for thy
ground shall be rich and fertile.   Thou shalt have wide
pasture-lands for thy cattle, and thy corn shall be so
abundant that thine oxen and thine asses shall feed on
salted provender and winnowed grain instead of hay
and chaff.   Even the summits of thy mountains and
the tops of thine hills shall be abundantly watered ;
thine enemies shall be slain with a great slaughter, and
all their fortresses shall fall.   Thy moon shall be bright
as the sun, and thy sun shall shine with seven-fold light,

when the Lord bindeth up and healeth the wounds of
His stricken people."

The glory of Hezekiah's deliverance (Isa. xxxvii.
33–38) was great ; that of the restoration from Babylon
was greater ; and the glory of Christ's gospel excelleth
all other glories that have yet been revealed (2 Cor. iii.
7–11). It doth not yet appear what shall be the glory
of the New Jerusalem.

" Behold, the Lord, whose name is a man of war,
cometh from afar. His wrath is as a fire that sendeth
up thick clouds of smoke. His lips overflow with indignation ; His tongue is as a consuming fire ; the
breath of His anger is as a stream that overfloweth its
banks and riseth above the plains even to the neck.
He will sift the heathen in the sieve of destruction, and
will put into their jaws a bridle that shall turn them to
ruin. But His own people shall sing as they sing in
the night of the passover ; their heart shall be glad as
those who go up with sound of music to worship the
Rock of Israel in His holy mountain. The Lord shall
thunder with the voice of His majesty, and shall smite
His foes with the arm of His strength in the fury of His
wrath, with lightning, whirlwind, storm and hail. The
voice of His thunder shall shatter the power of Assyria,
which smote the nations as a rod ; and at every stroke
of the staff of doom wherewith the Lord shall smite,
Judah shall rejoice with timbrel and with harp ; for
with a destroying onslaught will the Lord fight against
His people's foes. For Tophet hath been ordained
from of old to be the place of their perdition ; it is
made ready to receive their king. The Lord hath made
it deep and wide ; vast is the fire thereof, and the fuel.
The anger of the Lord, like a stream of brimstone, doth
kindle it."

Great is the Lord, and greatly to be feared ; and who
can stand in His sight when once He is angry ?

TWENTY-SIXTH HALF-HOUR

Chapters XXXI., XXXII.

IN the thirty-first chapter the prophet renews his denunciations of woe against those of his countrymen who sought help from Egypt, instead of looking for deliverance to the Holy One of Israel. He tells them plainly that they and their helpers shall perish together, and that the Lord of hosts will defend His own people by His own power. Let the men of Judah cast away their idols and return to Him against whom they have so deeply transgressed, and then the hosts of Sennacherib shall fall beneath the stroke of an unearthly sword, shall be devoured by the fire of God's wrath, which still burns as a furnace in Zion to consume the foes thereof.

" Woe unto the men who go down to Egypt for help, and rely upon its horses for deliverance from Assyria! Woe unto the men who trust in the multitude of Egypt's chariots and the might of its cavalry; who count it a vain thing to look to the Holy One of Israel, or to cry unto the God of their fathers! For remember, ye wise men, that He also is wise; it is He that hath brought this evil upon us, fulfilling His immutable word; and He will surely stretch out His hand against them that do evil in Judah, and will smite the Egyptian helpers of these workers of iniquity. [And why should ye trust in Egypt and its horses?] The Egyptians are men, and not God; their horses are flesh, and not spirit; and when the Lord shall stretch forth His hand to smite, your Egyptian helpers shall stumble (compare 2 Kings xxiv.

7), and ye who are holpen of them shall fall, and ye and they shall perish together.

"[The Lord of hosts is the defender of Zion;] for thus hath He said unto me : As a lion, or a lion's whelp, when he growleth over his prey, is undismayed at the attack of a multitude of shepherds which has been called together against him, and unmoved by the sound of their shouting ; so shall the Lord of hosts be when He shall come down to fight at Mount Zion, and to defend the hill thereof : [for what to Him is the tumult of Assyria's armies ?] Yea, as the eagle flieth swiftly to the defence of its nest, so will the Lord come to protect Jerusalem ; He will protect you, deliver you, pass over you [as when He brought you out of Egypt], and save you.   Therefore return ye to Him from whom ye have utterly revolted, ye children of Israel.   In that day [the day of your repentance and deliverance] ye shall each and all of you cast away your idols of silver and gold, the gods which your own hands have fashioned that they might lead you from sin to sin. And then, when ye shall have turned unto Me, saith the Lord (see 2 Kings xix. 1), then shall a sword not held in the hand of man strike down the Assyrian ; a sword not wielded by mortals shall devour him ; he shall flee from it, and his youthful warriors shall be subdued by it. All his might shall fail for fear, and his captains shall flee from the banner that shall dismay them, saith the Lord, whose anger goeth forth as a fire from Zion, and burneth as a furnace in Jerusalem against the enemies thereof."

It was a happy day for Judah when Hezekiah mounted the throne of David to begin his righteous reign of twenty-nine years. For though that reign was marked with more than one bitter trouble for himself and his people, and was not unstained by sin, it was yet the reign of a man who did that which was right in the eyes

of the Lord, according to all that his father David had
done.   He destroyed the idols of the land, and cast away
the gods of silver and gold which the hands of the
people had made.   (Compare Isa. xxxi. 7 with 2 Kings
xviii. 4.)   He trusted in the Lord, the God of Israel,
so that after him, with the exception of good Josiah,
there was none like him among all the kings of Judah.
For he clave to the Lord ; he departed not from following Him, but kept His commandments, which the Lord
commanded Moses.   And the Lord was with him ;
whithersoever he went forth, he prospered (2 Kings
xviii. 1–8).   It is quite clear that such a king would
surround himself, as far as was possible, with godly
counsellors and righteous officers of state ; a king who
thus reigned in righteousness would be encompassed
and upheld by princes who ruled in justice, and the
government of such a court would shelter the poor of
the land from the winds of wickedness, and the lowly
from the tempests of oppression.

"Yes," say the unbelieving Jewish expositors of
Isaiah, "this, and this alone, was the true historic
fulfilment of the prophecy : Behold, a king shall reign
in righteousness, and princes shall rule in judgment ;
and each of them shall be as a hiding-place from the
wind, a covert from the tempest ; as rivers of water
in a dry place, as the shadow of a great rock in a
weary land."

"Nay," say certain Christian commentators, jealous
for the honour of our Lord Jesus, "this prophecy refers
exclusively to the Messiah, and has been or will be fulfilled in the person, work and reign of that Son of David
who is the Son of God."

Let us listen to a wiser voice, which has often rightly
interpreted to us the mysterious word of prophecy :
"This prediction undoubtedly refers to Hezekiah and
his reign, under which the Church was reformed and

restored to its former splendour ; for previously it was in a wretched and ruined condition. Ahaz, who was a wicked and disgraceful hypocrite, had corrupted everything according to his own inclinations, and had overturned the whole condition of civil government and of religion (2 Kings xvi. 2–4). God therefore promises another king, whose power and righteousness shall restore the state of affairs which is thus wretched and desperate. In a word, he presents to us in this passage a lively picture of the prosperous condition of the Church ; and as this cannot be attained without Christ, this description undoubtedly refers to Christ, of whom Hezekiah was a type, and whose kingdom he foreshadowed. . . . While the prophet describes the reign of Hezekiah, he intends to lead us farther ; for he discourses concerning the restoration of the Church, which indeed was shadowed forth by Hezekiah, but has been actually fulfilled in Christ. We know that the Church is never in a healthy condition unless she be internally ruled by righteous and wise governors ; now this cannot be unless Christ reigns, and here, therefore, Christ and His reign are specially commended to us."

With this, which is the judgment of Calvin, we entirely agree, guided by the consideration that words spoken by the Lord with express reference to Solomon (2 Sam. vii. 14) are in the Epistle to the Hebrews (i. 5) expressly referred to Christ.

" But behold, in Zion there shall reign a king whose sceptre shall be a sceptre of righteousness, and all who bear rule in his kingdom shall rule in justice. He shall be unto his people a shelter from every wind, a covert from every tempest ; [he shall deliver them from the wrath of man, and from the wrath of God.] He shall refresh them as rivers of water refresh dry ground ; he shall shelter them as a great rock that throws its sheltering shade over travellers in a weary land. The eyes of the people shall no longer be blinded, as in former days (see Isa. vi. 10), and their ears shall no longer be deaf to the words of God. Yea, the inconsiderate shall be of an understanding heart (Prov. vi. 5), and stammering tongues shall be loosed to speak the praise of the Lord (see Mark vi. 32-37). In his days the fool shall no longer be had in honour as a prince, nor the churlish man be accounted bountiful. For the words of a fool are words of folly, and the fruits of his heart are works of iniquity ; he practiseth ungodliness, and uttereth falsehood against the Lord (Acts v. 4 ; 1 Tim. iv. 2) ; he robbeth the hungry of their bread, and the thirsty of their drink. The churlish man useth evil instruments and wicked devices, that he may destroy the poor with lying words, and pervert the course of justice unto the ruin of the needy. [Such shall not stand in the presence of the King of righteousness.] The bountiful man deviseth bountiful things, and in so doing he shall stand before the king."

It is evident that, as Calvin says, the adequate fulfilment of the above prophecy can only be found under the reign of Christ ; can only be found in that kingdom which is righteousness, and peace and joy in the Holy Ghost (Rom. xiv. 17).

The prophet now turns to the thoughtless and worldly women whom he has already rebuked in chap iii. 16-24, and again warns them of a time of distress which is speedily approaching. He may refer primarily to the Babylonian invasion under Nebuchadnezzar, and the desolation which should follow it—a desolation which, in some sense, stretched onward to the birth of Christ, and the days of the outpouring of the Holy Ghost, foretold by Joel and fulfilled at Pentecost. This long desolation was to be followed by the righteous reign of the Prince of Peace (Isa. xxxii. 15-20).

" Arise from your sloth, ye women of Judah that are

at ease, and hear my voice ; give ear unto my words, ye presumptuous daughters of Jerusalem. Yet a little while, and ye shall have trouble, ye that are now heedless and presumptuous ; for your foes shall rob you of your vintage, and your harvest shall be taken from you. [Is it famine or war that the prophet sees nigh at hand ? Apparently both.] Tremble and be troubled, ye slothful women, ye heedless daughters ; strip you of your ornaments, lay aside your robes, and gird your loins with sackcloth. For ye shall smite upon your breasts as ye lament the pleasant fields that are ruined, and the fruitful vines that are destroyed. Though ye are My people, and your land the gift of My covenant, yet shall it lie waste, overgrown with briars and thorns ; yea, briars and thorns shall cover the sites of all the houses of merriment in your merry city. The palace shall be emptied of its princes, and the streets shall be emptied of their crowds. [Fulfilled, Lam. i. 1 and 4]. For many a day shall hill and tower be as dens of wild beasts, a place where wild asses shall sport, and flocks shall roam undisturbed.

" Yet after those days the Spirit of the Lord shall be poured upon us from on high (Acts ii. 17 and 33), and shall turn the wilderness into a fruitful field, and shall make the fruitful fields such that their fruitfulness of former days shall be counted as the mere produce of a forest. Then shall the fertilised wilderness become the home of justice, and the fruitful field the dwelling-place of righteousness. Righteousness shall give peace, and the effect thereof shall be everlasting rest and everlasting safety (John xiv. 27 ; Rom. v. 1). And My people, saith the Lord, shall abide in a land of peace, in everlasting tabernacles, in quiet mansions (John xiv. 2). But the hail of My judgment shall overthrow the enemies of My people, as a storm overthrows the trees of the forest ; and their city shall be brought low in utter destruction. Blessed shall ye be who shall then till the richly-watered land, and send forth your oxen and asses to roam or to labour in peace and plenty."

Perhaps the vagueness of certain phrases which we have used in the above exposition is not altogether a defect. We dare not be too explicit where the best of men have differed, and where the words of the prophet seem to have such wide application and such manifold fulfilment.

Chapter XXXIII.

WE pray much before writing these Half-Hours, and add to our prayers a careful study of the portion of Holy Scripture which we are to explain. We compare English, French, and German translations of the Bible, and carefully consider the opinions of good commentators, rejecting without hesitation all that appears to us to be weak or fanciful. Finally, we submit our paraphrase to the kind criticism of a distinguished Hebrew scholar who is well known as an opponent of the rationalistic criticism of these latter days ; for we greatly desire that our interpretation of the prophets may be, as far as it goes, absolutely trustworthy.

Among commentators there are two whom we always consult for our own enlightenment, and for the confirmation or, if need be, the correction of our own views, namely, Calvin and Gill. And we must say that, much as we value Dr. Gill for his depth of learning and spirituality of thought, we find that Calvin excels him in correctness of exposition and sobriety of judgment. In proof of this we will lay before our readers short extracts from the writings of both, bearing on the well-known passage : " Thine eyes shall see the king in his beauty ; they shall behold the land that is very far off."

Calvin says : " This promise was highly necessary for supporting the hearts of believers, when the state of affairs in Judæa was so lamentable and so desperate.

When Jerusalem was besieged, the king shut up within the city and surrounded by treacherous counsellors, the people unsteady and seditious, and everything hastening to ruin, there appeared to be no hope left. Still the royal authority in the family of David was a remarkable pledge of the love of God. Isaiah, therefore, meets the danger by saying that though they behold their king covered with filthy garments (2 Kings xix. 1), yet he shall be restored to his former rank and splendour. . . . But it ought also to be observed that the kingdom of Judah was a type of the kingdom of Christ, whose image Hezekiah bore; for there would be but a slight fulfilment of this promise if we did not trace it to Christ, to whom all these things must be understood to refer. Let no man imagine that I am here pursuing allegories: I am averse to them; and that is the reason why I do not interpret this passage as relating directly to Christ. But because in Christ alone is found the stability of that frail kingdom, the likeness which Hezekiah bore leads us, as it were, by the hand to Christ. I am, therefore, disposed to view Hezekiah as a figure of Christ, that we may learn how great will be His beauty. . . . The restoration of the church consists of two parts: first, that the King shall be seen in His beauty; and secondly, that the boundaries of the kingdom shall be extended." This last remark is intended as an explanation of the phrase, " land of far distances." (Isa. xxxiii. 17, *margin*.)

Dr. Gill says: " Not merely Hezekiah in his royal robes and with a cheerful countenance, having put off his sackcloth upon the breaking up of the siege, but a greater than he, even the King, Messiah, in the glory of His person and office, especially as a king reigning gloriously before His ancients in Jerusalem. The apostles saw Him in His glory in the days of His flesh, corporeally and spiritually; believers now see Him by faith, crowned with glory and honour, as well as see His beauty, fulness, and suitability as a Saviour, and ere long their eyes shall see Him personally in His own and the Father's glory. . . . The heavenly country may be said to be a land afar off with respect to the earth on which the saints now are. . . . Of this now the saints have at times a view by faith, . . . though it may be that an enlargement of His kingdom all over the world to the distant parts of it may be here meant. . . . The words may be rendered ' a land of distances,' or, ' of far distances,' that reaches far and near, from sea to sea, and from the river to the ends of the earth ; which will be the case when the kingdoms of this world shall become Christ's."

We feel sure that, while the results obtained are, in this case, similar, Calvin's method is the safer of the two. We share his wholesome aversion to allegorising, believing that by means of it good men and bad men have continually engrafted their own fancies on the Word of God. It is our desire to discover for ourselves and to make plain to our readers the mind of the Spirit in His Word.

The ambassadors of peace, in verse 7 of this chapter, seem to be the envoys named in 2 Kings xviii. 18, 37, Eliakim, Shebna, and Joah, who returned in distress to Hezekiah, after hearing the haughty and cruel speech of the Assyrian general ; or the prophet may refer to some embassy which was sent to the invader, but has not been recorded. To understand aright verse 8, we must remember that Hezekiah had submitted to Sennacherib, and had paid the fine which that king had demanded—three hundred talents of silver and thirty talents of gold. By accepting this payment, Sennacherib entered into a covenant to spare Jerusalem the horrors of a siege. (See 2 Kings xviii. 13–16.) If our readers are familiar with the history of

Hezekiah's reign, they will easily understand the following paraphrase :—

"Woe unto thee, Assyria ! Thou gatherest spoil
from nations who have taken none from thee, and
breakest faith with those who have not broken faith
with thee : but when thou shalt no longer have the
power to despoil others, others shall despoil thee ;
when thou shalt no more be able to break faith with
others, others shall break faith with thee. [This threat
was fulfilled when Nineveh fell before the combined
forces of Babylonia and Media, which, as Nahum also
predicted, took away her spoil of silver and gold, and
her store of pleasant furniture, and made her empty,
and void, and waste—Nahum ii. 8, 9.] My people
cry to Me, saying, Lord, have mercy upon us ; for our
expectation is from Thee. Help Thou us morning by
morning, and save us in the time of our trouble. I will
cause their foes to hear the sound of a tumult and to
flee ; I will arise to deliver My people, and the heathen
shall be scattered (2 Kings xix. 34–36). And Judah
shall gather the spoil of their camp as caterpillars
gather their food ; the men of Jerusalem shall rush on
to spoil their fallen enemies as locusts rush on to strip
the fields. The Lord, whose throne is in heaven, hath
arisen to display His power ; He hath abundantly
executed judgment and justice for Jerusalem. Times
of stable prosperity shall be given to her, filling her with
salvation, and wisdom, and knowledge ; for the fear of
the Lord is the wealth of His people.

"But meanwhile our chief men wail in the streets ;
our ambassadors, insulted and rejected, rend their
clothes and weep (2 Kings xviii. 37). The highways of
our land are ravaged and deserted ; our enemy hath
broken the compact that he had made with us ; he
despiseth our cities and their inhabitants, [saying, Who
are they among all the gods of the countries that have

delivered their country out of my hand, that the Lord should deliver Jerusalem out of my hand?—2 Kings xviii. 33-35]. His forces have filled our land with sorrow and distress; our forests are shorn by him of the glory of their cedars; our orchards and vineyards are turned into leafless wildernesses. Therefore, thus saith the Lord, Now will I arise for the help of My people, now will I be exalted in the destruction of their foes. The designs of the Assyrian shall be as chaff, and the work of his hands as stubble; his own breath shall kindle a fire which shall devour him. The heathen shall be destroyed as stone in the heat of the lime-kiln; they shall perish as thorns that are hewn down and cast into the fire. Ye nations that are far off, hearken to the report of My judgment; and ye, My people, acknowledge My might in the destruction of your enemies. The sinners that are among you are panic-stricken, the ungodly in Jerusalem are smitten with terror; they say, Who among us can stand before Him whose wrath hath devoured an army in a night? Who among us can abide the flame of His everlasting anger? [But the Lord is good to them that fear Him.] They that follow after righteousness and speak words of uprightness, that scorn to get wealth by oppression, that close their hands against bribes, their ears against the counsel of the bloodthirsty, and their eyes from looking with favour on evil deeds—these shall be lifted above all their foes; their place of refuge shall be as a fortress on a rocky mountain, and their meat and drink shall never fail. They shall see their king clothed with honour and majesty, and the remotest parts of his dominions at peace. They shall muse on the terror of these days as a thing that is past, and say, Where are now the enemies that taxed us, exacted tribute, and marked out our towers for destruction? They shall no longer see their city surrounded by a people whose difficult speech they cannot comprehend, whose barbarous tongue they cannot understand. They shall see Zion thronged with worshippers at her holy feasts; and their eyes shall perceive that Jerusalem is a dwelling of peace, a tent which shall never be struck, a tent whose stakes shall never be plucked up, whose cords shall never be broken. For there the Lord of glory will be with us; His power shall surround and protect us, as broad rivers and streams surround and protect the mighty cities of our foes (see Nahum iii. 8, and Jer. li. 13). On the face of our protecting stream shall go no ship of war to destroy us, no gallant vessel to bring near our enemies; for the Lord is our Judge, the Lord is our Lawgiver, the Lord is our King, and He will save us.

" But as to thee, great vessel of Assyria's power, thy tackling is wrecked; thy mariners cannot set up thy mast nor spread thy sail. Thine abundant wealth is become the prey of My people, saith the Lord; even they that are lame among them shall take their portion of thy spoil. But the inhabitant of Zion shall no longer say, I am sick; for the iniquity of them that dwell therein shall be forgiven."

The historic fulfilment of these gracious promises in the day of Hezekiah's deliverance is a pledge of their more abundant accomplishment in the church of God, in the person of Christ, in the glories of heaven.

Chapters XXXIV., XXXV.

THE display of God's justice in the destruction of
Edom, and the display of His love in the salvation of His own people, are the themes of the two
chapters which we have now reached. The former
was brought about by the exterminating wars which,
between the days of Isaiah and Malachi, laid waste the
heritage of Esau (Mal. i. 3) ; the latter by deliverance
from Babylon, by the birth of the Messiah at Bethlehem,
by His mighty works of mercy (see Matt. xi. 4, 5, where
Christ claims to be the fulfiller of Isaiah's predictions),
by His atoning death, and by that eternal life which
His sacrifice procured for all the Israel of God.

While we ourselves have no doubt that this is the
true sense of the chapters before us, we shall now, as
often before, confirm our interpretation by referring to
the judgment of others. To this end we shall quote at
some length from Jenour's sober and learned commentary on Isaiah, and shall take from the Annotated
Bible a short sentence referring to chapter xxxv. Jenour,
writing on chapter xxxiv., says :

" After a very mature consideration of the prophecy,
I am inclined to think that the primary subject of the
threatening is Edom [Idumea], and its capital city,
Bozrah. No one could be more opposed to this view
of the prophecy at one time than myself. But upon
consideration, it appeared to me the most natural, and
encumbered with the fewest difficulties. . . . The
strongest argument in favour of a literal interpretation,
at least primarily, is that it has been literally accom-

plished. Edom, once a populous and flourishing kingdom, containing several large cities and possessing a numerous army, is now a perfect wilderness. Not only have the inhabitants disappeared, and its cities become heaps of ruins, but even its roads have been destroyed, and no person for many ages has passed through it. Those travellers who have recently [Jenour's book was published in 1830] explored the territory, in part, which once formed the country of Idumea, inform us that the eye discovers nothing in these regions but barren tracts of sand, among which are found, here and there, the ruins of large towns, of which nothing remains but broken walls and heaps of stones, and that these abound with serpents and scorpions, with wild beasts, and solitary birds. And so full of dangers do they represent these inhospitable wilds, that not even the wandering Arabs will venture into them ; and with difficulty can they be brought to conduct travellers even to the borders of what was once Idumea. These facts are amply sufficient to show that the prediction has been literally accomplished. . . .

" But has the prophecy no hidden meaning of more general interest ? Does the desolation of a single small kingdom like Edom form the sole subject of the latter part of these terrible denunciations, couched in such sublime and awful language ? I confess that I am loath to come to such a conclusion. Yet the application of the prophecy to any events yet future appears to me so vague and uncertain, and attended with so many difficulties, that no possible good can result from attempting it. . . . Upon the whole, therefore, I prefer adhering to the literal interpretation as being that which is both most natural and most profitable. What indeed can be more instructive to sinful and careless man than the contemplation of such a picture of the appalling effects of the wrath of an avenging God ? "

As to chapter xxxv., the reference which Christ makes
to it in Matthew xi. is sufficient to show that much of it
had a full and magnificent fulfilment in the days of His
own ministry, though the promise of a Zion filled with
everlasting joy evidently looks onward to that eternal
city whose builder and maker is God.   It is well said
in the Annotated Bible : "The prophecy seems to
unite in one beautiful picture the restoration of the
Jews from Babylon, the calling of the Gentiles into the
church, the glory of the Christian dispensation, the
safety and happiness of individual believers, and the
blessedness of heaven."

And now may the Lord guide our pen, so that it may
trace out a safe and sufficient exposition of this portion
of His Word.

"Come hither, ye nations, to hear the word of God
concerning you ; hearken thereunto, all ye kingdoms
of the world. [For the nations and kingdoms immediately concerned, see Jer. xxv. 15–38.] Let the earth
hear, and all that is in it ; the world, and all that cometh
forth of it. For the Lord is wroth with all the nations
[that have been wroth with His people], and His anger
is hot against all their host ; He hath devoted them to
destruction, and given them up to slaughter. Their
slain shall lie in unburied heaps ; the stench of their
putrefaction shall fill the air, and their blood shall run
in torrents down the mountains ; [for I will visit them
with the scourge of war.] Yea, the host of heaven
shall perish, and the heavens shall be rolled together
as a disused scroll. All their host shall fall, as the
leaves fall from a blighted vine or a withering fig-tree.
[Here the range of the prophet's vision seems to extend
to the day of doom foretold in 2 Peter iii. 10. Compare
also Rev. vi. 12–17.] For My sword is stretched out
from heaven to drink its fill of blood ; [that is, My
justice hath decreed that the nations shall be consumed

by the scourge of war ;] behold, My sword shall descend upon Edom, and shall execute judgment on those whom I have devoted to destruction. The sword of the Lord shall drink the blood of His enemies, and shall reek with the fat of His foes ; the common people shall fall before it, and their leaders shall not escape. For the Lord hath appointed that the men of Bozrah shall be sacrificed to His justice, and hath given up the land of Edom to be ravaged with the sword ; the fierce, the strong, the haughty, shall perish with the rest. Their land shall be soaked with their blood, and the dust thereof shall be saturated with their fat. For the day is come when the Lord will avenge His people, the time when He will repay those who have contended with Zion. And Edom shall be as Sodom, whose streams became pitch, her dust brimstone, and her whole land a burning furnace. The fire of My wrath shall never be quenched ; it shall smoke for ever. The land of Edom shall lie waste from generation to generation ; no foot of man shall pass through it for ever and ever. Unclean creatures shall make it their haunt, and birds of ill-omen shall build their nests therein ; for God shall mete it out unto confusion as by line, appoint it to desolation as by plummet. An heir to the throne of Edom shall be sought in vain, for the nobles shall be no more, and all the princes shall perish. The ruined palaces of the land shall be overgrown with thorns, its dismantled fortresses with nettles and thistles. Idumea shall become a home for jackals, a dwelling-place for owls ; the wild beasts of the desert and the howling creatures of the wilderness shall meet within her walls, and one hairy beast shall cry to another ; loathsome monsters of the night shall dwell in her, and shall find a settled rest. There shall the arrowsnake make her nest, lay her eggs, hatch, and gather her brood around her. Yea, the vultures shall assemble, each one with her mate. Search ye this book that the Lord hath written, and mark well its words ; not one of these evil denizens shall be missing in the land of Edom, and none of them shall be without her mate ; [they shall breed and multiply.] For the mouth of the Lord hath bidden them, and the breath thereof shall gather them. He hath appointed them their dwelling-place by lot, and His hand hath portioned it out unto them by line ; they shall possess the land for ever, and shall dwell therein from generation to generation."

From this awful picture of the effects of God's righteous curse upon Edom, a picture which reminds us of the eternal punishment of the wicked, it is a relief to turn to the promises of His grace in Christ, which fill the next chapter.

"Yet My blessing shall visit the wilderness [of banished Israel, of the desolate Gentile world, of the ruined hearts of sinners], and shall make glad for My people the solitary place : yea, it shall cause the desert to rejoice and blossom as the rose. The blossom shall be abundant, the rejoicing shall be with exceeding great joy and with the voice of praise. The wilderness shall be adorned as with the cedars of Lebanon, the vines of Carmel, and the bloom of Sharon : its glory shall be the glory of the Lord, its excellency the excellency of our God. Strengthen therefore the weak hands of My desponding people, and confirm their feeble knees. Say to those whose hearts fail for fear, Be strong, fear not : behold, your God shall come to take vengeance on your enemies ; God will recompense tribulation to your foes. (Compare Col. ii. 15.) He will come to seek and to save that which was lost. [Isaiah, looking forward through seven centuries, said : 'He will come.' We, looking back through nineteen centuries, say with John : 'We know that the Son of God is come.']

"[Found in fashion as a man, He will dwell among

you], opening the eyes of the blind, unstopping the ears
of the deaf, making the lame man to leap as an hart,
and the tongue of the dumb to sing. (See Acts iii. 8 ;
Mark vii. 34, 35.) For in the wilderness of the world
shall break out the waters of His grace, and in the
desert of fallen humanity the streams of His love.
Then shall the dry land of the desert become pools,
and the thirsty ground springs of water. That which
was once the haunt of jackals, the lair in which they
lived undisturbed, shall be green and fruitful as the
banks of the Nile. And a high-road shall be cast up in
the wilderness, a way for men to walk in, which shall
be called the way of holiness. (See John xiv. 6 ; Acts
ix. 2 ; xix. 9, 23.) The unclean shall not tread it ; it
shall be for those whom the Lord shall lead therein :
they that walk in it, though they be but fools, shall not
err. No lion shall be there to destroy, no ravenous
beast to devour ; they shall not be found there. (See
Luke x. 19.) The redeemed shall walk in it. And those
whom the Lord hath ransomed shall return from their
exile, and shall come with singing to the city of God.
Their heads shall be crowned with everlasting joy :
they shall obtain joy and gladness, and sorrow and
sighing shall cease for ever."

Only the blessings of the Gospel of Christ and the
heaven that awaits His ransomed flock can fully answer
to these glorious promises. God help us to believe them ;
to see by faith what He has already done to make them
good ; and to look for their complete fulfilment beyond
the resurrection of the dead.

Chapters XXXVI., XXXVII.

IN the fourteenth year of Hezekiah's reign the kingdom of Judah was brought to the brink of ruin, brought so near to destruction that nothing but a miracle could save it. Hezekiah and Isaiah cried to the Lord, and the needed miracle was wrought.

In comparison with the mighty empire of Assyria, the little kingdom of Judah must have seemed very insignificant to those who looked only at its area and population. Its size was approximately equal to that of Yorkshire, and a couple of hours on the railway would, in these days, take us from one end of it to the other. We may estimate its population from the fact that in the days of Uzziah, Hezekiah's great-great-grandfather, its fighting force was a little above 300,000 men. (See 2 Chron. xxvi. 13.) Taking this as one-eighth of the total number of the people, we have for the whole kingdom a population equal to that of a single modern city, such as Paris, or, roughly speaking, half that of our own London. Such a kingdom when, invaded by Assyria, was apparently as helpless and hopeless as Belgium would be if invaded by the combined armies of France and Germany.*

But God seeth not as man seeth. The land of Judah was His chosen land, and of the seed of David He designed to raise up Christ to sit upon his throne. It is well to remember that even in our own bodies it is the function of a member, not its size, that gives it

---

* This was written before the invasion of Belgium by Germany in 1914.

importance. We could part with one leg or with both, and live on ; but the loss of the heart or of the brain would mean instant death.

The prophet Isaiah has recorded these critical events in such simple language that our ordinary method of exposition by paraphrase would be out of place. It will be better to give a short summary of the two chapters under consideration, with a few explanatory remarks where they seem needful.

The Assyrian army, consisting probably of a quarter of a million of men, had besieged and taken most of the fortified towns of Judah, and was now in the west, laying siege to Lachish, a strong city distant about forty miles from Jerusalem. From that place Sennacherib sent one of his generals, (Rabshakeh is a title, not a name,) with a large force, to demand the surrender of the capital. He himself, in a boastful inscription which has been deciphered in our own times, says : " As for Hezekiah of Judah, who had not submitted to me, forty-six of his fenced cities and fortresses, and small towns in their neighbourhood without number, by casting down the ramparts and by open attack in battle, . . . I besieged and took. Himself I shut up, like a bird in a cage, in Jerusalem his royal city." And we know from Isaiah that the Assyrian commander approached the city wall to demand surrender, and that three of Hezekiah's nobles appeared upon the ramparts in answer to the summons.

Speaking in Hebrew, the Rabshakeh tells them that it is vain for them to look for deliverance from the power of his master, the great king ; Egypt cannot help them, and the Lord will not ; nay, the Lord has sent us to destroy the land. The three Jewish nobles request the general to speak to them in his own language, that the men on the wall may not understand his words ; but he, still speaking in the Hebrew tongue, goes on to vomit forth disgusting and insulting threats, and endeavours by every possible argument to move the men of the city to rebel against their king and open their gates. He tells them that Hezekiah is a deceiver, altogether unable to deliver them ; that Sennacherib will take them away to a peaceful and fruitful land as good as their own ; that the gods of all other cities have been powerless against the great king, and therefore it is clear that the god of Jerusalem, (we drop the capital letter, because a blasphemer is speaking who knows not the difference between the true God and false gods,) will be unable to deliver his city. With this blasphemy the summons ends, and the three envoys retire from the ramparts in silence, and with rent garments take the evil message to their master.

On receiving it, Hezekiah laid aside his royal robe [his " beauty," Isa. xxxiii. 17], clothed himself in sackcloth, sought his God by prayer, and asked Isaiah to join him in his supplications : " Lift up thy prayer for the remnant that is left." Then came the word of the Lord through the prophet to the king : " Be not afraid : I have heard the blasphemer ; I will drive him back to his own land, and there he shall fall by the sword." Thus encouraged, the good king meets the summons with silent refusal, and the Assyrian returns to his master. Meanwhile, the latter has stormed Lachish, and gone thence to lay siege to Libnah. Here he receives tidings that the Ethiopian king of Egypt is advancing against him, and moves onward into that land to meet the new foe. At the same time he sends to Hezekiah a threatening letter couched in terms very similar to the message already delivered by the Rabshakeh before the walls of Jerusalem : " Let not thy god deceive thee ; as I have prevailed against the gods of other cities, so shall I prevail against the god of Jerusalem."

This letter sealed the doom of him who sent it. It drove the godly king once again to the temple courts to spread it before the Lord and to cry for help to Him who filled the mercy-seat between the cherubim. Thence came the answer of the Holy One of Israel: "The virgin city hath laughed thee to scorn, Sennacherib; Jerusalem hath shaken her head at thee! Thou boastest of thy deeds of might, and knowest not that in them thou art but an instrument in the hand of God to accomplish the things which He hath purposed from of old. I know thy rage against Me; I will lead thee whithersoever I will, as a bull is led by the ring in its nose, or as a mule is led by the bridle between its lips. Thou shalt return to thy city by the way that thou camest, without shooting arrow or casting up mound against the city which I have chosen; for I will defend it for the sake of Mine anointed."

What followed is best told in the prophet's own words: "Then the angel of the Lord went forth, and smote in the camp of the Assyrians a hundred and four-score and five thousand; and when men arose early in the morning, these were all dead corpses. So Senna-cherib, king of Assyria, departed, and went and re-turned, and dwelt at Nineveh. And it came to pass [after a lapse of some twenty years, during which he never again troubled Judah], as he was worshipping in the house of Nisroch his god, that Adrammelech and Sharezer his sons smote him with the sword; and they indeed escaped into the land of Ararat; but Esarhaddon his son reigned in his stead."

As the Lord said that the Assyrian king should not shoot an arrow at Jerusalem, nor come before it with shields, nor raise up an earthwork against it, we may perhaps infer that the destruction of his mighty men of valour and leaders and captains (2 Chron. xxxii. 21) took place at a distance from that city. Indeed, we have from an Egyptian source, through the Greek historian Herodotus, a distorted account of the miracle, which seems to imply that after the visitation from heaven the remnant of the Assyrian army was routed by the forces of Egypt. As the writings of Herodotus are inaccessible to many of our readers, we will close this Half-Hour with an extract from his pages :—

"Sethos, king of Egypt, despised and neglected the warrior class of the Egyptians. . . . Therefore, when Sanacharibos, king of the Arabians and Assyrians, marched his vast army into Egypt, the warriors refused to help their king against him. Thereupon the monarch, greatly distressed, entered into the inner sanctuary of Vulcan, and before the image of the god bewailed the fate that impended over him. As he wept he fell asleep, and dreamed that the god came and stood at his side, bidding him be of good cheer and go boldly forth to meet the Arabian host, which would do him no hurt, as he himself would send helpers. Sethos, relying on the dream, collected such of the Egyptians as were willing to follow him—not warriors, but traders, artisans, and market people. With these he marched to Pelusium, which commands the entrance into Egypt, and there pitched his camp. As the two armies lay here opposite to one another, there came in the night a multitude of field mice, which devoured all the quivers and bow-strings of the enemy, and ate the thongs with which they managed their shields. Next morning they commenced their flight, and great multitudes fell, as they had no arms to defend themselves."

With the book of Isaiah in our hands, it is not difficult to make the necessary corrections in this Egyptian story.

THIRTIETH HALF-HOUR

Chapters XXXVIII., XXXIX.

SINCE fifteen years of life were given to Hezekiah
after his recovery from sickness, and the whole
duration of his reign was twenty-nine years, it is evident
that the sickness came upon him in the fourteenth year of
his reign—that is, in the year of Sennacherib's invasion
(Isa. xxxvi. 1). But did this affliction come during the
siege or after the great deliverance ? It is hardly possible
to speak with certainty on this point. The prophet's
words, " In those days was Hezekiah sick unto death,"
leave the question open.

When God sent a healing message to the sick monarch,
He said, " I will deliver thee and this city out of the
hand of the king of Assyria"; and hence some commentators have argued that the king's sickness must
have preceded the destruction of Sennacherib's army ;
but this reasoning is not conclusive. Even after that
signal deliverance Hezekiah may well have felt that he
still needed the power of God to protect him from his
baffled foe. Calvin's words on this point are worth
quoting : " Those who think that Hezekiah was sick
during the time of the siege found an argument on this,
that otherwise the promise (xxxviii. 6) would appear to
be superfluous. But there is little force in that reasoning ; for the Assyrian might have recruited his forces
and mustered a fresh army at a later period for the
purpose of again invading Judæa, and attacking Jerusalem. The very defeat of which we have now read
(xxxix. 36, 37) might have been a provocation to his rage
and cruelty ; so that the Jews had good reason for

being continually alarmed at any reports which they heard. The promise, therefore, is far from being superfluous, because along with life it promises protection from the enemy."

We know from Assyrian monuments that Merodach Baladan was finally deposed by Assyria shortly after the return of Sennacherib from Judæa ; and this has been used with some force as an argument that the events recorded in chapters xxxviii. and xxxix. must have taken place before the Assyrian invasion. It is said that after that date Merodach Baladan was not in a position to send an embassy to Hezekiah ; but we hardly know enough of the history of the times to speak with certainty on this point.

On the whole, we incline to the belief that Hezekiah's sickness and recovery were subsequent to the deliverance from Sennacherib ; but remembering that the writings of the prophets are not always arranged in chronological order, we cannot speak with certainty here. The question is discussed at length in an instructive book written by a dear friend of the author of these Half-Hours, to which we have already directed enquiring readers ; but on this point the conclusion arrived at differs from our own.*

The question may be asked, " Why was a godly king so terrified at the approach of death ? " Some writers account for it by supposing that he looked upon death as the end of all things, that he had no hope beyond the grave. It has been well answered that his great teacher, Isaiah, was not ignorant of the truth of the resurrection. Even if the resurrection referred to in xxvii. 19 is a figurative one, the prophet could not have used the figure if he had been ignorant of the fact of the resurrection of the body. No ; we believe that Hezekiah's

---

* " Hezekiah and his Age." By Robert Sinker, D.D. Eyre & Spottiswoode.

distress can be otherwise explained. When we remember the words of the psalmist, "Bloody and deceitful men shall not live out half their days," and reflect that the king was not only sick unto death, but had received a death sentence from the Lord Himself, we need not wonder at his consternation. Moreover, any Christian who knows his own weakness knows that it is far easier to look at death as an event in the dim distance than to look it in the face when it is really close at hand. It is a solemn thing to die. Another thing which must have greatly troubled the king was the fact that as yet he had no heir. Manasseh was born three years later.

A few words about the miracle of the dial. Whatever was done, the Almighty did it. Whether He stayed for a season the rotation of the earth, or altered in some mysterious way the laws of light, is a vain and, perhaps, impious enquiry. Let us rather ask ourselves the two important questions: Who by searching can find out God? Is anything too hard for the Lord?

We shall now endeavour to set Hezekiah's psalm of confession and thanksgiving before our readers in such a form as shall interest their minds, assist their memories, and guide them into the true spirit of the king's words.

HEZEKIAH'S PSALM

My sun goes down at noon; the darksome grave
   Swallows the remnant of my clouded day;
My God no longer shows His face to save;
   The light of man's sweet friendship fades away.

As shepherd strikes his tent, as from the loom
   The weaver cuts the work his hands have made;
So sinks this frail clay dwelling to the tomb,
   So breaks my God to-day life's brittle thread.

Through the long hours of tardy-gaited night
   I waited for the coming dawn in dread;
The terrors of God's wrath my soul affright,
   To-day His hand will break life's brittle thread.

My restless groans, my broken prayers, are vain
  As crane's or swallow's cry, as dove's low moan;
My aching eyeballs faint with upward strain;
  I am oppressed: Lord, make my cause Thine own.

*   *   *   *   *   *

How shall I thank Thee for these words of grace,
  Or bless the hand that lays aside the rod?
My rescued feet shall softly tread Thy ways;
  My chastened soul shall humbly walk with God.

Thus dost Thou hold our souls in life, O Lord;
  Thy frowns correct us, and Thy smiles revive;
Diseases fly before Thy healing word;
  Thy loving-kindness bids the dying live.

With bitterness Thine hand did fill my cup,
  But bitter woe hath brought me sweet delight:
Thy love from hell's dark gate hath raised me up,
  And cast my sins for ever from Thy sight.

The grave's still chambers ring not with Thy praise,
  No hope in Thy sure promise there is known;
Thy living saints their living psalms shall raise,
  And sires to sons shall hand Thine honours down.

My Saviour, unto Thee my praise belongs,
  Through all the added years Thy love has given;
Thy temple courts shall echo to my songs,
  And glad thanksgivings shall ascend to heaven.

The Assyrian power, with mighty Nineveh for its
capital, was an offshoot from Babylon, and in process
of time overshadowed and subjugated the city from
which it sprang. In the days of Hezekiah, Nineveh
was all-powerful, and Babylon had sunk into weakness;
and yet Isaiah tells Hezekiah that his posterity shall be
carried captive to Babylon, and there serve as slaves.
Generations passed away, Nineveh was destroyed,
Babylon rose to fresh power, and the prophecy was
accomplished. (See Daniel i. 1–4.) The Lord confirmed the word of His servant, and performed the
counsel of His messenger; known unto Him are all His
works from the beginning.

There is an interesting reference to Merodach Baladan in an inscription of Sargon, king of Assyria, the father of Sennacherib ; we transcribe from it a sentence or two : " Merodach Baladan, king of Chaldea, stirred up against me all the nomad tribes, and prepared himself to the battle, and advanced against me. During twelve years he stirred up the countries of the Sumerians and Accadians (*i.e.*, the provinces of Babylonia). In honour of the god Asshur, the father of the gods, and the great august lord Merodach, I aroused my courage and prepared for the battle, and resolved on an expedition against the Chaldeans, that rebellious and impious nation. Merodach Baladan heard of my approach and fled from Babylon." It appears from other inscriptions that Merodach Baladan afterwards regained his throne in Babylon and reigned there for about six months till he was finally deposed, as we have said, by Sennacherib, shortly after the ignominious return of that king from his expedition against Judæa and Egypt.

These facts throw light on Merodach Baladan's embassy to Hezekiah ; his real motive was to secure the assistance of Judah in his struggle with Assyria. And Hezekiah was glad of the alliance ! Instead of trusting in the God who had changed the course of the sun's beams to show His love to him, he was ready to trust in an arm of flesh. What is man ?

We see the godliness of the king in his humble acceptance of the punishment with which he was threatened ; nor must we consider that his words, " There shall be peace and truth in my days," imply selfish indifference to the sufferings of posterity. He acknowledges that God, in delaying the punishment of his own sins and the sins of the nation, was merciful and long-suffering beyond what could have been expected.

Chapter XL.

AS we pass from the first thirty-nine chapters of Isaiah to the last twenty-seven, we observe a marked difference in style and subject. The language of the prophet in the latter section is more simple and direct. Some of it is so transparently clear in its own grand and glorious form that any attempt to make it clearer would be an attempt to paint the lily white. Moreover, many of the sentences are so enshrined in the memories and hearts of Christians, that we should almost seem to be committing a sacrilege if we endeavoured to modify them even for the purpose of exposition. We confess that we are greatly perplexed, therefore, with the task that lies before us ; and we pray that we may have such guidance from the Holy Spirit as shall enable us to lead the readers of our pages into a true understanding of this part of the Scriptures, the most exalted (if it is right to make such a comparison) of all the utterances that came from the mouth of God before He sent His Son into the world.

Many of our readers may be happily ignorant of the fact that certain modern theologians look upon these twenty-seven chapters as the work of an unknown author who lived a century and a half later than Isaiah— that is to say, at the time of the Babylonian captivity. Yet so it is ; and this wild theory has been supported with such a show of learned reasoning that some well-meaning Christian people have been carried away with it. Indeed, the " critical " folly of certain writers has gone so far as to invent some twelve or thirteen unknown authors of various parts of Isaiah's prophecy. As a preservative from these erroneous speculations, it will be enough for the ordinary Christian to remember that Christ and His apostles treated the book as one undivided whole. For an example, we may refer to John xii. 38–40, where in the compass of three short verses the evangelist quotes Isa. liii. and Isa. vi., and adds : " These things said Isaiah, when he saw His glory, and spake of Him." We cannot, and need not, discuss this question here. It is ably handled in the book to which we referred in our last Half-Hour. (" Hezekiah and his Age." By Robert Sinker, D.D. Eyre & Spottiswoode.)

There is another point of difference between these chapters and what has gone before. The historic references of the prophet are for the most part vague. He seems often to be addressing not so much the men of his own days as the world at large : his eye sweeps down the vistas of time to the portals of eternity. Of course, this is the case more or less with all God's prophets ; but especially is it so with Isaiah. He is a seer whose eyes are opened, in the visions of God, to look through the night of earth to the day of heaven. He sees the first streak of dawn in the restoration of Jerusalem and Judæa after the then future Babylonian captivity : he sees this brighten rapidly into the golden light of the Baptist's ministry : then he sees the Sun of Righteousness rising in all the splendour of God manifested in the flesh, and setting in the blood-red cloud of Calvary : he sees the glory that should follow in the Redeemer's gospel kingdom among the nations : and beyond all this his eye penetrates to the new heavens and the new earth wherein shall dwell righteousness. Such is the range of the magnificent prophecy contained in the last twenty-seven chapters of this book, chapters which may justly be entitled, The Gospel according to Isaiah. And now let us turn our attention to the fortieth chapter.

We have seen that Isaiah foresaw and foretold the desolation of Jerusalem by the armies of Babylon, though at the time then present Babylon itself was overshadowed and crushed by the all-conquering empire of Assyria. He said to Hezekiah: "Hear the word of the Lord of hosts: Behold, the days come that all that is in thine house, and that which thy fathers have laid up in store until this day, shall be carried to Babylon: nothing shall be left, saith the Lord." In view of this impending trouble, Isaiah and his colleagues or successors in the prophetic ministry are commissioned to speak words of comfort to the people of God, words designed not only to support the Lord's true worshippers who had such tribulations in prospect, but to afford consolation when the blow should have fallen. In proof of this we need only compare with Isaiah's words the opening message of Zechariah to the returning exiles: "And the Lord answered the angel that talked with me with good words and comfortable words. . . . I am returned to Jerusalem with mercies: My house shall be built in it, saith the Lord of hosts: My cities through prosperity shall yet be spread abroad: and the Lord shall yet comfort Zion, and shall yet choose Jerusalem." It is quite clear from this and similar passages that Isaiah's "Comfort ye, comfort ye," had an immediate reference to the times that should follow the captivity, and were obeyed by the prophets of those days—Haggai, Zechariah, Malachi. But this is not all: it is evident from the whole scope of Isaiah's own message that his prophecy of "comfort" contains in germ the substance of the gospel of Christ, and is a warrant to gospel ministers to comfort those who are in any trouble with the com-

fort wherewith they themselves are comforted of God
(2 Cor. i. 4). It is well to remember also that all effectual
comfort is given by the great Comforter who, according
to the promise of Christ, will abide with the flock of God
for ever.

We have the authority of Matthew, Mark, Luke, John,
and John the Baptist himself for referring the third,
fourth and fifth verses of this chapter to the Baptist's
ministry ; though we can see that they had a previous
and typical fulfilment in that decree of Cyrus which
levelled mountains and exalted valleys for the returning captives of Judah. Moreover, we learn from Luke
that the glory of the Lord which should be revealed to
all flesh was the salvation of God. (Compare Isa. xl. 5
with Luke iii. 6.) Seven centuries before the coming
of Christ the prophet said : " The glory of the Lord
shall be revealed, and all flesh shall see it together."
When the Saviour had come, and had accomplished the
salvation of God by His life, death, and resurrection,
His apostles said : " The mystery which was kept
secret since the world began is now made manifest,
and by the scriptures of the prophets, according to the
commandment of the everlasting God, made known
unto all nations for the obedience of faith : our Saviour
Jesus Christ hath brought life and immortality to light
through the Gospel, and by reason of the excelling
glory thereof that which was previously made glorious
hath no glory." (Rom. xvi. 25, 26 ; 2 Tim. i. 10 ;
2 Cor. iii. 10.)

Again the word of the Lord comes to the prophet :
" Cry." The prophet answers : " What shall I cry ? "
The divine voice bids him proclaim that all the strength
and excellency of man is as the grass of the meadow or
the flower of the field, that nothing is eternally stable
but the word of the Lord ; and the apostle Peter
leaves no doubt as to the nature of that word : " This

is the word which by the Gospel is preached unto you "
(1 Pet. i. 25).

The humble believer in Christ's Gospel will not regard
as fanciful the interpretation which refers verse 9, " O
Zion, that bringest good tidings, etc.," to the preaching
of the apostles, who began their work at Jerusalem
(Luke xxiv. 47–49), and said first to the cities of Judah,
then to Samaria, then to the ends of the earth, Behold
your God : and he who reads John x. with a spiritual
consciousness that the voice which saith, " I am the
Good Shepherd," is the voice of the Son of God, will
have no difficulty in understanding Isaiah's prediction,
" He shall feed His flock like a shepherd." The minor
fulfilment of the words in the days of Ezra will not
blind the eyes of such a one to their truest and greatest
accomplishment in the Redeemer's work and person.

The remainder of this wonderful chapter needs to be
read, not explained. It sets forth in language which
has never been equalled outside the Holy Scriptures,
never surpassed within their compass, the infinite
greatness and wisdom of God, the infinite tenderness
of His love to His weak and weary people, and the
infinite folly and wickedness of the makers and worshippers of idols. In its sublime words the apostle
Paul twice finds expression for his own admiration
of the wisdom and knowledge of God (Romans xi. 34 ;
1 Cor. ii. 16).

A few phrases in this chapter call for a special word of
explanation.

It seems, on the whole, safest to say that the " double "
of verse 2 means such a measure of chastisement as the
Lord in His grace considered to be sufficient, though it
was by no means more than Jerusalem deserved. In
lxi. 7 the word " double " is used in a different sense.

Verse 10 is explained by Hebrews xii. 2. Christ
wrought the work of redemption with His own eternal

reward of exaltation and of satisfied loving-kindness ever before his eyes.

In verse 20 we have an instance of that holy sarcasm which the prophets of God occasionally used, as did their royal Master after them. (Mark vii. 9, " Full well ! ") Here Isaiah asserts that the poverty-stricken wretch who cannot afford to have a god of gold and silver will have one made of the best wood that he can procure !

Verse 23 is more easily understood if we adopt the translation : " Hardly are they planted, hardly are they sown, hardly hath their stock taken root in the earth, when He bloweth upon them and they wither, and the whirlwind taketh them away as stubble." It is well illustrated by the overthrow of Nineveh and Babylon, and by such events as are referred to in Daniel ii. 35.

Ponder our words, dear readers, and then turn with fresh docility and fresh expectation to the words of God's holy prophet, " Comfort ye, comfort ye, My people, saith your God." May it be yours to prove the truth of his prediction : " They that wait upon the Lord shall renew their strength ; they shall mount up with wings as eagles ; they shall run, and not be weary ; and they shall walk, and not faint."

Chapter XLI.

"GIRD up now thy loins like a man ; for I will demand of thee, and answer thou Me." Thus, after long silence, God spake out of the whirlwind to His servant Job (Job xxxviii. 1–3).

This is not the only occasion on which the Creator has condescended to reason with a creature concerning the Creator's righteousness and the creature's sin,

> " And justify the ways of God to man."

He said a second time to His humbled servant Job : " Gird up now thy loins like a man ; I will demand of thee, and declare thou unto Me." He said to Micah : " Arise, and plead My cause against Israel in the presence of the mountains of their land ; and let the hills which have seen My dealings with them, and theirs with Me, from generation to generation—let those same hills hear thy voice and bear their testimony to My righteousness." And again in later days by His servant Ezekiel : " Hear now, O house of Israel ; is not My way equal ? are not your ways unequal ? " (Ezek. xviii. 25, 29).

Similarly, in this forty-first chapter of Isaiah, the Lord condescends to come into court, as it were, before the nations of the world, and to vindicate the honour of His Godhead against the claims of the gods of the heathen. He calls to the lands beyond the seas [such is often the sense of the word " islands " in the writings of the prophets], and bids them listen in silence while He proves His own glorious existence by His knowledge of the future and His power to shape that future at His will ; He will raise up one from the East who shall do His righteous bidding, and shall overthrow the enemies of Israel, so that captives fainting with poverty and thirst shall be restored to miraculous prosperity ; the change shall be as wonderful as if a dry desert were planted from end to end with graceful and stately trees. Who among the gods of the heathen can promise and perform such things ? Let them prove their own existence by foretelling the future, and by sending prosperity or adversity ; then shall their claims be admitted. But behold ! no answer is forthcoming from them, and thus it is proved to all that they are vanity and confusion.

Such, in outline, is the meaning of this chapter. But who is " the righteous man " from the East, the servant whom the Lord of hosts summons to victory ? Some commentators, both Jewish and Christian, and among them the learned Calvin, say that the man referred to is Abram, who was called by God from Ur of the Chaldees, and by whom the armies of the five kings were dispersed like stubble. (See Gen. xiv. 14, 15.) In spite of the great names which support this interpretation, we believe that it is wrong. The victory of Abram, an event which was then twelve hundred years old, would hardly be brought forward in the days of Isaiah to furnish the heathen world with proof of God's foreknowledge and power. Moreover, this same prophet mentions by name a conqueror before whom God would subdue nations, loose the loins of kings, and open the double gates of mighty cities. We believe, therefore, that the predicted conqueror from the east, in the present chapter, is Cyrus, king of Persia. (See xliv. 28, and xlv. 1-4.)

It may not be out of place or unprofitable to glance at the life of Cyrus as recorded in profane history. We read much of him in the two Greek writers Herodotus and Xenophon ; and though their accounts differ in some particulars, they agree in representing Cyrus as a military genius who extended his conquests in all directions, a king whose career was such as Isaiah had foretold ; though, of course, these writers knew nothing of the oracles of God.

According to Herodotus, Cyrus was the son of a Persian father and a Median mother. His grandfather on the mother's side was Astyages, king of Media. Astyages dreamed two significant dreams, and his wise men interpreted them to mean that a child born of his daughter Mandane would, in course of time, rise up against him and usurp his throne. Accordingly, when Mandane gave birth to Cyrus, Astyages commanded that the babe should be exposed upon the mountains and left to perish. By a chain of events which we need not sketch, the child's life was preserved, and he afterwards became king of Persia, overthrew the power of Media, and took his grandfather prisoner. He then turned his victorious arms in various directions, and became master of Babylon, and of what had formerly been the great empire of Assyria. He fell fighting against the Scythians in B.C. 529. If these statements of Herodotus are true, and we have no reason to question their substantial accuracy, Cyrus lived about seven years after giving freedom to the captive Jews.

It has been argued that Cyrus was not " a righteous man," being, at the best, a fire-worshipper. But this is no real objection to our interpretation. The word which our translators have rendered " righteous man " really means righteousness. It forms the second part of the well-known word Melchi-zedek, king of righteousness. Perhaps we ought to render the question thus : " Who raised up one from the east in righteousness ? " This would agree with Isa. xlv. 13. Besides, we do not know how far this man's heart was affected by God's dealings with him. Who shall say that he was not one of the lost whom Christ came to save ?

We think that the present chapter is of such a nature that we can best explain it by a running paraphrase, taking care to leave some of the most familiar parts unaltered.

" Listen to Me in silence, ye lands beyond the seas, saith Jehovah ; ye nations that dwell therein, gird up your loins, draw near to the bar of justice, and plead for your gods. Let them defend their own cause against the Holy One of Israel, that men may know who is God.

" Who raiseth up from the east one whose footsteps are attended with righteousness ? [That is, one whose career is ordained for the execution of God's righteous judgments.] Who subdueth the nations before him, giving him dominion over kings, and making their swords to be as dust before him, and their bows as driven stubble ? He pursueth his foes, and passeth on safely into lands hitherto untrodden by his feet. Who hath brought it to pass? Who hath done it ? Who calleth into being generation after generation from the beginning of the world ? I, Jehovah, the same yesterday, and to-day, and for ever. I am God !

" [Yea, My servant shall come from the east, and] distant lands shall see his approach, and shall fear ; the ends of the earth shall tremble. Behold, they draw near to one another, and come together [to resist his progress] ; they help every one his neighbour, and encourage every one his brother [if so be they may withstand him with the help of their idols]. The wood-carver encourageth the gilder, and one smith exhorteth another ; they say, The image is now plated, and the soldering is good. Then they nail their god to his throne, lest he should fall ! But fear not thou, O Israel My servant (Deut. vi. 13), O Jacob My chosen, O seed of Abraham, My friend; thou whom I have fetched from the ends of the earth, and called from the farthest bounds thereof, saying, Thou art My servant; I have chosen, not rejected thee. (See Deut. xiii. 4; vii. 7, 8.) Fear thou not, for I am with thee; be not dismayed, for I am thy God; I will strengthen thee; yea, I will help thee; yea, I will uphold thee with My faithful right hand. All thine enemies shall perish, for I will help thee.

" Fear not, O Jacob, though thou be but a worm, though thy men be but a feeble remnant; I will help thee, saith the Lord; I, the Holy One of Israel, am thy Redeemer. I will cause thee to thresh thy foes, as a new threshing-wain with sharp edges thresheth corn. Thou shalt thresh kingdoms that stand as mountains in thy path, and shalt make the hills as chaff. They shall flee before thee; the wind shall carry them away; the whirlwind shall scatter them. But thou shalt rejoice in the Lord, and shalt glory in the Holy One of Israel. Ye are poor and needy, ye seek water and find none, your tongue faileth for thirst; but I the Lord will hear you, I the God of Israel will not forsake you. I will make rivers flow from the dry mountain-tops to slake your thirst, and will open fountains for you in the valleys through which you pass; I will make the desert a pool of water, and the dry land a place of watersprings. In the desert shall flourish trees strong and stately, trees of fragrance and beauty, the planting of My right hand. And men shall see, and know, and consider, and understand that this is the handywork of the Lord, the creation of the Holy One of Israel."

Without pretending to limit these promises to any particular period of the history of the church of God, we may safely say that they had respect in the first place to the coming restoration of Israel in the days of Cyrus, and that they are sweetly and gloriously fulfilled whensoever and wheresoever the gospel of Christ triumphs in the desert of fallen humanity.

From these promises to His chosen people the Lord turns again to plead His own cause against all idol gods :

" State your cause, saith the Lord ; defend yourselves as best ye can, saith the King of Jacob. Bring forth your proofs of godhead by telling of things to come. Show us what ye have foretold in time past, and point out to us the fulfilment of your words, or show us things which are yet to come. Reveal the future, that we may know that ye are gods ; send prosperity or adversity, that we may fear you when we see it. Behold, ye are of no account, ye can do nothing ; he that chooseth you for his god is like unto you, an abomination.

" [But I am the true God.] I tell of one that shall be raised up from the north, and he cometh ; yea, from the east he cometh, and acknowledgeth My name. (See Ezra i. 2.) He shall tread down rulers as one treadeth mortar, as the potter treadeth clay.

" Who hath declared such things from the beginning, that we may know that he is God ? Who hath fore-told them, that we may say that he is true ? There is none that declareth such things, none that foretelleth them. Yea, no man hath heard the gods of the heathen say what things shall be hereafter.

" But I, the living God, have said unto Zion from of old, Behold them, behold them ! And I will send to Jerusalem one who shall bring tidings of the fulfilment of My words. But when I look to the idols, there is none that can thus declare the future ; there is none wise among them that can answer a word to My challenge. Behold, the gods of the heathen are all vanity ; their works are nought ; their idols are empty as the wind, and confused as chaos."

It is worthy of note that the word here translated

" confusion " is the same as that used by Moses to describe the state of the earth at the beginning of the creation, " without form."

All the worshippers of images will one day be put to everlasting shame ; but the worshippers of the Holy One of Israel, who rejoice in Christ Jesus, and have no confidence in the flesh, will then see God with joy.

Chapter XLII.

' GOD, who at sundry times and in divers manners spake in time past unto the fathers by the prophets, hath in these last days spoken unto us by His Son." If any man believes the principal part of this statement, namely, that God has spoken by His Son, he will have no difficulty in believing the subordinate part, that God spoke by the prophets. And conversely, those who cannot see Christ in Isaiah xlii. and liii. do not really see Him in Matt. xii. and xxvii. The prophet foretold His coming, the evangelist recorded it ; the prophet foretold His death, the evangelist recorded it ; but the voice in both cases is the same : it is the voice of God, a voice which can only be heard by the ear of faith.

One single sentence from the mighty pen of Calvin puts the matter very clearly : " The prophet now speaks of Christ as the Firstborn and the Head, for to no other person could the following statements be applied ; and the evangelists place the matter beyond all controversy " (Matt. xii. 17–21). This being the case, it is not worth our while to dwell on the theories advanced by unbelieving Jews and sceptical critics that the servant of the Lord mentioned at the beginning of this chapter is the Israelitish nation, or the righteous part of it, or the prophet Isaiah himself. If we are asked, " Of whom speaketh the prophet this ? of himself or some other man ? " we will endeavour to follow Philip's example, and preach Jesus to the enquiring reader (Acts viii. 34, 35). For it is clear to us that

the Father here speaks of Jesus Christ, saying, Behold,
My Son cometh into the world to serve Me and to save
sinners (ver. 1); He shall be gentle with the gentleness
of infinite love, and strong with the strength of infinite
power; He shall establish My law by revealing My
gospel (2–4); I, the Almighty, will appoint Him to
His office and uphold Him in it; in Him Israel shall
find a new covenant of grace and peace, and the Gentiles
shall see the light of eternal life (5, 6). He shall enlighten the blind and release them that are in bondage,
and My glory shall be revealed in Him (7–9). Remotest
nations shall hear tidings of great joy, and shall sing
My praise (10–12). I have long seemed silent and
inactive, saith the Lord; but at the appointed time I
will speak and act, I will destroy My foes and deliver
My sons (13–16). But who is so blind as Israel, the
nation to whom I have written the great things of My
law? (17–21; compare Hosea viii. 12). I pour out
judgments upon them for their sins, but they see not
who smiteth them; neither do they lay to heart the
chastisements of their God.

Such is the purport of this chapter, which we shall
now with the utmost reverence attempt to paraphrase,
being convinced of the usefulness of that method; our
reverence will cause us to leave many words unaltered,
and to use, as far as possible, other parts of Scripture
where it seems necessary to change or to modify for the
purpose of explanation.

But let us first say a few words about two or three
passages which seem to us to have a different meaning
from that which is ordinarily attached to them.

Let the inhabitants of the rock sing. It would be easy
for a heedless person to suppose that the rock here is
Christ; and if he were a preacher he might found on the
words an interesting sermon, showing what cause men
have to praise God when He has set their feet on the

Rock of Ages. But this is not the prophet's meaning ;
the villages of Kedar mentioned just before are the
tents of the wandering Arabs, to whom in after-days
Paul carried the gospel (Gal. i. 17) ; and the inhabitants
of Sela (Rock) are the Edomites, apparently mentioned
as a type of the heathen to whom the apostles should
preach Christ.

Who is blind but My servant ? Among many views
of the meaning of these and the following words, the
right one seems to us to be that which is adopted both
by Calvin and by Gill, namely, that the servant of God
in this passage is not Christ, but Israel, the peculiar
nation called to the service of God (Deut. vi. 13) ; the
nation whose priests and prophets were God's messengers to men (Mal. ii. 5–7), " perfect " in knowledge by
the possession of the divine law, or, as others render this
word, " at peace " with God by virtue of the covenant
made with Levi (Mal. ii. 5).

*The Lord is well pleased for His righteousness' sake ;
He will magnify the law and make it honourable.* This
is often understood to mean that the Father would be
well pleased with the righteousness of His Son Jesus
Christ, and that the Son would honour the Father's
law by His own obedience unto death, so bringing in
an everlasting righteousness to be imputed to all His
people. Now the truth which this interpretation con-
nects with this verse is the very essence of God's gospel,
as we learn from Rom. iii. 21–31, and from many other
parts of the New Testament. Yet this does not appear
to us to be a correct exposition of this passage. We
fear that in saying this we may offend or startle some
who truly love the gospel ; but no consideration must
induce us to swerve from our task of setting forth the
mind of the Spirit in the Word of God. Without
asserting positively that the above interpretation is
wrong, we can tell our readers that a very different one

is given by Calvin and Gill, who will certainly not be suspected of denying imputed righteousness. We mention their names here, not that we may appeal to them as infallible interpreters, but that we may reassure our readers, if necessary, as to our own orthodoxy. Now let the prophet speak, or rather let God speak by him.

"Behold, He cometh; My Son shall be My Servant, and I will be His strength; My well-beloved shall do My will; in Him My soul delighteth. I will anoint Him with My Spirit, and He shall reign in righteous mercy over the nations. He shall not cry aloud in the streets, nor cause His voice to be heard among men (Matt. viii. 4; ix. 30; xii. 16, 17, 19; Mark v. 43; Luke viii. 56). The contrite heart shall be accounted by Him for a bruised reed that He will not break, a dimly-burning lamp that He will not quench; He shall speak in faithfulness and reign in righteous loving-kindness. Himself shall be no bruised reed nor dimly burning lamp; [He shall be strong and shine as the sun] until He have established righteousness in the earth, until the farthest lands receive His words and trust them. [It is worthy of special notice that in the Hebrew the word 'bruised' in ver. 3 is akin to 'fail' in ver. 4, and 'smoking' akin to 'discouraged.']

"Thus saith God the Lord, who created the heavens and stretched them out, who spread abroad the earth and caused it to bring forth, who giveth breath to them that people it, and spirit to them that walk upon it; I, the Lord, in My righteousness have called Him to be My Servant (Heb. v. 4, 5). I will uphold Him and keep Him, and will give Him unto Israel for a covenant, and unto the heathen for a light (Acts xiii. 46, 47). He shall give sight to the blind, liberty to the captive, light to them that sit in darkness and in bondage. My name is Jehovah; My glory will I not give to another, nor My praise to idols; [it shall be revealed in the person

of My Son].   Behold, I have made promises aforetime,
and have fulfilled them (Josh. xxi. 45), and now I make
new promises and greater ; before they come to pass I
tell you of them, and My words shall be fulfilled in due
season (Luke i. 20).

" Let men sing unto the Lord a new song for His new
mercy ; let the ends of the earth declare His praise ;
those that go down to the sea in ships, and all that
dwell upon its waters, the lands beyond the sea, and
their inhabitants.   Let the wilderness and its cities
take up the song ; let the Arabs sing in their tents, and
the Edomites shout from their rocky heights (Jer. xlix.
16 ; Obad. 3) ; let them praise the Lord for His goodness, and sing unto Him in their far-off lands.   For the
Lord shall arise to His work as a mighty man ariseth
to the fight ; His zeal shall flame forth like the fury of
a warrior ; He shall utter His mighty battle-cry, and
shall prevail against His enemies.   (See Eph. i. 19–21 ;
Col. ii. 15.)

" After long silence I will speak (Acts xiv. 16 ; xvii.
30) ; after long forbearance I will cry aloud, as a woman
when her travail cometh ; I will destroy My foes, and
My wrath shall devour the enemies of My people.
Mountains of power and hills of difficulty shall disappear
before Me, for I will wither up all their strength.   The
waters of rivers shall be parted, and the depths shall
be dried up [as in the days of Joshua and Moses].
I will guide the blind in unknown ways, and lead them
in unknown paths ; I will make darkness light before
them, and crookedness straight ; I will do for them
that which I have promised, and will not forsake them.
But confusion and utter shame shall be to those who
trust in graven images, and call molten images their
gods.

" Hear, O Israel, and be not deaf ; see, and be not
blind.   Who so blind as this nation that I have chosen

to serve Me? Who so deaf as the priests to whom I have entrusted My law? Who so blind as the people with whom I have made a covenant by sacrifice, the people whom I have called to serve Me? They see My many works, but heed them not; they hear My words, but understand them not. Out of My own righteous lovingkindness I have given them good statutes and a glorious law; [but they have rejected them—compare Deut. iv. 5–8.] Now therefore they are a prey to robbers and spoilers; they are snared as wild beasts by the hunters, and cast into prison by their captors; there is none to deliver the prey or restore the spoil (Lam. iv. 17–20).

"But who is there among you, O Israel, that will hear and understand? Who will hearken, that he may be wise in days to come? Is it not the Lord that hath done this? He hath given up Jacob to the spoilers, and Israel to the robbers, because they have sinned against Him, because they have refused to walk in His ways, and have disobeyed His law. (See 2 Chron. xxxvi. 16, and Jer. xl. 2, 3.) For this cause hath He visited us with the heat of His anger, and fought against us with His strength. The fire consumeth us on all sides, but we know not that the Lord hath kindled it; it burneth us, but we lay not to heart the lesson that it teacheth."

Reader, turn now to the Lamentations, and behold the fulfilment of God's threatenings; turn to the four gospels, and see the work of His Son and Servant.

Chapters XLIII. 1–XLIV. 5.

WE believe in election. It is clearly taught in Holy
Scripture; and the words therein spoken concerning it have been deeply engraved on our heart by the
Spirit of God. We have learned to believe John xvii. 2
and Rom. ix. 16 as firmly as Isa. lv. 7 and Rev. xxii. 17.
Even in the darkest periods of Israel's history there has
always been among that nation "a remnant according
to the election of grace" (Rom. xi. 5). And it is clear
to us that the words of eternal love which the Lord
spake unto Israel by the prophets were designed particularly for the elect remnant, though they were wisely
published to the nation at large. Hence come those
wonderful interminglings of judgment and mercy which
we find in the prophecies, such as: "I have given
Jacob to the curse, and Israel to reproaches; yet now
hear, O Jacob My servant, and Israel whom I have
chosen: fear not." It seems impossible to understand
the Word of God unless we perceive that He determined
to save some with an everlasting salvation, and to leave
others to answer at His righteous bar for their own
sins. "Is there then unrighteousness with God? God
forbid!"

But in due season it was revealed that the Holy One
of Israel has His elect among the Gentiles as well as
among the sons of Jacob. Christ said, in the days of
His flesh, "Other sheep I have which are not of this
fold; them also I must bring"; and after His return
to heaven He soon began to bring in these other sheep

by the voice of His gospel, especially by the ministry of His servant Paul. We see now that God has chosen out of all mankind a number that no man can number, and that these constitute the church of Christ, the ransomed host that shall people heaven. In Christ Jesus there is neither Greek nor Jew, circumcision nor uncircumcision (Col. iii. 11). Hence all truly spiritual promises made of old to Israel belong equally to us, who are fellow-heirs with them of the grace of life. In so saying we do not rob the Jews ; we simply assert that God has called us to share in all their spiritual blessings.

This being the case, we agree with the reformers, and with our own divines and teachers of more recent times, in their use of the term, " The Israel of God," to denote the universal church of Christ. Indeed, it appears to us that this is the sense in which Paul uses the words in Gal. vi. 16. We see no validity in the arguments which assign a strictly literal sense to the word " Israel " in that passage ; but even if those arguments were valid, we should still employ such terms with respect to the church at large, and should consider the usage to be in harmony with the teaching of the New Testament. (See especially Gal. iii. 28, 29.) On this point, as on many others, Calvin's words are words of wisdom which can hardly be improved. Writing on Isa. xliv. 5, he says : " He describes a change (regeneration) which surpasses nature and all the conceptions of men, when out of the accursed race of Adam is formed a spiritual Israel."

The principles stated above guide us to the conclusion that this portion of Isaiah, like many others, had a first fulfilment in the deliverance of the Jews from Babylon by Cyrus, and a second fulfilment, infinitely more glorious, in the gospel of Christ. On this point we cannot forbear to quote again from one who has justly

been called the prince of commentators. Calvin says,
"The return of the people [from Babylon] is closely
connected with the renewal of the Church. For what
God began by bringing His people out of captivity He
continued till Christ, and then brought to perfection;
and thus it is one and the same redemption. Hence it
follows that the blessings which are here mentioned
ought not to be limited to so short a time"; that is,
the prophet's words foretell not only the escape from
Babylon under Zerubbabel and Ezra, but the deliverance of a greater Israel by the Christ of God.

With this view we cordially agree. The same Spirit
who enabled the prophet to foresee the approaching
captivity and its happy issue, enabled Him to foresee
the day of Christ; and, like Abraham, "he saw it and
was glad." Let us once more attempt to explain his
his words in detail.

"Yet now [notwithstanding all thy sin and all My
chastisement], thus saith the Lord, who created thee
for Himself, O seed of Jacob, the Lord who formed
thee for His own, O house of Israel. Fear not; for I
redeemed thee of old time, and will still redeem thee
(Ex. xx. 2; Lev. xxvi. 44, 45). I have called thee by
name, and made thee Mine own people (Deut. vii.
6–8). Thou shalt pass through the waters of affliction,
but I will be with thee; thou shalt pass through
floods of calamity, but they shall not overflow thee;
thou shalt walk through the fire of tribulation, but shalt
not be burned, neither shall the flame thereof consume
thee. For I am the Lord thy God; I am the Holy One
of Israel; I am thy deliverer. I gave up Egypt to
destruction that thou mightest go free; Ethiopia and
its allies, that thou mightest escape. [See especially
Ex. iv. 22, 23; xii. 29; xiii. 14, 15; 2 Chron. xiv. 12;
2 Kings xix. 9. In the last passage we find that God
gave Hezekiah relief by turning the arms of Sennacherib

against Egypt and Ethiopia. It is also worthy of note that after Cyrus had liberated the Jews he overran Egypt. Compare Ezek. xxix. 18–20.] Thou art precious in My sight ; I have raised thee to honour, and set My love upon thee ; therefore will I destroy thine enemies that thou mayest be delivered, and give nations over unto death that thou mayest live. Fear none of those things which thou shalt suffer (Rev. ii. 10), for I am with thee ; I will bring thy seed from the east, and gather thee from the west ; I will say to the north, Give up, and to the south, Keep not back ; bring My sons from afar, and My daughters from the ends of the earth, all who are called the people of Jehovah, whom I have created for My glory, have formed and fashioned by My power, that they may show forth My praise."

Since these promises were made, the Jews have been recalled to their native land under Zerubbabel, and great numbers of them have been saved in apostolic times. (See Acts ii. 41 ; iv. 4, 32 ; v. 28 ; vi. 7 ; and Gal. ii. 8, 9.) Moreover multitudes of God's Gentile sons and daughters have been gathered in from the ends of the earth ; and we have a renewed promise in Rom. xi. that Israel shall yet be received into the believing Church of Christ. Beyond this interpretation we dare not go. We have arrived by independent and prayerful study of God's Word at the same conclusion as Dr. Kay in his commentary on Isaiah : " In the notes on Isaiah no attempt will be made to determine the question how far a literal restoration of Jerusalem is to be looked for. The writer does not see that Scripture supplies material out of which a definite judgment on this point can be formed." (The Students' Commentary, Vol. IV., p. 9. This book, abridged from the Speaker's Commentary, is a work which we greatly value.)

Two distinct interpretations of ver. 8 are possible, and both are consistent with other parts of Scripture. The blind people that have eyes, the deaf that have ears, may be Israel, as in Isa. vi. 10; or they may be idolatrous Gentiles, as in Psa. cxv. 5, 6, 8. We incline to the latter view. We thus join this verse to the following passage (verses 7–13), in which the Lord again challenges the heathen to prove the divinity of their false gods.

" Come forth, ye nations, blind and deaf as the idols that ye worship; gather yourselves together, assemble yourselves to plead the cause of your gods. Which of them can declare the future, or show us predictions that have been accomplished? Let them produce their witnesses and prove their divine fore-knowledge; or let them listen to My claims and pronounce them true. Ye, My people, are My witnesses, saith the Lord; the nation whom I chose to serve Me, that ye might know Me, and believe Me, and perceive that I am God. No god that has been formed was before Me, neither shall any succeed Me. I, I, am Jehovah; neither is there salvation in any other (Acts iv. 12). I have spoken to you, O Israel, I have delivered you; I have fore-told you things to come when no strange god was named among you. (See Jer. ii. 2, 3.) Therefore ye are My witnesses, saith the Lord, that I am God. Yea, from everlasting I am God; none can deliver out of My hand; I will work, and who shall hinder? "

Next follows a definite promise of the overthrow of Babylon for Israel's deliverance from the then future captivity. The word translated " nobles " more probably means " fugitives."

" Thus saith the Lord, your deliverer, the Holy One of Israel. For your sakes I have determined to send the Medes to Babylon, to bring down its power and drive its people into exile, even the Chaldeans, who glory in their ships; for I am the Lord, your Holy One, the Creator of Israel, your King.

"Thus saith the Lord, who divided the Red Sea and made a passage through its mighty waters; who drew forth the chariots and horses of Egypt, Pharaoh's army and all its might, and made them lie down together, never to rise again; who quenched the fire of their wrath as the flame of an extinguished lamp. Remember not those former deeds of power, dwell not upon those things of old; [ye shall see greater things than these—John i. 50.] Behold, I will do a new thing; quickly shall it come to pass, and ye shall surely know it. I will again make a way for My people through the wilderness, and will give them rivers to drink in the desert. The beasts of the field shall see it and bear witness to My power, the jackals and ostriches shall testify of My glory; for I will cause waters to flow in the wilderness, and rivers in the desert, to give drink to My people, My chosen, the people whom I formed for Myself, that they might show forth My praise."

Let the reader compare Ezra viii. 21–23, but let him not limit the fulfilment of these glorious promises to the return from Babylon.

We have next a severe reproof of Israel for its incessant departures from the Lord; but in the very midst of these reproaches is a promise of God's sovereign forgiveness and unchanging love, and the reproaches are followed by a passage of unmixed comfort (xliv. 1–5); Israel's Creator and Father will pour out the Holy Spirit upon Israel's seed; the Lord will acknowledge them as His people, and they shall acknowledge Him as their God.

"But [though I am thy God] thou hast not called upon Me, O Jacob; thou hast been weary of My worship, O Israel. Thy sheep and lambs have been offered on the altars of other gods, and thou hast honoured them instead of Me with thy sacrifices. *I have not burdened thee* with offerings, *nor wearied thee* with the burning of incense, to impoverish thee or to feed Myself ; *but thou hast burdened Me* with thy sins, *and wearied Me* with thine iniquities. (Compare Amos ii. 13, and Isa. i. 14.) [Yet I will have mercy on whom I will have mercy.] For I, even I, am He that blotteth out thy transgressions for Mine own sake, and will not remember thy sins. Remind Me of thy good works, if thou hast any ; plead thy cause, and justify thyself if thou canst. Thy leaders have sinned [' first father ' may refer to Jacob], and thy teachers have transgressed against Me ; therefore I give up the princes of My sanctuary to profanation, Jacob to the curse, and Israel to reproaches. (Read Lam. v. 7–12.)

" Yet now hear My words of love, O Jacob My servant, O Israel My chosen ; thus saith the Lord thy Maker, who formed thee for Himself from thy birth, and will deliver thee from all trouble. Fear not, O Jacob My servant, thou whom I have chosen to be a righteous people : for I will pour water upon thee in thy thirst, and streams when thou shalt be as dry ground ; yea, I will pour the living water of My Spirit upon thy children, and My blessing upon thine offspring : then shall they spring up as from a fruitful soil, as the willows spring up by the water-courses. One shall say, I am the Lord's ; another shall claim Jacob as his father ; another shall subscribe himself a servant of the Lord, and shall take unto himself the name of Israel."

We thank God that the sovereign grace and unchanging love here revealed do not belong exclusively to the seed of Jacob ; we thank God that He has since sent His Son to tell us that " God so loved the world, that He gave His only begotten Son, that whosoever believeth in Him should not perish, but have everlasting life."

Chapters XLIV. 6–XLV. 13.

IN this passage the Lord declares again that He is the only true God, and that this is proved by His foreknowledge of the future and by His government of the affairs of men (verses 6–8). He shows the folly of idol-makers and idol-worshippers, who procure their firewood and their god from the stock of the same forest-tree (9–20) ; and bids Israel rejoice in His redeeming power and love (21–23). He then predicts the restoration of Jerusalem and the temple after the coming Babylonian captivity ; and promises to raise up a prince, Cyrus by name, who shall overthrow many nations in his victorious career, and shall let go captive Israel without price or reward (xliv. 24–xlv. 13).

The words of the prophet may be singularly illustrated by two quotations from heathen writers. We will lay these before our readers, and then, without further preface, give our exposition.

The Latin poet Horace ridicules idolatry in language which reminds us of Isaiah's words, though it proceeds not from the same holy source :

> I was a fig-tree's trunk, a useless log.
> The workman wavered : ' Shall I make a stool,
> Or my pet god ? ' He chose to make the god,
> And thus a god I am.

Let us remember that, however men may defend the use of images in worship, as Rome does by various specious arguments, all such use is idolatrous and sinful, and deserves alike the derision of the heathen poet and the denunciation of the holy prophet.

In a previous Half-Hour we have given a short account of Cyrus: let us now supplement that account with a few further particulars taken from the Cyropædia of the Greek writer Xenophon. After speaking in the highest terms of the king's genius as a conqueror and administrator of nations, he says: " We know that Cyrus was willingly obeyed by some who lived at a distance of many days' journey, by some who were distant a journey of several months, by some who had not even seen him, and by some who well knew that they would never see him, and yet were willing to obey him. . . . Starting with a small army of Persians, he received willing obedience from the Medes and Hyrcanians. He subdued the Syrians, the Assyrians, the Arabians, the Cappadocians, the inhabitants of both the Phrygias, and the Babylonians. He ruled over the Bactrians, the Indians, the Cilicians, and likewise the Sacians, the Paphlagonians, the Mariandynians, and very many other nations which we cannot even name. He also governed the Greeks in Asia, went down to the sea, and became master of Cyprus and Egypt."

We have thought it worth while to give Xenophon's list of the conquered nations without abridgment, because it forms a striking comment on Isaiah xlv. 1: " Cyrus, whose right hand I have holden, to subdue nations before him; and I will loosen the loins of kings; " a prediction uttered and recorded about 140 years before Cyrus was born.

" Thus saith Jehovah, Israel's King; the Lord of hosts, Israel's Redeemer: I am from everlasting to everlasting, and beside Me there is no God. Who as I, can call future things into being, and declare them before they come to pass? Let him set them in order for Me [and foretell them], even as I have done since I took unto Me the seed of Abraham in the days of old.

If any can, let him foretell the things that are coming, the things that shall be. Fear not, O My people, nor be afraid : have not I declared unto your fathers the future from of old, and shewn it unto you before it came ? (See Gen. xv. 13–16 ; and similar passages.) Is there a God beside Me ? There is no other Rock ; I know not any.

" The makers of graven images are all vanity ; the idols in which they delight shall not profit them. The witnesses to their gods have neither sight nor knowledge : their blindness and ignorance shall fill them with confusion. Behold, he that hath fashioned a god, that hath cast or engraved a useless image, shall be confounded, and all his fellow-worshippers with him. The makers of the idols are themselves but men : though they band themselves together and stand up for their gods, they shall be filled with fear, and shall all be confounded.

" [Behold, they make their god on this wise !—] The smith maketh an axe, heating it in the fire and hammering it on the anvil ; he worketh with his strong arm till he is weak for want of food, and faint for want of water : [an exhausted god-maker !] Then the carpenter useth rule and pencil to mark out the form of his god, whom he shapeth with chisels, measureth with compasses, and fashioneth to the figure and comeliness of a man, to stay in his house [because it cannot walk]. For this purpose one man heweth down a cedar ; another taketh an ash or an oak, or strengtheneth for his use some other tree of the forest. Another taketh a fir which he himself hath planted, and which the rain has caused to grow : part of it serveth for fuel, with which he maketh a fire that he may warm himself ; yea, on the fire which he hath kindled he baketh his bread ; yea, of the same tree he maketh his god, and worshippeth it ; he maketh a graven image, and falleth down to it. With part of it he maketh a fire to seethe the flesh that he shall eat, and to roast the savoury meat that shall satisfy his hunger. The remnant of the wood he maketh into a graven image to be his god : he falleth down before it, worshippeth it, and prayeth to it, saying, Deliver me, for thou art my god.

" They know nothing, neither do they understand : for God hath closed their eyes that they should not see, and hardened their hearts that they should not understand. (Compare Isa. vi. 9, 10 ; 2 Thess. ii. 11, 12.) None remembereth [that it is but a log] ; none hath knowledge or understanding to say, I have burned part of it in the fire ; I have cooked my food with it ; and shall I make the remnant of the tree an abomination, and worship a log of wood ? They feed on ashes : their heart hath deceived them and led them astray, so that none of them can deliver his soul and say, Am I not holding fast to a lie ?

" O house of Jacob, remember these things ; O Israel, remember that thou art My servant : I will never leave thee nor forsake thee. I have blotted out thy transgressions as the sun scattereth a thick cloud : I have removed thy sins as the wind driveth away a mist. Turn again to Me with all thine heart, for I have redeemed thee. Let the heavens above sing, for the Lord hath done it ; let the earth beneath shout ; let its mountains break forth into song, and the forest with all its trees : for the Lord redeemeth Jacob, and will glorify Himself in the deliverance of Israel [from Babylon and from the curse. Ezra i. 1–4 ; Gal. iii. 13, 14.]

" Thus saith the Lord unto thee, O Israel ; He that redeemed thee from Egypt, He that formed thee in the womb : I the Lord am the Maker of all things ; I am He that stretcheth forth the heavens above and spreadeth out the earth beneath them ; that frustrateth the tokens of false prophets, and giveth up soothsayers

to madness; that establisheth the words of His prophets, and performeth the counsels revealed by His
messengers; that saith, Jerusalem shall again be inhabited, the cities of Judah shall be rebuilt, and the
desolations thereof shall be restored; that saith of
Cyrus, he shall serve Me as a shepherd, and shall do all
My pleasure; he shall command that Jerusalem be
rebuilt, and that the foundation of the temple be laid
(2 Chron. xxxvi. 22, 23).

" Thus saith the Lord to His anointed servant Cyrus :
I will strengthen thy right hand and give thee victory
over nations; I will smite down kings before thee,
opening to thee the doors of their fortresses and the gates
of their cities. I will go before thee and will remove
all hindrances from thy path. I will break in pieces
before thee the brazen gates and iron bars of the cities
of thy foes, and will give into thine hand the treasures
which they have stored in dark places, the riches which
they have hidden in secret vaults : that thou mayest
perceive that I the God of Israel, who have called thee
by thy name, am the living God. For the sake of
Jacob My servant, Israel My chosen, I have called thee
by thy name ; and though thou knowest Me not, I have
named thee My shepherd and Mine anointed. I am the
Lord : there is none else ; there is no God beside Me.
I will strengthen thee and uphold thee, though thou
knowest Me not, that all the world from east to west
may learn that I alone am God : I am the Lord, and
there is none else. I form light and create darkness :
I make peace and create trouble (Amos iii. 6) : I the
Lord do all these things.

" The heavens shall drop My mercy from above, and
the skies shall pour down My righteous loving-kindness :
the earth shall open to bring forth salvation, and shall
cause righteousness to spring up with it : I the Lord am
the author thereof.''

On this eighth verse Calvin makes a beautiful comment which we must quote, because it explains so
wisely the prophet's words, and expresses so exactly
our own view of the use of the word "righteousness" in
many passages of the Psalms and of the Prophets:
" By the word righteousness he means nothing else than
the fidelity with which the Lord defends and preserves
His people. The Lord thus drops down from heaven
righteousness, that is, well-established order, of which
salvation is the fruit. For he speaks of the deliverance
of the people from Babylon, in which the Lord shews
that He will be their protector. Yet while we understand the natural meaning of the prophet, we must
come down to the kingdom of Christ, to which these
words undoubtedly bear a spiritual reference ; for God
does not limit these promises to a few years, but continues His favours down to the coming of Christ, in
whom all these things were abundantly fulfilled. There
can be no doubt therefore that he likewise celebrates
that eternal righteousness and salvation which is brought
to us by Christ ; but we ought first to observe the simple
interpretation with respect to the return from the
captivity in Babylon." Let us return to Isaiah.

" [And do ye murmur at My ways, O house of Israel ?]
Woe unto him that contendeth with his Maker, for-
getting that he is but a potsherd among the potsherds
of the earth ! Shall the clay say to the potter, What
makest thou ? Or the work to the workman, Thou
hast no hands ? Woe unto him that saith to his father,
What hast thou begotten ? or to his mother, What
hast thou brought forth ? Thus saith the Lord, the
Holy One of Israel, and his Maker : Ye may ask Me of
things to come ; but will ye dare to tell Me how to deal
with My sons, how to deal with the work of My own
hands ? I made the earth and created man upon it :
I with My own hands made the heavens, and My word

marshalleth all their hosts. And in My faithfulness I will raise up My anointed servant, and will prosper him in all his ways. He shall build My city, and shall release My captives without price and without reward, saith the Lord of hosts."

By sending Cyrus after an interval of 140 years, and Christ after the lapse of seven centuries, the Lord has confirmed the word of His servant Isaiah, and has given proof of His own foreknowledge and Godhead.

Chapter XLV. 14–25.

"THE things which are seen are temporal; the things which are not seen are eternal" (2 Cor. iv. 18). It follows that whenever we read in the prophets of everlasting mercies, whether promised primarily to Jew or to Gentile, these mercies must be of a spiritual nature. A careful remembrance of this self-evident truth will preserve us from gross and materialistic interpretation of the figurative language of prophecy; everlasting blessings must be spiritual blessings. When we read, as in the passage now under consideration, that Israel shall be saved in the Lord with an everlasting salvation, we shall, if we remember the above-mentioned principle, know that the prophet is referring to Christ's salvation, and that his words are not to be limited to Israel after the flesh.

We have already drawn attention to this point, the interest of the Church at large in all spiritual promises made to Israel. It seems to us that this truth is obscured by those who give an exclusively literal meaning to the term Israel as employed by the prophets. The more we consider this question, the more we are convinced that godly preachers have been right in claiming for the Church at large the promises made to the people of God under the name of Israel. Some words of Calvin on this point are well worth quoting: " As to the greater part of Israel having been rejected by God, this did not set aside God's covenant; for the adopted remnant were always the true and lawful Israel; and although they were few in number, yet they were the first-born in the Church. Besides, all those among the Gentiles who had been engrafted into the body began also to be accounted children of Abraham : One shall say, I belong to Jacob ; another shall subscribe with his hand, I am a descendant of Israel (Isa. xliv. 5). And on this ground we are now reckoned the genuine Israel of God, though we are not the descendants of Israel."

It is difficult to assign an historical fulfilment to the promise that the wealth obtained by Egyptian manufacturers and Ethiopian traders, " the labour of Egypt and the merchandise of Ethiopia," should be placed at the disposal of Jerusalem, and that the stalwart warriors of Seba, " the Sabeans, men of stature," should become the bond-servants of Israel (verse 14). We have found no better explanation of this difficulty than that given by Calvin, who says : " The prophet alludes to the contributions made by Cyrus to the building and adorning of the temple. (See Ezra i. 4 ; and compare the decree of Darius, Ezra vi. 8.) At that time was fulfilled what he says, that the labour of Egypt and the merchandise of Ethiopia should come to the Jews ; for Egypt and Ethiopia were tributaries and subjects of the king of Persia, and from this tribute the temple of Jerusalem was rebuilt. But as that restoration was only the prelude to that which was accomplished by Christ, so likewise the homage which foreign nations then rendered to the people of God was only the beginning of that homage which various nations rendered to the church of God after Christ had been revealed to the world. . . . The Lord redeemed His people from Babylon in order that He might preserve some church till the coming of Christ, to whose authority all nations should be subject ; and therefore we need not wonder if the prophet, when speaking of the return of the people from Babylon, directs his discourse at the same time to God's end and design, and makes it to be one redemption."

We think that if our readers will compare Isaiah's

words in verses 18–23 with Paul's address to the men of Lystra (Acts xiv. 15–17), it will be clear to them that the prophet is foretelling that which the apostle accomplished, and which the preaching of the Gospel to the heathen always accomplishes when it is attended by the power of the Holy Ghost.

ISAIAH. "Thus saith the Lord that created the heavens and the earth: They have no knowledge that set up the wood of their graven image, and pray to a god that cannot save."

PAUL. "We preach unto you that ye should turn from these vanities unto the living God, which made heaven and earth, and the sea, and all things that are therein."

The section which we have marked off for our present exposition is short; but it is full of the Gospel, and constitutes a rich revelation of "the love of God our Saviour toward man" (Titus iii. 4). Let us endeavour to read, mark, learn, and inwardly digest it.

' Thus saith the Lord, The wealth of Egypt and Ethiopia shall be thine, O Jerusalem; the tall warriors of Seba shall come over unto thee and shall submissively follow thee: yea, they shall come to thee as bond-servants, doing obeisance unto thee and entreating thy favour, saying: ' Only in Zion is God to be found; there is none other, no God beside; verily, though Thou hast been hidden from us Gentiles (see Psa. cxlvii. 20), Thou art God, O God of Israel, the only God that can save.'

"All worshippers of idols shall be ashamed and confounded; they and the makers of their idols shall sink into despair together: but the seed of Israel shall be saved in the Lord with an everlasting salvation; they shall not be ashamed or confounded, world without end; [for the God of Israel is the true and living God.]

"For thus saith the Lord, who created the heavens:

[He is the true God :] the Lord who formed and made the earth : He established it ; He created it not to remain without form and void ; He formed it to be inhabited : I am the Lord, and there is no God beside Me. My words have been uttered openly, not in the secrecy of dark places, like the oracles of the heathen : not in vain have I commanded the seed of Jacob to worship Me ; My words are righteous words, and My doctrine is right doctrine.

" Assemble yourselves together, and come before Me, ye nations, to plead for your gods ; draw near, such of you as have escaped My judgments ; know ye that all they are ignorant who pray to a god that they make of wood, and carry upon their own shoulders, a god that cannot save. Publish ye My challenge, and bring forth the defenders of idols : let them all take counsel together, that they may prove the godhead of their gods. Which of them hath showed beforehand the things that now are ? Who hath declared them from of old ? I, the Lord, have done it ; and there is no God beside Me who is righteous and able to save. Turn from your vain idols and look to Me, all nations unto the ends of the earth : for I am God, and there is none else. By myself have I sworn, the word is gone forth from My mouth in righteousness, and shall neither be recalled nor frustrated, that every knee shall bow to Me, and every tongue shall acknowledge that I am God. It shall be said of Me, In the Lord alone is to be found righteousness and strength. Unto the God of Israel shall all men come, and all that have rebelled against Him shall be ashamed. In the Lord shall all the chosen seed be justified, and in Him alone shall they boast : [he that glorieth shall glory in the Lord.]"

The records of the Acts and the doctrine of Paul's Epistle to the Romans form the best commentaries on these wonderful words of God.

Chapters XLVI., XLVII.

BEL was one of the idols worshipped in Babylon; he is twice mentioned as such by the prophet Jeremiah (l. 2 and li. 44) : "Babylon is taken, Bel is put to shame, Merodach is dismayed. . . . I will do judgment upon Bel in Babylon." But who was Nebo ? He is not elsewhere mentioned in Scripture, except that he evidently supplies the first two syllables of each of the names Nebuchadnezzar, Nebushasban, Nebuzaradan (Jer. xxxix. 13). But we have in the British Museum a statue of Nebo, which was brought from Nimroud, and also an inscription of King Nebuchadnezzar found amid the ruins of Babylon in 1862, which begins as follows : " Nebuchadnezzar, king of Babylon, the elect of Merodach the supreme lord, the worshipper of Nebo. I have restored the sanctuaries of the god; for Merodach is the great king who created me, and I have extolled all his great works. Nebo his son sustains my royalty, and I have always exalted the worship of his majestic, divinity. Nebo, the guardian of the hosts of heaven and earth, has committed to me the sceptre of justice to govern men." Thus, although the name of this idol is only once mentioned in Scripture, modern times have supplied us with abundant proof of its existence, and of the worship which was paid to it at Babylon. We may here remark that the true sense of the expression translated "your carriages" in Isa. xlvi. 1, seems to be " the things (that is, the idols) which ye Babylonians are accustomed to carry about your streets " in solemn processions; these, saith the prophet, shall form a heavy load for the horses and mules of those who shall despoil your temples. He speaks as if he already saw the conquering Medes and Persians loading their wagons with the wealth of the temples of the doomed city.

We read in the pages of Xenophon that when Cyrus was about to do battle with Crœsus, king of Lydia, " he commanded his men to observe the standard, and to follow it in even line. Now his standard was a golden eagle with outspread wings, mounted on a long lance." These words of the Greek historian remind us of Isaiah xlvi. 11, " calling a ravenous bird from the east " ; the man who is here likened to a bird of prey was the king who had an eagle for his standard, a fitting emblem of his swift and terrible progress.

In our English version of this chapter occur the remarkable words, " Israel My glory." If they are a correct rendering of the prophet's words, they are well explained by his previous utterance, " For the Lord hath redeemed Jacob, and glorified Himself in Israel " (xliv. 23). God's people are His glory, because He glorifies Himself in their redemption. But there is another rendering of this verse which deserves consideration, and is adopted by Calvin and by other competent translators : " And I will place salvation in Zion, and My glory upon Israel." If rightly understood, both versions give the same sense.

We hope that our paraphrase will be suggestive enough, and clear enough, to make further introduction unnecessary.

" The gods of Babylon totter and fall, their images are placed by the spoiler upon beasts of burden, and are packed in wagons to be drawn away by oxen. Once they were carried in procession with divine honours, now they are a load and a burden to the weary beasts that drag them from their shrines. They totter and fall together ; they cannot save their own images from the plunderer ; they themselves go into captivity.

" [Not such a one is the living God !] Hearken unto Me, O house of Jacob, all ye that remain of the house of Israel. I, your God, have borne you from your infancy, and carried you from your birth. [I have never been carried from place to place by you.] Down to old age ye shall find Me the same ; when ye are grey-headed I will still carry you ; I made you, and I will bear you ; I will carry you in your times of weakness, and deliver you in your times of trouble. Will ye then be dismayed at the gods of Babylon, as if I were like unto them ? Will ye compare Me to them, or regard them as My equals ? Idolaters pour their gold out of the bag, and weigh their silver in the scale-pan ; they hire a goldsmith to fashion the metal into a god ; then they fall down before it, yea, they worship it. They lift their god upon their shoulders, carry him, and set him in his place ; there he standeth, for he cannot move. When his worshipper crieth unto him, he cannot answer, nor give deliverance from trouble.

" Remember these things, O Israel, and show your-selves men ; [be not dismayed at false gods.] Bring to mind the word of the Lord, ye that are prone to turn aside. Remember the mighty works that I have done of old, saith the Lord ; for they show that I am God, and that there is none else ; I am the true God, and there is none like Me. Known unto Me are all My works from the beginning of the world. I say, My counsel shall stand and I will do all My pleasure. I will sum-mon from the east one who shall come as swiftly as a bird of prey ; I will summon from a far country a man who shall fulfil My counsels. I have said it, and I will bring it to pass ; I have spoken it, and I will do it. Hearken unto Me, therefore, ye rebels among My people, who have removed your hearts far from Me and from

My righteousness. I will bring near My righteousness [in the ruin of My foes and the deliverance of My people]. (Compare Isa. xxix. 13, 14.) My righteousness shall not be far off, and My salvation shall not tarry. I will give salvation unto Zion, and My glory unto Israel." [By Cyrus and by Messiah.]

Thus far the prophet has spoken of the downfall of Babylon's gods ; he now proceeds to foretell once more the destruction of the city, and he does it in language which compels attention and admiration. He seems to see Babylon as a virgin-empress seated on a throne of magnificence and power ; he takes his stand before her as the messenger of the King of kings, and commands her to descend from her throne and sit in the dust ; to depart into exile, slavery, shame, silence and darkness. This is to be the end of her vain expectations of eternal sovereignty, and it is to come suddenly and unexpectedly ; her magicians, with all their pretence of reading the future by stars and moon, shall be unable to foresee her calamity or to give her warning thereof, for they themselves shall perish as stubble perishes in the flames, and all her mercenaries and allies shall flee in terror and leave her to her fate. Do not the prophet's words foreshadow also the ruin of that mystic Babylon whose fall is predicted in the Revelation ? In the days of her pagan power it was the boast of her great national poet that Jupiter had given her *Imperium sine fine*, " Dominion without end," a boast which reminds us of Isa. xlvii. 7. 8. But God has said that her seven-hilled throne shall fall.

" Get thee down into the dust, O Babylon, proud virgin queen : sit throneless on the ground, daughter of Chaldea. Thy effeminacy and luxury shall be no more. Take thy place among the bond-maids that grind meal for their masters. Lay aside thy veil, strip off thy robes, wade bare-legged through the rivers on thy way to exile. God shall show the nations thy nakedness, and the kingdoms thy shame. (Compare Nahum's address to Nineveh, Nah. iii. 5.) I will execute vengeance upon thee, and will show thee no mercy, saith our Redeemer, whose name is the Lord of hosts, the Holy One of Israel. Sit down in silence and depart into darkness, daughter of Chaldea ; for thou shalt no longer be called the empress of the nations. When I was angry with My people Israel, when I gave up My chosen sons to dishonour and delivered them into thine hand, thou showedest them no mercy, thou sparedst neither age nor weakness (Lam. v. 12, 13). Thou saidst, I shall be a queen upon my throne for ever, and consideredst not that thou shouldest see adversity, nor thoughtest that thine own end should come.

" Now therefore hear this word, thou pleasure-loving city, secure and careless. Thou sayest in thine heart, ' I am : [my life is divine and independent :] I have no peer. I shall never know widowhood nor loss of children.' Behold, suddenly in one day shall both these things come upon thee, loss of children and widowhood (Dan. v. 30) : thou shalt know all their bitterness, in the midst of thy manifold sorceries and endless enchantments. Thou hast trusted in thine evil ways, and hast said, ' They are hidden from the light of heaven ' (Psalm x. 11). Thine own wisdom and knowledge have led thee astray, till thou hast said in thine heart, ' I am God, and there is none else.' [Yea, thou hast trusted in evil ;] therefore shall evil come upon thee : but thou shalt not perceive its dawn. It shall be a ruin from which thou shalt not be able to escape ; a sudden desolation, which shall come upon thee at unawares.

" Stand therefore amidst thine enchantments and the manifold divinations which thou has practised from of old : peradventure they may profit thee ; peradventure

by their means thou mayest save thyself! (Compare
1 Kings xviii. 27.) But nay; thy many schemes
shall end in weariness. Let thine astrologers, thy
readers of the stars, thy diviners that prophesy at each
new moon, arise and save thee from the ruin that
hangeth over thee. Behold, they shall be as stubble
that perisheth in the fire; they shall not be able to
save themselves from the flame that shall destroy their
dwellings: it shall be no fire of coals before which a
man may sit to warm himself.

"Such shall be the end of all thy toil. And the
merchants who have trafficked with thee from thy
youth shall flee to the four winds, each for his own life.
There shall be none to save thee."

> A mound of ruins by Euphrates' side:
> Behold the dark still tomb of Babel's pride.

Chapter XLVIII.

TO an ordinary reader, the chapter before us may seem to consist of disconnected utterances which he cannot understand, and he may therefore feel inclined to turn from it to easier and more familiar passages. But is this wise ? Must we not admit that every part of God's Word teaches its own peculiar lesson, and that no part can be neglected without real loss ? We think that those who are wise enough to believe that all Scripture is given by inspiration of God will acknowledge this. Let us, therefore, endeavour to understand this chapter. We shall not dwell too minutely on the difficulties presented by certain of its phrases. Some of these difficulties arise, we believe, from faulty translation. For instance, verse 7, which is scarcely intelligible as it stands in our Authorised Version, becomes quite plain when we read it thus : " They [that is, the things which I am about to do] are created now : they were not created of old, and before this day thou hast not heard of them ; lest thou shouldest say, Behold, I knew them." We write thus without the slightest desire to find fault with our Authorised Version, one of the best translations that the world has ever seen ; we simply wish to take all unnecessary stumbling-blocks out of the way of our readers. Perhaps we shall best attain this end by giving a short clear summary of the whole chapter before we attempt a more detailed exposition.

" There are those who pride themselves on their

descent from Jacob, and look to his God for protection, while they worship idols, and live ungodly lives (verses 1, 2). Knowing your obstinate unbelief, I have often foretold by My prophets things that should come to pass, and have in due season fulfilled My words : that ye might acknowledge Me to be the true God, and not attribute My work to your idols (3–5). [This the Jews continued to do down to the time of Jeremiah, when they said, ' We will worship the queen of heaven as our fathers did in Jerusalem : for then had we plenty of victuals, and were well, and saw no evil,' thus attributing to their idols the blessings given by their God. Jer. xliv. 17, 18.] And now, in order to deliver you from the same obstinate unbelief, I foretell unto you fresh things [captivity in Babylon, and deliverance by Cyrus], whereof ye have not yet heard (6–8). Ye are most rebellious, but for the glory of My own great name I will not cast off My people (9–11). (Compare Ex. xxxii. 12 ; Num. xiv. 13–16 ; Joshua vii. 9.) Hear, O Israel : I am the true God, the Creator. What god of the heathen can thus foretell the future ? There shall arise a man chosen by Me for this service, Cyrus by name, who shall take Babylon and release My captive people (12–15). Listen to Me, your God : I have spoken plainly from of old, and now by My Spirit I have sent My servant Isaiah to instruct you ; how would it make for your peace to hear My voice ! (16–19). Notwithstanding all your unworthiness, I will deliver you from Babylon, that ye may be a source of blessing to the nations ; and My ancient power shall supply your needs in your homeward march. But there is no peace to the wicked " (20–22).

Let us now endeavour to expound the chapter with more fulness and precision.

" Hearken to this proof of My Godhead, O house of Jacob ; ye who are called by the name of Israel and are

of the lineage of Judah ; ye who swear by the name of
Jehovah, and claim the God of Israel for your God,
while ye walk in falsehood and unrighteousness ; ye who
boast yourselves citizens of the holy city, and look for
the protection of the God of Israel, the Lord of hosts.
[Thus saith the Lord unto you :] I declared to you
beforehand the things which are now past ; I foretold
them and revealed them by the mouth of My prophets ;
and afterwards I did them suddenly, and they came to
pass. For I knew the hardness of thine heart, the stiff-
ness of thy neck, and the shamelessness of thy brazen
brow ; and therefore I disclosed those things from of
old, before they came, lest, when I had wrought deliverance for thee, thou shouldest look upon it as the work
of thine idols, thy graven and molten gods. Thou
didst hear My predictions—behold their fulfilment ; will
ye not acknowledge it ? [An event to which these words
may specially point is the past deliverance of Jerusalem
from Sennacherib, Isa. xxxvii. 33–38.]

" And now I foretell new and hidden things, which
thou hast not known ; My power performeth them in
days now near at hand, not in the days of your fathers :
yea, until this day thou.hast not heard of them ; so
that thou canst not say, Behold, I knew them. Thou
hast not before heard of them nor known them, nor
have they ever entered into thine ear. [I foretell them
now, to give thee fresh proof that I am God ;] for I
know that thou wilt deal treacherously, and that from
the womb thou hast gone astray, and hast been rightly
called a transgressor. Yet for My great name's sake I
will not pour out My wrath ; for My own glory will
I spare thee. Thou art not silver, but dross ; yet will
I refine thee : in the furnace of affliction will I prove
thee. For Mine own sake, for Mine own sake will I
deliver thee ; for I have pity on My holy name, and will
not give My glory to another. [The destruction of the

city by the Chaldeans must come, and ye must go to Babylon ; but for My covenant's sake I will preserve you and bring you back thence, humbled and instructed by My chastisements.]

"Hearken unto Me, O house of Jacob, children of Israel whom I have called My own : I am the same for ever ; I am the first and the last. Mine hand laid the foundations of the earth, and My fingers stretched out the heavens : by the word of My power I uphold them all. Come hither, ye worshippers of idols ; which of your gods hath foretold these things ? There shall arise one whom the Lord hath chosen unto this honour, that he should do the Lord's will upon Babylon, and execute His justice upon the Chaldeans. I, I have spoken it. I have named him beforehand, and will raise him up ; he shall march on from victory to victory.

"Draw near to Me, ye sons of Jacob, and hear these My words : I have ever spoken plainly by My prophets ; from of old I have been present with them : and now by My Spirit I send My servant Isaiah. It is Jehovah that speaketh, thy Redeemer, the Holy One of Israel : I am the Lord thy God, who teacheth thee for thy profit, and leadeth thee in the way which thou shouldest go. O that thou wouldest hearken to My commandments ! Then should thy peace flow on as a mighty stream, thy prosperity as the waves of the sea ; thou shouldest multiply as the sand upon the shore, and thine offspring as the grains thereof ; Israel should not be driven from his heritage, nor destroyed from before Me.

"[But for your sins ye shall go to Babylon ; yet will I be your God and your deliverer ; and it shall be said :] Go forth from Babylon ; hasten homeward from the land of the Chaldeans ; declare it with the voice of song, and publish the good tidings to all nations, saying, The Lord redeemeth His servants, the children of Jacob. As in the days of old, so shall it be now : they shall not thirst while He leadeth them through the wilderness : their God will cause water to flow, as He did aforetime from the rock ; it shall be as if the rock again were cleft, and the waters again gushed forth.

" [My people shall have peace ; but] there is no peace, saith the Lord, to the wicked."

Here ends that portion of " The Vision of Isaiah the son of Amoz," which tells of the approaching captivity and of the subsequent deliverance from Babylon ; the following chapters look on to the times of Messiah and beyond.

We have seen that the Spirit of God, speaking through the prophet, foretells the events of the near future with minutest accuracy, and this with the express purpose, repeatedly proclaimed, of proving the eternal power and Godhead of Jehovah, and the vanity of the gods of the heathen.   The living God challenges the dead gods over and over again in such language as this : " Produce your cause, saith the Lord ; bring forth your strong reasons, saith the King of Jacob. Let them bring them forth, and show us what shall happen ; let them show [that they have foretold] the former things, that we may [might] consider them and know the latter end of them ; or [let them] declare us things for to come. Show the things that are to come hereafter, that we may know that ye are gods ; yea, do good or do evil, that we may be dismayed, and behold it together. Behold, ye are of nothing, and your work of nought ; an abomination is he that chooseth you.   I have raised up one from the north, and He shall come ; from the rising of the sun shall He call upon My name, and He shall come upon princes as upon mortar, and as the potter treadeth clay. Who hath declared [such things] from the beginning, that we may know ? and before time, that we may say, He is righteous ?   Yea, there is none that showeth ; yea, there is none that declareth ;

yea, there is none that heareth your words" (Isa. xli.
21–26). [Similar passages, which the reader would do
well to find at once, and read attentively, are : xli. 1–4 ;
xlii. 9 ; xliii. 9 ; xliv. 7, 8 ; 24–28 ; xlv. 4–6 ; 19–21 ;
xlvi. 9–11 ; xlvii. 11–13 ; xlviii. 3–8 ; 14–16.]   In
view of this, it is not too much to say that those who
assign these utterances of Isaiah to an unknown writer
who lived at Babylon during the exile, are guilty of
making God a liar (1 John v. 10).   On the other hand,
this unknown writer, this "Deutero-Isaiah," if he had
existed elsewhere than in the imaginations of theorists,
would have been an impious deceiver, passing off as
proofs of the foreknowledge of the Lord of hosts mere
historic records of past events.   We have not so learned
to read the Holy Scriptures ; we have learned from
them to say, " Let God be true, but every man a liar."

Chapter XLIX.

IT will greatly help us to understand this chapter if we first endeavour to answer two questions which it suggests :

1. Who is the speaker ?

2. To what events, future in Isaiah's day, does he refer ?

1. The writer is Isaiah, the son of Amoz. We have already said enough about the recent attempts of "critics" to dismember this prophet's writings, and to assign them to various unknown authors ; and if the closing words of our last Half-Hour do not convince our readers of the folly and wickedness of such theories, it would be idle to discuss the subject further. The writer is Isaiah. But who is the speaker who says, "Hearken, O isles, unto me"? Does the prophet here speak in his own person, or in the person of another ? Happily, we can give to this question an answer which must be decisive for every true Christian. Follow our simple argument attentively, dear reader, and it will convince your mind. God grant that it may also profit your soul.

The Lord Jesus said, before He suffered, "This that is written must yet be accomplished in Me, And he was reckoned among the transgressors : for the things concerning Me have fulfilment" (Luke xxii. 37). Here we have Christ's express statement that He Himself is the Servant of the Lord whose sufferings and triumph are predicted in Isa. liii. But that chapter and this, and those that come between, are so closely connected that they necessarily refer to the same person when they speak of the Servant of the Lord. Let us write down a few passages which will set this connection clearly before our eyes.

" Thou art my servant; [thou art that] Israel in whom I will be glorified. And now saith the Lord that formed me from the womb to be his servant, . . . It is too light a thing that thou shouldest be my servant to raise up the tribes of Jacob, and to restore the preserved of Israel : I will also give thee for a light to the Gentiles, that thou mayest be my salvation unto the ends of the earth. The Lord God hath opened mine ear, and I was not rebellious, neither turned away backward. I gave my back to the smiters, and my cheeks to them that plucked off the hair : I hid not my face from shame and spitting. . . . Who is among you that feareth the Lord, and obeyeth the voice of his servant ? . . . Behold, my servant shall deal prudently, He shall be exalted, and extolled, and be very high. Who hath believed our report ? and to whom is the arm of the Lord revealed ? For he shall grow up before him as a tender plant. . . . A man of sorrows and acquainted with grief, wounded for our transgressions, bruised for our iniquities : the chastisement of our peace was upon him, and with his stripes we are healed. He is led as a lamb to the slaughter. . . . He had done no violence, neither was any deceit in his mouth : yet it pleased the Lord to bruise him. . . . By his knowledge shall my righteous servant justify many ; for he shall bear their iniquities. . . . He was numbered with the transgressors."

We repeat that to a disciple of Christ, who receives his Master's interpretation of the words last quoted, the conclusion is absolutely clear and certain that Christ is the speaker who says, in chap. xlix., " Listen, O isles, unto Me." And why should it be thought a thing incredible with any who believe in the Godhead of our

Lord Jesus that He should speak out plainly in His own person, by the mouth of Isaiah, seven centuries before His own coming in the flesh ?

2. The second question is not so easily answered. What are the events, yet future in Isaiah's day, to which the divine speaker refers ?   Are they still future, or have they been partially or completely accomplished ? We will endeavour to give an answer in accordance with the teaching of the New Testament.

We find the apostles Paul and Barnabas saying to the Jews assembled in the synagogue at Antioch in Pisidia : " It was necessary that the word of God should first have been spoken to you : but seeing ye put it from you, and judge yourselves unworthy of everlasting life, lo, we turn to the Gentiles. For so hath the Lord commanded us, saying, I have set thee for a light to the Gentiles, that thou shouldest be for salvation unto the ends of the earth " (Acts xiii. 47). Clearly, therefore, the apostles saw in their own preaching to the Gentile world the fulfilment of Isaiah xlix. 6. We draw a similar conclusion from Paul's comment on verse 8 : " Behold, now is the accepted time ; behold, now is the day of salvation " (2 Cor. vi. 2). These two instances show that the apostles of Christ regarded this chapter as a prophecy which had its fulfilment in Gospel days and in Gospel blessings. But does it look beyond to a second and more literal fulfilment ? For instance, do the promises contained in verses 14–26 refer to some exaltation and restoration of Israel which still lie in the future, after the lapse of twenty-six centuries ? If it is so, we must seek the nature of that deliverance in Romans xi. ; and we there find that it is spiritual, and consists in the reception by faith of that Messiah whom they have hitherto rejected : " They also, if they abide not still in unbelief, shall be grafted in : for God is able to graft them in again. And so all Israel shall be saved." As we Gentiles have obtained mercy through their unbelief, so through our mercy they also shall obtain mercy. On the temporal future of the Israelitish nation our plan of exposition does not allow us to enter : we leave it an open question.

Three quotations from Calvin shall close our introductory remarks.

Writing on verse 6, he says : " The Jews read this verse as a question : ' Is it a small thing ? ' As if the prophet had said that it is enough, and that nothing more or greater ought to be desired. But they maliciously corrupt the natural meaning of the prophet, and imagine that they will one day be lords of the Gentiles, and will have wide and extensive dominion. The true meaning of the prophet is, this work in itself indeed is magnificent and glorious, to raise up and restore the tribes of Israel which had fallen very low ; for He will add the Gentiles to the Jews, that they may be united as one people, and may be acknowledged to belong to Christ. . . . In this, as well as in other passages, Isaiah foretold that the Church would be greatly extended when the Gentiles should be received and united to the Jews in the unity of faith."

Again, on verse 8, he says : " These predictions should not be limited to a certain age, since they belong to the whole church in all ages. For if we begin with the deliverance from Babylon, we must go on to the redemption of Christ, of which it must be regarded as the commencement and forerunner. And since there are still found among us many remnants of slavery, we must proceed forward to the last day, when everything shall be restored." That is, the fulfilment of these wonderful promises to Jew and Gentile stretches onward to the great day of God, where earth ends and heaven begins.

Finally, on verse 22, Calvin says : "When he

promises that the sons of the church shall be brought in her arms and on her shoulders, the language is metaphorical, and means that God will find no difficulty when He shall wish to gather the church out of her dispersion, for all the Gentiles will assist Him. Although this refers in the first instance to the Jews who had been banished and scattered, yet it undoubtedly ought to be extended to all the elect of God, who have become partakers of the same grace."

And now let us come to the words of the prophet, or rather to the words of the Christ who was not yet incarnate.

"Listen unto Me, ye lands beyond the seas, saith the Servant of the Lord : hearken, ye nations that are far off, saith the Messiah of God ; from My birth the Lord calleth Me unto His service ; from My mother's womb He giveth Me the name that seemeth Him good (Matt. i. 21 ; Luke i. 31 ; ii. 21). He maketh the word of My mouth like unto a sharp sword sheathed in the hollow of His hand : He maketh Me to be as a polished arrow hidden in His quiver, to be shot forth at the time appointed as a shaft from the bow of the Almighty (Gal. iv. 4). He saith to Me, ' Thou art My Servant ; Thou art the true Israel, in whom I will be glorified ; [for Thou shalt finish the work which I give Thee to do." John xvii. 4.] But Mine own nation will reject Me, so that My labour among them shall seem to be in vain, and My strength shall appear to have been spent for nought and without profit ; yet will I leave My cause with the Lord, and will look for My reward from My father and My God. (See John i. 11 ; Acts xiii. 46 ; Rom. iii. 3 ; Heb. xii. 2.)

"Now, therefore, thus hath the Lord said unto Me, the God who fashioned Me in the womb that I might be His Servant, that I might bring Jacob to Him again, and might gather Israel together to be His people ; the

Lord in whose eyes I am honourable, the God who is
My strength : [in verse 5 we adopt the marginal translation for reasons which we cannot give here :] yea,
thus saith He unto Me : It is too small an honour for
Thee that Thou shouldest serve Me by raising up the
tribes of Jacob, and restoring to My favour the remnant
of Israel. I will also give Thee to the Gentiles, that
Thou mayest be their light ; and Thy name shall be
proclaimed throughout the world as the name whereby
men must be saved.

"Thus saith the Lord, the Redeemer of Jacob, the
Holy One of Israel, to Him who is despised and rejected
of men, against whom the kings of the earth set themselves and the rulers take counsel together : Kings
shall see Thee and shall do Thee reverence ; princes
shall fall down before Thee ; for faithful is the Lord
that honoureth Thee, the Holy One of Israel who hath
chosen Thee to be His Servant. [Fulfilled at various
times by the submission of kings to the sceptre of the
Gospel.]

"Thus saith the Lord : When Thou callest upon Me,
I will accept Thee and will answer Thee ; when Thou
seekest My help I will save Thee. (See Heb. v. 7–9.)
I will make Thee victorious, and will give Thee unto
men for a covenant of salvation, that Thou mayest
restore the earth and repeople with living heirs the
wastes of the heathen. (See Acts xv. 14–18.) Thou
shalt preach deliverance to the captives and recovery
of sight to the blind. Thy flock shall find food in their
passage through the wilderness, and pastures even on
bare mountain tops, [not merely when they shall return
from Babylon, but in later days when they shall journey
from the prison-house of sin to the paradise of God.]
They shall neither hunger nor thirst ; for Thou, their
Shepherd, shalt have mercy upon them, and shalt lead
them to springs of living water. And I the Lord will

make all the mountains that lie in My path to be as a level road, and will throw My highways across the valleys. Lo, My flock shall come from far ; these from the north, these from the west, and these from the eastern wastes of the Sinites. [This probably means China.] Let the heavens sing, let the earth be glad, and let the mountains break forth into praise ; for the Lord comforteth His people with the message of His grace, and showeth mercy to His poor by the good tidings of His love " (Matt. v. 3).

Between Isaiah's times and these blessed days of the Son of man were to come the horrors of the Babylonian captivity and the dark centuries from Malachi to John the Baptist. We can, therefore, well understand that the people of God would have their faith sorely tried, and would often think that the Lord had forsaken and forgotten them. To this the prophet's next words seem to refer.

" But Zion will say, ' Jehovah hath forsaken me ; the Lord hath forgotten me.' Can a mother forget the child at her breast, so as to show no pity to the infant that she brought forth ? She may forget : but I will not forget Zion, saith the Lord. Behold, I have graven thee, O My city, upon the palms of My hands, and thy walls are thus ever before Me. Thy children shall speedily return to thee, and thy destroyers and ravagers shall depart. Gaze around thee and behold : these that flock together unto thee are thy children. By Myself have I sworn, saith the Lord, that they shall be to thee as a robe and an ornament ; thou shall deck thyself with them as a bride decketh herself with her nuptial garment. Thy cities lie waste and desolate, and thy land hath been ravaged by the destroyer ; [see the Lamentations ;] but, in the time when I shall restore thee, thy bounds shall be too small for thine inhabitants (Zech ii. 4) ; and thine oppressors shall be removed far from thee. The children that I will give thee after thy bereavement shall cry to thee: ' There is not room for us; enlarge thy walls that we may dwell in thee.' Then shalt thou wonder, and shalt say in thine heart: ' Who hath given these unto me, unto me who have been bereft of children, solitary, an exile, and a wanderer? Who hath reared these? Behold, I was alone. And where, meanwhile, were these?' "

This wonderment of the Jewish Church at the calling of the Gentiles reminds us of Peter's vision (Acts x.), and of the astonished cry of the Church at Jerusalem: " Then hath God granted to the Gentiles also repentance unto life " (Acts xi. 18).

" Thus saith the Lord God: Behold, I will stretch out to the nations the hand of My power, and will lift up to the peoples the banner of My word; and they shall bring thy sons and daughters to thee as parents carry their infants in their bosom or on their shoulder. [Both are common modes of carrying children in the East.] The kings and queens of the nations shall protect thee as if they were thy foster-fathers and foster-mothers; they shall bow down to the earth before thee and kiss the ground on which thou standest; and when thou shalt thus receive their homage and their love, then shalt thou know that I am the Lord, and that they who wait for Me shall not be put to shame.

" [But ye look with dismay at your approaching captivity, and ye say,] We are to be the prey of the mighty; and how can we be taken from them? We are to be carried captive by the terrible; and how can we be delivered? But thus saith the Lord: Even the captives of the mighty shall be taken from them, and the prey of the terrible shall be delivered. For I the Lord will fight against them that fight against thee, and I will deliver thy children from their captors. I will cause them that oppress thee to destroy every one his brother (Haggai ii. 22), so that they shall feed, as it were, on their own flesh, and be drunken with mutual bloodshed as with new wine ; and all men shall see that I the Lord am the Mighty One of Jacob, thy Saviour and thy Redeemer.''

It is ever a just display of God's wrath when He causes the enemies of His people to rise up against each other and mutually destroy themselves, as in the days of Gideon and Jehoshaphat (Judges vii. 22 ; 2 Chron. xx. 22, 23). So in modern times, in France, the massacre of St. Bartholomew's Day was followed in due season by the Reign of Terror.

FORTIETH HALF-HOUR

Chapters L. 1—LI. 8.

IN our second Half-Hour with Hosea we wrote as
follows: "When the Lord took the Israelitish
nation by the hand to bring it out of the land of Egypt,
He entered into a marriage covenant with it. (See
Jer. xxxi. 32.) In this wonderful wedding Jehovah
was the husband and Israel his wife. For a season the
young wife was, so to speak, comparatively faithful to
her high and holy husband. 'Israel served the Lord
all the days of Joshua, and all the days of the elders
that overlived Joshua, and which had known the work
of the Lord that He did for Israel' (Joshua xxiv. 31).
But 'Joshua, the son of Nun, the servant of the Lord,
died; and also all that generation were gathered unto
their fathers; and there arose another generation after
them which knew not the Lord, nor yet the work which
He had done for Israel. And the children of Israel did
evil in the sight of the Lord, and served Baalim: they
forsook the Lord God of their fathers, which brought
them out of the land of Egypt, and followed other gods,
of the gods of the people round about them, and bowed
themselves unto them, and provoked the Lord to anger.
And they forsook the Lord, and served Baal and
Ashtoreth' (Judges ii. 8–13). In the just and holy
language of Scripture, so true and forcible that we
shrink from reading it in our pulpits, the wife played
the harlot and committed foul adultery against her
heavenly husband." (See "Half-Hours with the Minor
Prophets," pp. 8, 9.) These words throw upon Isaiah
l. 1 the same light as upon Hos. ii. 2; and two further

quotations, taken from the Bible itself, will fitly complete our present introductory remarks.

In Deut. xxiv. 1 we read : " When a man hath taken a wife and married her, and it come to pass that she find no favour in his eyes, because he hath found some unseemly thing in her, then let him write her a bill of divorcement, and give it in her hand, and send her out of his house." We learn from the New Testament that this kind of divorce was allowed because of the hardness of men's hearts.

In 2 Kings iv. 1 we read : " Now there cried a certain woman of the wives of the sons of the prophets unto Elisha, saying, Thy servant my husband is dead ; and thou knowest that thy servant did fear the Lord ; and the creditor is come to take unto him my two sons to be bondmen." We see from this that a poverty-stricken parent was sometimes compelled to sell his own children to pay his debts.

Let us now endeavour to explain Isaiah's words in our usual manner.

" Thus saith the Lord : Have I divorced thee, O Zion, as a hard-hearted husband divorceth a wife whom he loveth not ? Or have I sold My children into bondage because I cannot pay My debts ? Behold, thou hast been sold into bondage because of thine own iniquities ; and by thine adultery against Me thou hast wrought thine own divorce. I have sent My prophets to warn thee : why hath no man given heed to them ? I have sent thee many a summons to return to Me : why hast thou not obeyed ? Dost thou despise My words because thou thinkest that My redeeming hand can no longer reach thee, or that My arm of power can no longer deliver thee ? Hast thou forgotten that I rebuked the Red Sea and divided it for thy deliverance ? That I dried up the Jordan before thee, so that its fish died for thirst and stank ? That I clothed the sky of Egypt with darkness as with a covering of sackcloth ? [Why then dost thou doubt My power and despise My word ?]"

The voice of the Lord God now melts, if we may so say, into the voice of Messiah, whom we may recognise as the speaker, at least as far as verse 7.

" The Lord God is My Teacher : He teacheth Me as a master teacheth them that learn of him, that I may know how and when to speak words of comfort to the weary. [Compare carefully John viii. 38, and Hebrews ii. 18.] Morning by morning He wakeneth Mine ear ; yea, He wakeneth it to learn of Him as disciples learn of their master. [During His life on earth Messiah was to receive constant instruction from His heavenly Father.] He hath spoken in Mine ear, [saying, Go, learn obedience by the things which Thou shalt suffer ;] and I am not rebellious, neither do I turn away from the work that He giveth Me to do. I am resolved to give My back to the scourge of the Gentile, and My cheeks to the buffeting of the Jew ; nor will I hide My face from insult and spitting. For the Lord God will help Me ; therefore I despise the shame : therefore also do I set My face like a flint against My foes, and I know that in the end I shall not be put to confusion. My God is near, and will pronounce Me just : therefore will I hasten to meet Mine accusers, and to close with Mine adversaries. (See Col. ii. 14, 15.) Behold, the Lord God will give Me victory ; who then shall condemn Me ? Behold, Mine adversaries shall perish like a garment that waxeth old and is eaten up of moths."

Our warrant for referring the above passage so directly to the sufferings of the Lord Jesus Christ is to be found in His own words : " Then He took unto Him the twelve, and said unto them, Behold, we go up to Jerusalem, and all things that are written by the prophets concerning the Son of man shall be accomplished. For He shall be delivered unto the Gentiles, and shall be mocked, and spitefully intreated, and spitted on ; and they shall scourge Him, and put Him to death : and the third day He shall rise again " (Luke xviii. 31–33).

The Father now speaks again, bidding the faithful in Israel listen to the voice of His prophets and His Messiah ; He speaks as if the faithful in those days were few, a hidden remnant.

" Who is among you that feareth Me ? saith the Lord : let him hearken to the voice of My servant. [So the Seventy translators, and the structure of the passage seems to justify them.] Though such a one walk in the darkness of affliction, and be bereft of the light of joy, yet let him trust in Me, and stay himself upon Me ; for I am the Lord his God. But as for you, ye that forsake My fear and walk in the light of your own inventions, [ye that worship false gods and trust in them], walk on in the light of your inventions ; Mine hand shall requite you with a just reward ; for your end shall be shame and misery " (Dan. xii. 2).

Having thus referred to the faithful remnant in Judah, who fear the Lord amidst the darkness, and are commanded to listen to the voice of His Servant (l. 10, as in the Septuagint), the Lord goes on to address to them a threefold promise of salvation (li. 1–3, 4–6, 7, 8). Those readers who, like Simeon, have seen God's salvation in the Babe of Bethlehem, will find no difficulty in acknowledging that this glorious threefold promise is fulfilled in the Gospel of Christ.

It is worthy of notice that the word " obey " in l. 10, and the word " hearken " in li. 1 and 7, are the same in the Hebrew original. This seems to bind together the whole passage l. 10–li. 8.

" Hearken to My words of comfort, ye that walk in the paths of righteousness and seek My face, saith the Lord. [Ye are discouraged because ye are few ; but] consider your origin, and look back at the quarry from which I took you : look back at your father Abraham and your mother Sarah. He was but one man, and I called him, blessed him, and multiplied his seed as the stars. Even so will I comfort Zion and restore her desolate land : from a wilderness she shall become an Eden ; from a desert, the garden of the Lord. Joy and gladness shall be found in her ; thanksgiving and the voice of melody."

The Lord delights in the thanksgiving which His people send up to Him through Christ ; by Him, therefore, let us offer the sacrifice of praise to God continually, that is, the fruit of our lips giving thanks to His name ; speaking to ourselves in psalms and hymns and spiritual songs, singing and making melody in our heart to the Lord (Heb. xiii. 15 ; Eph. v. 19).

" Attend unto My words, O My people ; give ear to My promise, O My nation ; a new law of love shall go forth from Me ; I will establish it, that it may give light to the nations. (See 2 Tim. i. 10.) The revelation of My righteousness is at hand ; My salvation goeth forth ; My power shall establish righteousness among the nations : remotest lands shall wait for My mercy, and shall trust in Me as in One that is mighty to save. Look up at the heavens, and look down upon the earth. The heavens shall vanish like a mist, the earth shall decay like a worn-out garment, and its inhabitants shall perish with it : but My salvation shall endure for ever, and My righteous loving-kindness shall never pass away."

In like manner Christ said, " Heaven and earth shall pass away, but My words shall not pass away."

" Hearken unto My words of encouragement, ye that know the paths of righteousness and have My law in your hearts. Fear not them that reproach you, nor be dismayed at their revilings. They shall perish as a garment that is moth-eaten, or as wool that is devoured by worms. But My righteous love to you shall endure for ever, and the salvation which I shall give you shall be an eternal salvation."

Eye hath not seen, nor ear heard, neither have entered into the heart of man, the things which God hath prepared for them that love Him. But God hath revealed them unto us by His Spirit. For God, who commanded the light to shine out of darkness, hath shined in our hearts, to give the light of the knowledge of the glory of God in the face of Jesus Christ. If we are indeed thus enlightened, it will be clear to us that these prophecies have received in the Gospel of Christ the highest fulfilment that they can have short of heaven.

Chapters LI. 9—LII. 12.

WITH a stretched-out arm did God deliver Israel from Egypt (Ex. vi. 6). Plague after plague fell upon that proud land, known to the prophets of after-days as Rahab, or Haughtiness. Finally its mighty force was drowned in the Red Sea and left to rot upon its shores, like a huge alligator that had been dragged from the depths of the Nile to die (Ezek. xxix. 1–5); while the bed of the sea formed a road along which the redeemed of the Lord passed to the land flowing with milk and honey, the inheritance which God had promised to their fathers.

But, alas! Israel forsook God, and so deeply and wilfully rebelled against Him that at last His wrath arose, and there was no remedy. In Isaiah's day the time was drawing near when they were to be uprooted from the land which God had given them, and delivered up to seventy years' bondage among the heathen. Little more than a century was now to pass before Jewish exiles should sit by the waters of Babylon, their harps silent, and their hearts fearing continually because of the fury of the oppressor. With the eye of a prophet Isaiah saw all this affliction as a present reality; and, personating the captive Church, pleaded with God for a fresh manifestation of the power that had smitten Egypt in days of old. He saw too that the outstretched arm of the Lord would speedily bring the exiles back to their native land, raise them to fresh happiness and honour, and cause their enemies to drink of the cup that had been put to the lips of

Jerusalem. He saw a messenger coming over the
mountains to announce in Zion the glad tidings of the
fall of the oppressor, and the deliverance of the oppressed, and foretold it in language which applies with
equal, or rather with greater, force to the proclamation
of the gospel of Christ.   We do not pretend to give an
exhaustive explanation of these glorious predictions,
nor to define with precision the limits of their fulfilment ;
but we do pray to be kept from assigning to them any
meaning at variance with the mind of Christ.

"Awake, awake, O Lord ! stretch forth Thine arm,
and deliver us by Thy strength ; awake to help us as
Thou didst help our fathers in the days of old. Didst
Thou not break down the pride of Egypt, and destroy
his dragon power in the Red Sea ? [Compare the
language of Ezek. xxix.] Didst Thou not dry up the
sea, and divide the waters of the deep, making its bed
a road for the passage of Thy redeemed ones ? [Even
so, when Thy power shall be put forth anew,] the ransomed of the Lord shall return from the land of their
captivity, and come with songs to Zion. They shall
be crowned with everlasting joy ; they shall be filled
with gladness and rejoicing, and sorrow and sighing
shall fly away. [Compare carefully Neh. xii. 43 ; Luke
ii. 10 ; Rev. xxi. 4.]

Such is the prophet's cry for help ; and it relates
primarily, as it seems to us, to the then approaching
Babylonian captivity. Then the Lord Himself speaks
to His afflicted people with special reference to the same
crisis, but in words which are pregnant with the promise
of eternal salvation by Christ.

"I, even I, saith the Lord, am thy comforter, O
Israel : why then shouldest thou fear man that shall
die, or the son of man that shall wither like grass ?
In thy distress thou forgettest the Lord thy Maker,
the God that created heaven and earth, and fearest

continually the rage of the oppressors who threaten to destroy thee. And where is their rage ? [It is quickly quenched in death.] My banished people shall speedily be delivered from their bonds ; they shall not die and go down to the grave in captivity, neither shall they lack bread. For I the Lord am the God of Israel ; I rule the raging of the sea : the Lord of hosts is My name. I have put My words into the mouth of Mine Anointed, and have hidden Him in the shadow of Mine hand, that I may send Him forth in due season to create new heavens and a new earth, and to make the inhabitants of Zion a people unto Me for ever."

Now follows another address to Jerusalem from the God whom she has invoked. She has cried, " Awake, awake, O arm of the Lord, and put forth Thy strength for our deliverance : " He answers, " Awake, awake, O Jerusalem ; arise from the despondency, despair, and misery of thy captivity. The Assyrian and the Chaldean have taken thee for a slave without paying a price for thee, and they shall let thee go free without receiving a ransom." These promises are akin to those previously made concerning Cyrus : " He shall let go My captives, not for price nor reward, saith the Lord of hosts " : like them they have a second and grander fulfilment in the salvation of Christ, and the freedom wherewith He makes His people free.

" Awake, awake, O Jerusalem, and arise from the stupor of despair. Thou hast drunk the cup which I put into thine hand, the cup of My indignation. Thou hast emptied it, and it hath made thee stagger ; thou hast drained its bitter dregs. [Let the reader pause to read Lam. v.] Among all the sons of thy womb there is not one that can lead thee out of trouble ; among all thy citizens there is not one that can hold forth to thee a helping hand. Two evils have befallen thee, and none pitieth ; desolation by famine and destruction by the sword; how canst thou be comforted? Thy sons faint with weakness and fear at the corners of thy streets, like unto prey in the net of the hunter. They have drunk deep of the Lord's anger, of the rebuke of their God. Hearken therefore to this message of My pardoning love, saith the Lord Jehovah, thy God, that defendeth His people: Behold, I will take from thine hand the cup that maketh thee to stagger, the deep cup of My indignation; thou shalt no longer drink thereof, but I will cause them to drink thereof who have afflicted thee, saying to thy soul, ' Lie down, that we may walk over thee,' who have made thee give them thy back as the ground, as a beaten road to tread upon."

This transfer of the cup of wrath from Jerusalem to Nineveh and Babylon was soon effected. They drank of it, and departed into darkness; but Jerusalem lived on to hear good tidings of good, to hear the voice of one that said, Thy God reigneth; His kingdom is at hand; repent ye, and believe the Gospel.

" Awake, awake, O Zion! Arise from thy weakness, and gird thee with the strength that I will give thee: clothe thee with garments of beauty, O Jerusalem, thou city of the Holy One. No longer shall the heathen enter thy gates to oppress thee. Shake off the dust of thy captivity, and sit upon thy throne, O Jerusalem; cast off from thy neck the yoke of slavery, thou captive city of David. For thus saith the Lord: Your captors paid no price for you, and they shall receive no price for your discharge. For thus saith the Lord God: In days of old My people went down into Egypt to sojourn there, and were brought into bondage; and I delivered them: and now the Assyrian and the Chaldean have taken them violently away from their own land, and oppress them without a cause. What then shall I do, seeing that My people have been taken away by violence, and that their captors howl forth blasphemies against

My name continually, [saying, Who is the Lord, that
He should deliver you out of our hand?] Therefore
My people shall again know that I am God: in the day
when I shall deliver them they shall know that it is I
who have spoken, Behold, it is I, the Lord!"

By comparison with Nahum i. 15, we see that the
words which come next may have a first reference to
the overthrow of Jerusalem's old enemies, Assyria
and Chaldea; and it was indeed good tidings of peace
when the downfall of these cruel foes was announced,
for then, according to Isaiah's words elsewhere (xiv.
7, 8), the whole earth was at rest and was quiet: they
broke forth into singing: yea, the fir trees rejoiced,
and the cedars of Lebanon, saying, "Since thou wast
laid down, no feller is come up against us." But by
comparison with Romans x. 15, we also know that the
spirit of prophecy is here foretelling that preaching
of the Gospel which was to begin with the ministry of
the Baptist, and to pass on into that of the apostles
and their successors.

"How beautiful are the feet of them that come over
the mountains to Zion bringing good tidings, publishing
peace; good tidings of good things, the message of salvation, saying unto her, The kingdom of God is at hand!

"Hearken! The voice of the prophets of God!
(Ezek. ii. 17; 2 Cor. v. 20.) They lift up their voice,
and sing together with joy, for they see with their own
eyes that the Lord returneth to Zion. [They behold
Messiah's glory, the glory as of the only begotten from
the Father, John i. 14.] Break forth into joy, and join
in a song of praise, ye ruins of Jerusalem: for the Lord
hath awaked to comfort His people and to deliver
Jerusalem. He stretcheth forth His holy arm in the
sight of all the nations, and all the ends of the earth
shall see the salvation of our God. (Compare Luke ii.
30–32.)

" Go forth, go forth, ye captives : depart from the
land of your captivity, and defile not yourselves with
its abominations ; depart from the midst of it, and
sanctify yourselves, for ye are the priests of the Lord
and bear His holy vessels. Ye shall not depart in haste,
as ye did from Egypt, neither shall ye flee by stealth ;
the Lord shall march before you as your captain, the
God of Israel shall guard your rear."

Two phrases which occur in this portion of Isaiah's
prophecy are often used by readers of the Bible in a
sense which the words were not intended to bear, and
cannot bear. In li. 20 the words " as a wild bull in a
net " naturally suggest to the English reader the picture
of a rebellious and desperate struggle amid the meshes
of calamity ; the fact is that " wild bull " is a mis-
translation, and should have been " antelope " or
" stag," and the picture is one of helpless and hopeless
entanglement. Again, in lii. 8 the expression " eye
to eye " means " face to face " ; the watchmen of
Zion shall be eye-witnesses of the Lord's return to her :
it is curious that these words should ever have been
understood to mean agreement of views.

We believe that our double interpretation of this
portion, as referring both to the deliverance from
Babylon and to the Gospel of Christ, is far from being
fanciful ; we believe that we have therein the mind
of the Spirit. By way of confirmation, not of proof,
we quote again from the soberest of all sober interpreters.

Writing on lii. 8, Calvin says, " This extends indeed
to spiritual conversion ; but let us not on that account
depart from the literal sense, so as not to include also
the benefit which the Lord conferred on the ancient
people. For when He restored the Jews to liberty,
and employed the ministry of Zerubbabel, Ezra and
Nehemiah, these things were fulfilled. [That is, the

promise was fulfilled that the Lord should bring again Zion.] Yet at the same time the fulfilment of these words ought to be continued down to the coming of Christ, by which the Church was gathered out of all parts of the world. But we ought also to go forward to His last coming, by which all things shall be perfectly restored."

Again, on verse 10 of the same chapter, he says : " The extension of this magnificent spectacle to the ends of the earth [before the eyes of all nations] makes it evident that the prophet does not speak merely of the return of the people which should take place a few years afterwards [about a century], but of the restoration of the whole Church. This prophecy is maliciously restricted by the Jews to the deliverance from Babylon, and is improperly restricted by Christians to the spiritual redemption which we obtain through Christ ; for we must begin with the deliverance which was wrought under Cyrus, and bring it down to our own time. Thus the Lord began to display His power among the Medes and Persians, but afterwards He made it visible to all the world."

If we want God's help for ourselves, for our country, or for the church of Christ, let us cry with the prophet, Awake, awake, put on strength, O arm of the Lord ! Hast Thou not miraculously delivered Thy people of old ? Then to us also shall the Lord return answer, Awake, awake : put on thy strength : My strength shall be made perfect in thy weakness.

FORTY-SECOND HALF-HOUR

Chapters LII. 13—LIII. 12.

THIS portion of Isaiah's writings renders such a distinct testimony to the person and work of Jesus Christ that it has been justly called the Fifth Gospel. Before, however, we consider its testimony to Christ, we will consider His testimony to it; we shall then be better able to understand and receive the testimony which it bears to Him. Nor will this be " reasoning in a circle "; for even if this passage had never been written, we should have known from other Scriptures that Jesus is the Christ, the Son of the living God. As He says Himself, the Scriptures are they that testify of Him.

In the third Gospel we find Christ saying, " This that is written must yet be accomplished in Me, And He was reckoned among the transgressors " (Luke xxii. 37). It is evident that, in thus claiming the closing words of this prophecy as written concerning Himself and fulfilled in Himself, He claims the whole of it as similarly written and similarly fulfilled. Hence Christians have their Lord's authority for so understanding it.

This view is confirmed by the testimony of evangelists and apostles. Instead of merely giving references, we will quote their words at length, and the reader can then at once compare them with those of the prophet.

" To whom He was not spoken of, they shall see : and they that had not heard shall understand." " Lord, who hath believed our report ? and to whom hath the arm of the Lord been revealed ? " " Lord, who hath believed our report ? " " Himself took our infirmities and bare our sicknesses." "By whose stripes ye were healed ; for ye were as sheep going astray." "He was led as a sheep to the slaughter, and like a lamb dumb before His shearers, so opened He not His mouth : in His humiliation His judgment was taken away : and who shall declare His generation ? for His life is taken from the earth." "Who did no sin, neither was guile found in His mouth." (Rom. xv. 21 ; John xii. 38 ; Rom. x. 16 ; Matt. viii. 17 ; 1 Pet. ii. 24, 25 ; Acts viii. 32, 33 ; 1 Pet. ii. 22.) And, in addition to these direct quotations, we find that the substance of the prophet's words is often reproduced in the New Testament. For instances of this, let the reader carefully compare Philip. ii. 9–11 with Isaiah lii. 13–15, and Philip. ii. 6–8 with Isaiah liii. 2–5.

It is not difficult to prove from this prophecy that the Christian religion is of God ; but this is not our present object : we merely wish to point out to Christians that they have the authority of Christ and His apostles for regarding it as fulfilled in His person, history and work. The language is so direct that little explanation is needed ; yet there are one or two expressions which admit of various interpretations, and are, therefore, somewhat hard to understand ; they occur in the seventh and eighth verses of the fifty-third chapter. It will not be necessary to notice all the meanings that have been assigned to them ; we may safely take as a guide to their true sense the quotation from the Septuagint, given in Acts viii. 32, 33. But even so, what are we to understand by the words, " Who shall declare his generation ? " We think that the word here translated " generation " is such that it cannot refer to the Sonship of Christ. Indeed, Calvin, who believed as we do that Christ is in His Divine nature, and independently of His incarnation, the Son of God, co-equal and co-eternal with the Father, expresses regret that this passage was ever used in support of that sacred truth. He says very wisely, " The ancients abused this passage when, in reasoning against the Arians, they wished to prove by it Christ's eternal generation. They ought to have been satisfied with clearer testimonies of Scripture, that they might not expose themselves to the mockery of heretics, who sometimes take occasion from this to become more obstinate ; for it might easily have been objected that the prophet was not thinking about that subject." It seems to us that the words are a prediction that Messiah should be taken away in His prime, so that the record of His life on earth should be cut short, so to speak, at its beginning.

This prophecy is couched in such simple language that very little change is needed to make its meaning clear. Moreover, the expressions are so well known and so sacred that we should fear to offend the Christian reader if we did not to a great extent leave them untouched.

" Behold, the Messiah shall be My servant, saith the Lord ; He shall accomplish in wisdom the work which I have given Him to do ; and I will reward Him by exalting Him above all principalities and powers. As there will be many who will wonder at His degradation, when they shall see His face more marred with grief and suffering than that of any of the sons of men ; so shall there be many nations who shall feel the virtue of His blood ; for [the tidings of His salvation shall be carried to the heathen, and] that which had not been told them shall they see, that which they had not heard shall they consider.

" But who, hearing our testimony, believeth us ? To whom is it revealed that Messiah is the power of God ? For He shall grow up before the Lord like a weak and tender plant, feeble as a root that springeth out of dry ground. [Not merely the Jewish race but human nature at large, was indeed dry ground when the Word was made flesh.] He will have no outward comeliness ; and when He shall appear there will be no worldly pomp to commend Him to us. He will be despised and rejected of men, a Man of sorrows, and acquainted with grief [having grief for His constant companion], one whom men despise as not fit to be looked upon, one whom we esteem not.

"But surely the grief which He beareth, He beareth for us, and the sorrow which He carrieth, He carrieth for us ; yet we esteem Him stricken for His own iniquities, smitten of God with affliction for His own transgressions. But He is wounded for our transgressions, bruised for our iniquities : the chastisement which brings us peace with God is upon Him, and by His stripes we are healed. All we like lost sheep have gone astray ; every one of us hath turned to his own evil way ; and the Lord hath laid upon Him the iniquity of us all.

"He is oppressed, but He humbleth Himself, and openeth not His mouth ; He is led as a lamb to the slaughter, and as a sheep before her shearers is dumb, so He openeth not His mouth. By oppression and injustice He is cut off, and who shall write the record of His days ? For [in the midst of His years] He is cut off out of the land of the living ; for the transgression of Israel is He stricken. He is put to death with the wicked, but buried with the rich ; and yet He hath done no violence, neither hath deceit been found in His mouth.

"Yet the Lord saw fit to bruise Him, and put Him to grief, and to make His soul a sacrifice for sin : and when all is finished, He shall see in His ransomed seed the fruit of His own death ; He shall live for evermore, and the pleasure of the Lord shall prosper in His hand. [His hand shall sway the sceptre of God's grace.] In the persons of His ransomed ones He shall see the result of the travail of His soul, and shall be satisfied ; [it shall be His sufficient reward.] By His doctrine shall My righteous Servant make many righteous, saith the Lord, for He shall bear their iniquities. Therefore will I recompense Him as the victorious are recompensed ; He shall take the prey as conquerors after the battle. (See Col. ii. 14, 15.) For He hath poured out His soul unto death ; He hath been numbered with the transgressors ; He hath borne the sin of many, and He intercedeth for the transgressors."

What is known as the orthodox doctrine of atonement could not be more distinctly stated than it is in these words of Isaiah ; and those who reject it would do well to consider the prophet's complaint, "Who hath believed our report ? and to whom is the arm of the Lord revealed ? " It is an awful thing to live and die an unbeliever.

In consulting Calvin's exposition of this passage, we were almost startled by the following remark, because it so exactly defines our own mind and method in these humble labours : " Here we might bring forward many things about the blessed consequences of Christ's sufferings, if we had not determined to expound rather than to preach ; and therefore let us be satisfied with a plain exposition." If we can lead our readers into a clear understanding of the prophet's words, we shall have accomplished our purpose.

Chapter LIV.

WE believe that we shall guide our readers into a true understanding of this beautiful chapter if we can give correct and authoritative answers to three questions.

1. Who is the woman addressed by the prophet, or rather, by the Lord?

2. What is the nature of the promises made to her?

3. To what time did the Spirit of Christ point? (1 Pet. i. 11).

Happily we are not left in this enquiry to the conjectures and interpretations of uninspired men: the New Testament supplies us with the answers that we need.

1. Cities and nations are often spoken of in Scripture as the mothers of their citizens, and very wisely so; for the city or nation in which a man is born may in many respects be fitly called his mother. Now the apostle Paul tells us that there are two Jerusalems: the Jerusalem which now is, and is in bondage with her children; and the Jerusalem which is above, which is free, and is the mother of all the children of promise; and he justifies this statement by quoting the first verse of this very chapter. The apostle concludes his argument with the words, " So then, brethren, we [believers] are not children of [that Jerusalem which is] a bondwoman, but of [that Jerusalem which is] a free woman. Stand fast, therefore, in the liberty wherewith Christ hath made us free, and be not entangled again in the

yoke of bondage " (Gal. iv. 25–v. 1). We, therefore, who accept Paul as a man sent from God to be our teacher in faith and verity (1 Tim. ii. 7), conclude with certainty that the desolate wife addressed by the prophet is the Church of Christ, the city within whose holy ramparts neither circumcision availeth anything, nor uncircumcision, but a new creature.

2. The nature of the promises addressed to this city is the same as that of the city itself ; they are heavenly promises, promises of blessings which, in Isaiah's day, were " good things to come " (Heb. x. 1). But though this is an obvious inference from the answer to the first question, we have here also the direct guidance of the New Testament. " It is written in the prophets," saith Christ, " that they shall all be taught of God : every man, therefore, that hath heard, and hath learned of the Father, cometh unto Me " (compare John vi. 35 with Isa. liv. 13). Here is the testimony of Jesus Christ that the children of the city built of goodly stones, and standing on foundations of sapphire, are those who learn of the Father, and therefore fly for salvation to the Son ; the blessedness of the instruction given to them culminates in this, that they come to Christ, in whom there is neither Jew nor Gentile, seeing that all His are one in Him (Gal. iii. 28). To our second question we answer therefore : The blessings here promised to Zion are the blessings of the Gospel.

3. We cannot answer the third question by pointing to another verse in this chapter which is actually quoted in the New Testament ; but we think that we may safely say that the times referred to by the prophet are the days of which Peter speaks in Acts iii. 24 : " Yea, and all the prophets from Samuel, and those that follow after, as many as have spoken, have likewise foretold of these days." Let our readers consider

well the promise in Isa. liv. 17 : " Every tongue which shall rise against thee in judgment thou shalt condemn : this is the heritage of the servants of the Lord, and their righteousness is of Me, saith the Lord " : and then let him ask himself if it is not adequately fulfilled in the Gospel which entitles all true believers to say with Paul : " Who shall lay anything to the charge of God's elect ? It is God that justifieth. Who is he that condemneth ? It is Christ that died, yea, rather, that is risen again, who is even at the right hand of God, who also maketh intercession for us " (Rom. viii. 33, 34).

It is our aim in these expositions to give our readers a sound knowledge of the general scope of Holy Scripture, without entering into the discussion of details which, after all, can only be of interest to those who are sufficiently equipped with scholarly attainments to be able to grasp both the difficulties and the proposed solutions. We think, therefore, that we have now said enough by way of introduction, having shown that the prophet, after speaking in the previous chapter of the sufferings of Christ, now passes on to foretell the glory that should follow (1 Pet. i. 11), a glory which actually did follow from Pentecost and onwards.

" Sing, O city, that hast been as a barren woman ; break forth into songs of joy and shouts of triumph, thou that hast ceased to bring forth : for the children of thy widowhood (Lam. i. 1) shall be more numerous than those of thy married life, saith the Lord. [That is, the citizens of the Church of Christ shall exceed in number the sons of Jacob in the palmiest days of old, for instance, in the times spoken of in 1 Kings iv. 20.] Enlarge the compass of thy tent, O Zion : stretch wide the curtains of thy dwelling-place : stint not thy children for room : lengthen the cords of thy tabernacle, and strengthen the stakes thereof. For thy sons shall spread abroad on every side ; they shall people all lands, and shall fill with citizens the cities that have long been desolate. [Let us pause here, and think of Judæa, Samaria, and the uttermost part of the earth (Acts i. 8) ; let us think of Ephesus, Corinth, Athens, Rome ; of the distant regions of Africa and Europe ; of Britain, of China, of the then undiscovered Western continents, and the islands lying beyond them in the remote Pacific : all to be admitted in due season to the freedom of the heavenly Jerusalem.] Fear not, O Zion, for thou shalt not be ashamed ; be not dejected, for thou shalt not be put to confusion : for thou shalt forget the shame of thy former days, and shalt no more remember the reproach of thy divorce. (See Isa. l. 1.) For I, thy Maker, am thy husband (Eph. v. 23, 31, 32), the Lord of hosts is My name ; I, the Holy One of Israel, am thy Redeemer ; the God of the whole earth will I be called. [The one God of Jew and Gentile. Rom. iii. 29, 30.] For I will take thee back again (Jer. iii. 1), though for thy sins thou hast been as a divorced wife that is grieved in spirit, as a young wife cast off by her husband, saith the Lord. For a small moment have I forsaken thee [for instance, during the seventy years' captivity, and much of the sad and silent interval between Malachi and John the Baptist], but with great mercies will I gather thy children unto Me. (See John xi. 52.) In an outburst of Mine anger against thy idolatries I hid My face from thee for a moment ; but with everlasting kindness will I have mercy on thee, saith the Lord thy Redeemer. (See 2 Thess. ii. 16.) For this covenant that I make with thee is as that which I made with Noah concerning the waters of the flood : for as I sware unto Noah that I would not again destroy the earth with a flood, so have I sworn that I will not be wrath with with thee nor rebuke thee.

[Seeing that this promise is made to the true children of Zion, and is of a spiritual nature, we need not stumble at the second destruction of Jerusalem in the days of Vespasian and Titus.] For though [the heavens depart, and] the earth with its mountains and hills be removed, My kindness shall not depart from thee, neither shall My covenant of peace be removed, saith the Lord that hath mercy on thee."

In the light of these promises, we, who have entered into Gospel rest, may well be persuaded that neither height, nor depth, nor any other creature, shall be able to separate us from the love of God, which is in Christ Jesus our Lord (Rom. viii. 39).

" O Zion, who art and shalt be afflicted, tossed with tempest, and not comforted (see Lam. i. 16, 21), behold, the days come, saith the Lord, when I will build thee anew, comely with the comeliness that I will put upon thee, and safe within the walls which My love shall throw around thee. [Thou shalt be built upon the foundations of My messengers and prophets, Messiah Himself being the chief corner-stone, in whom the whole building shall be fitly framed together for a habitation of God. (Eph. ii. 20–22.)] All thy citizens shall be taught of the Lord, and their peace shall be great under the reign of the Prince of Peace. In My righteousness will I establish thee: no oppressor shall put thee in fear, no terror shall make thee afraid. When thy foes gather together against thee they shall not have My help as in former days (see Jer. xxi. 4, 5 ; xxxvii. 10) : they shall perish that thou mayest be safe. Behold, the smith that bloweth his fire of coal to form a weapon of war is himself but My creature, and I have created another to destroy his work of destruction. (Compare Zech. i. 20, 21.) No weapon that is formed against My people shall prosper : they shall condemn every tongue that shall seek to condemn them. (See Zech. iii. 1, 2 ; Rom. viii. 31–34.) This is the inheritance of My servants, and this is the righteousness which I will bestow upon them, saith the Lord."

Remember, reader, that as the ocean is made up of drops, so the Church of Christ is made up of individual souls. Hast thou proof of thine own interest in these exceeding great and precious promises ?

Chapter LV.

"I WILL make an everlasting covenant with you, even the sure mercies of David": thus said the Lord to the thirsty and the poor some seven centuries before David's greater Son was born at Bethlehem. About fifteen years after He had ascended from Olivet, the same God spake again by His servant Paul, saying: "And as concerning that He raised Him from the dead now no more to return to corruption, He said on this wise, I will give you the sure mercies of David." We are thus distinctly taught to regard the fifty-fifth chapter of Isaiah as a prophecy which referred to the times of Christ and His apostles, had its fulfilment in their days, and is still fulfilled in that everlasting Gospel which is sent to every creature under heaven. And how fitly such a chapter, full of Gospel invitation, Gospel exhortation, Gospel promise, is placed after two which speak of the sufferings of Christ, and the glory that should follow! Christ died and rose again; the Church was beautified as with jewels and fair colours by the descent of the Spirit at Pentecost; and then the voice of God went forth to all nations, crying, "Ho, every one that thirsteth, come ye to the waters."

We think that Acts xiii. 34, to which we have just referred, is the only place in the New Testament where this chapter is directly quoted: and yet well nigh the whole of the chapter may be re-written in language taken from the New Testament. We will endeavour to do this, and afterwards, for the sake of uniformity of treatment, we will endeavour to paraphrase the chapter, though the clearness and the simplicity of the prophet's words render a paraphrase almost superfluous.

" If any man thirst, let him come unto Me and drink : he that drinketh of the water that I shall give him shall never thirst. When they had nothing to pay, He frankly forgave them both. Labour not for the meat that perisheth, but for that meat which endureth unto everlasting life, which the Son of man shall give unto you : for Him hath God the Father sealed, (given by an everlasting covenant to be a Saviour). To this end was I born, and for this cause came I into the world, that I should bear witness unto the truth. Every one that is of the truth heareth My voice. A Prince and a Saviour, the Captain of our salvation. Ye shall receive power, after that the Holy Ghost is come upon you : and ye shall be witnesses unto Me both in Jerusalem, and in all Judæa, and in Samaria, and unto the uttermost part of the earth." (See Isa. lv. 1–6.)

Again. " We preach unto you that ye should turn from these vanities unto the living God ; repent ye, therefore, and believe the Gospel : for through this Man is preached unto you the forgiveness of sins, and by Him all that believe are justified from all things. How unsearchable are His judgments, and His ways past finding out ! The words that I speak unto you, they are spirit and they are life. Heaven and earth shall pass away, but My words shall not pass away. Peace I leave with you, My peace I give unto you : your heart shall rejoice, and your joy no man taketh from you. I send thee to the Gentiles, to turn them from darkness to light, and from the power of Satan unto God," that in the waste places of the heathen world firs and myrtles may grow instead of thorns and briers. (See Isa. lv. 6–13.)

Let the reader carefully compare the above cento of extracts from the New Testament with the chapter which we have now under consideration, and he can hardly fail to agree with the interpretation of it given by our translators in their admirable summary : " The prophet, with the promises of Christ, calleth to faith and to repentance. The happy success of them that believe."

Verses 5 and 13 demand some special notice before we pass on. The former has received two interpretations, which differ in appearance rather than in reality. Some consider that the person addressed is the Messiah, the Witness, Leader and Commander spoken of in the third person in the previous verse. Such abrupt changes of person are not uncommon in the prophets, and it is quite possible that this view of the passage (which, by the way, is Calvin's) is correct ; if so, the words mean that Christ should call to Him those whom He had hitherto treated as though He knew them not. But other expositors, with whom we are inclined to agree, consider that this promise is addressed to Israel, that is, to the Church of God, and that it was fulfilled in the preaching of the apostles, who were all Jews, and did indeed call the unknown Gentiles to fellowship with them in Christ. There is but little practical difference between these two interpretations, inasmuch as the Gospel in the mouth of the apostles was in fact the voice of Christ.

It is interesting to know that the meaning which we have assigned to verse 13 was assigned to it many centuries ago by the Jews themselves. In the Targum, or Chaldee translation, of Isaiah the passage stands thus : " Instead of the ungodly shall come up righteous persons, and instead of sinners shall rise up such as fear to sin." Dr. Gill quotes this, and wisely agrees with it ; his words are : " Those who are like briers and thorns in their nature state, being no better than others, but children of wrath even as others, shall by the grace of God be made like firs and myrtle trees ; as great a change shall be wrought in them as if briers and thorns were changed into firs and myrtle trees, to which the saints were sometimes compared." We account that the good doctor is here anything but fanciful. Saul of Tarsus was a brier: Paul the apostle was a myrtle, whose fragrance still floats upon the morning breeze wheresoever the day of salvation dawns upon the dark deserts of heathendom.

" [And when Messiah shall have made His soul a sacrifice for sin, and shall have beautified the city of His abode with the glories of salvation, then shall this call go forth from Judæa unto the ends of the earth :] Ho, every one that thirsteth, come to the fountain of living waters, even every one that hath nothing to pay. Come, buy bread for the asking, and eat (Matt. vii. 6–11) ; yea, come, buy the wine of My love and the milk of My gracious word, without money and without price (Rom. xi. 6). Wherefore do ye seek to buy as bread that which is but a stone ? Wherefore do ye spend your toil to get food that satisfieth not ? [Wherefore would ye feed your immortal souls on husks that the swine do eat, the things of this perishing world, or schemes of salvation devised by man ?] Hearken diligently to the voice of God, eat the good bread of His Word, and feast your souls on the riches of His grace. Give ear unto Me, saith the Lord, and come hither ; hearken unto Me, and ye shall live ; for I will bring you into an eternal covenant with Me, and ye shall inherit the mercy which I have promised to David and to his seed for ever. Behold, I will cause the Son of David to bear witness unto My truth among all nations, to be a Prince of life and a Captain of salvation among all peoples. Behold, his messengers shall go forth from Jerusalem (see Luke xxiv. 47) to call nations which hitherto they have not known ; and nations which have been strangers to them shall hasten to join themselves unto them ; for it shall be seen that the Lord is their God, and the glory of the Holy One of Israel shall rest upon them (Luke xxiv. 49).

" [And they shall preach to every creature, saying :] Seek ye the Lord while He may be found [while He calleth to repentance] ; pray to Him while He is near [while the voice of His gospel is still heard]. Let the wicked forsake his way, and the unrighteous man his thoughts : let him return unto the Lord, for He will have mercy upon him, and to our God, for He will abundantly pardon. [Repent ye, and believe the gospel.] For My thoughts are not your thoughts, nor your ways My ways, saith the Lord. [My thoughts are thoughts of love to My enemies; yours are thoughts of enmity against God (Rom. viii. 7, 8). Your ways are ways of evil ; Mine are ways of triumphing goodness.] For as the heavens are higher than the earth, so are My ways higher than your ways, and My thoughts than your thoughts. For so surely as the rain and snow descend from heaven and return not thither until they have watered the earth and made it fruitful, that it may produce seed-corn for a future crop and bread for the passing year, so surely shall My word not go forth from My mouth in vain : it shall not return unto Me void, but shall accomplish all My pleasure, and prosper in the thing whereto I sent it. Exiles shall return with joy from banishment, and prisoners shall be brought out of the prison-house in peace. The mountains and the hills that lie in their path shall resound with the voice of praise, the very trees of the field shall share in the gladness of My redeemed. Thorns shall give place to fir-trees, and briers to myrtle-trees. Thus shall the Lord get unto Himself a name and great glory : for the work of His hands shall be an everlasting wonder that shall not pass away."

I thirst : I come : I drink : I live. Hallelujah.

Chapter LVI.

" REPENT ye, for the kingdom of heaven is at
hand : and bring forth fruits meet for repentance." So preached the Baptist, acting as the immediate forerunner of Christ ; and his message was confirmed by Christ Himself, who shortly afterwards
" began to preach, and to say, Repent, for the kingdom
of heaven is at hand." Thus God, when about to
reveal His great salvation, called for a repentance
which should be shown by suitable fruits of godliness
and righteousness.

The same message had been delivered by Isaiah
seven centuries before, with reference to the same
salvation, which even then was nigh at hand in the eyes
of Him with whom a thousand years are as one day.
The chapter which we have reached opens with the
words, " Do justice, for My salvation is near to come " ;
that is, " Repent, for the kingdom of heaven is at
hand." The two messages are one.

After thus summoning Judah to repentance, because
of the near approach of God's salvation, the prophet
passes on to foretell the admission of the Gentiles into
the kingdom of God. Neither the son of the stranger
nor the degraded slave, though formerly excluded from
the sanctuary of Jehovah (see Deut. xxiii. 1–3), should
be excluded from the courts of the temple which Messiah
was to build ; no national or personal disqualifications
should shut out such from the true City of God, the walls
whereof were to be Salvation, and her gates Praise.
In gospel days the house of the Lord should become a

house of prayer for all peoples, and the outcasts of the Gentiles should be gathered unto the gathered outcasts of Israel (verses 1–8).

Then the prophet seems to turn back, so to speak, to his own days, when the downward course of the nation under Ahaz, after being temporarily checked by Hezekiah's reformation, was resumed amid the idolatries and murders of Manasseh. Isaiah tells the watchmen—that is, the princes, priests, and prophets of Judah—that they are no better than dumb sheep-dogs, or ignorant shepherds; that they are greedy, self-indulgent, besotted revellers. Therefore, in the Lord's name he summons the armies of the heathen, whom he addresses as beasts of the field and of the forest, to come and devour the wicked: a call which was terribly obeyed, about a century later, by the cruel hordes of Chaldea. (See 2 Kings xxiv. and xxv.)

Such is our own view of the scope of this chapter: let us confirm it by quoting Calvin. Writing on verse 7 he says: "By these modes of expression he describes what he had formerly stated, that foreigners who were formerly excluded from the Church of God are called to it, so that henceforth the distinction between circumcision and uncircumcision shall be abolished. . . . He testifies that the grace of God shall be diffused throughout the whole world; and this cannot be accomplished without uniting the Gentiles to the Jews, so as to form one body, which happened when the difference between circumcision and uncircumcision was taken out of the way. There is, therefore, nothing now to prevent Gentiles from ministering to God, seeing that they have been called into the temple, that is, into the assembly of believers."

Let our readers observe carefully what Calvin here says about the temple, "that is, the assembly of believers." It may help to preserve them from a

mischievous literalism which, while it professes extreme
faithfulness to the language of Scripture, really misses
the mind of the Spirit in His word. A few further
words of Calvin on this point are so instructive, and
put the matter so clearly, that we will transcribe them
here before we attempt our usual paraphrase : " By
the word sacrifices he means such spiritual worship of
God as is enjoined in the Gospel ; for the prophet spoke
in accordance with what was customary in his time,
when the worship of God was wrapped up in a variety
of ceremonies. But now, instead of sacrifices, we offer
to God praises, thanksgivings, good works, and finally
ourselves. When He declares that they shall be
acceptable, let us not imagine that this arises from their
own value or excellence, but from God's undeserved
kindness ; for He might justly reject them if He looked
at them in themselves."

Let our readers bear this principle carefully in mind :
" The prophets spoke in accordance with what was
customary in their time, when they described the
spiritual worship of God which is enjoined in the Gospel."
If we neglect to apply this principle, and fall back into
uniform literalism, we shall do violence to the spirit
of those prophecies unto the very letter whereof we
profess to cling. Let us now come to the words of
Isaiah.

" Thus saith the Lord [to the princes of Judah and
the inhabitants of Jerusalem] : Execute judgment
with integrity (Ex. xviii. 21), and deal righteously
every man with his neighbour (compare Luke iii.
7–14) ; for My salvation cometh quickly, and My
righteousness shall shortly be revealed. (Compare
Mal. iii. 1–5.) Blessed is the man that keepeth My
sabbaths and profaneth them not ; blessed is the son
of man that cleaveth to My word and refraineth his
hand from doing evil. And let not the stranger from

among the Gentiles, who would share in the worship of
the God of Israel, say, ' The Lord will reject me from
the number of His people '; nor let the eunuch say,
' I am as a withered and fruitless tree.' [For those
who have been hitherto excluded from My sanctuary,
shall have admission to My holy courts.] For thus
saith the Lord concerning the eunuchs that worship
Me and choose the things that I delight in, and cleave
to the precepts of My word: Even unto them will I
give among My priests and within My kingdom a place
and a name better than that of sons and of daughters.
[They shall have a place in Messiah's heart, and a name
upon his breastplate—Ex. xxviii. 21, 29.] They shall
be known for ever as the sons of the Lord Almighty,
and their name shall never perish (2 Cor. vi. 18;
John x. 27–29). Also the Gentiles who shall seek unto
the Lord, that they may minister unto Him, love His
name, and be His servants, every one that shall worship Me in truth and cleave to the precepts of My word,
all such will I bring into My holy presence, and will
make them joyful in My house of prayer, [at My throne
of grace.] Their prayer and praise, their gifts and their
persons, shall be like unto accepted sacrifices offered
upon Mine altar; for My house shall be called a house
of prayer for all peoples, [My throne of grace shall be
open unto all nations.] The God who hath gathered
Israel from all his captivities saith, I will gather others
unto Israel from among the Gentiles, beside the outcasts of Israel whom I shall have brought back from their
captivities.

" [But now hearken unto me, ye godless princes,
priests, and prophets of Judah:] I will summon all
the beasts of the field, yea, all the beasts of the forest
(see Hab. i. 6–9); I will summon the hosts of the
heathen, and they shall devour you. The watchmen
of Judah are blind; none hath knowledge: they are

like unto dumb sheep-dogs that cannot bark, but dream, lie down, love to slumber. In their avarice they are as dogs, greedy dogs that can never be satisfied: they are shepherds that have no understanding: they have turned each to his own way, seeking his own gain, all of them on every side. Yea, one feasteth another, saying: 'Come ye; I will fetch wine, and we will take our fill of strong drink; we will be merry to-day, and much merrier to-morrow.'"

God's salvation is now come, and His righteousness is revealed in Christ. He still demands repentance of those who would share in such blessings; and His grace bestows the repentance which His holiness demands. When Israel and Judah became hopelessly corrupt, He used as His besom first Assyria, then Chaldea, then Rome. He is the same God now: may He keep us as a nation from provoking His wrath till there shall be no remedy.

Chapter LVII.

ISAIAH tells us that he prophesied in the reigns of Uzziah, Jotham, Ahaz, and Hezekiah; and this statement seems to imply that his ministry and his life ended in the days of the last-named king. Yet this is not a necessary or certain inference from the prophet's statement: and unless we are prepared to attribute to some later sacred historian the reference to Sennacherib's death, we must conclude that Isaiah lived till at least the seventh year of Hezekiah's son and successor. (See Isa. xxxvii. 38.) If this was the case, Isaiah must have witnessed the idolatry and bloodshed which are referred to in 2 Kings xxi. 1–16. The Jews have a tradition that this prophet was sawn asunder in the reign of Manasseh: it is possible that this was really the case, and that his martyrdom is alluded to in Hebrews xi. 37.

It seems to us that the prophecy now before us was delivered in those sad days, probably soon after the death of the good king, with whom the prophet had walked so long and so lovingly. We will therefore transcribe here some part of the history, in order that our readers may have it freshly before their minds as they enter on the study of the prophecy. Even if our conjecture is wrong, if the prophecy belongs to the days of Hezekiah, its truths find a terrible illustration in Manasseh's reign.

" And Manasseh did that which was evil in the sight of the Lord, after the abominations of the heathen whom the Lord cast out before the children of Israel.

For he built up again the high places which his father had destroyed, and he reared up altars to Baal, and made an Asherah, as did Ahab, king of Israel, and worshipped all the host of heaven, and served them. And he built altars in the house of the Lord, of which the Lord said, In Jerusalem will I put My name. And he built altars for all the host of heaven in the two courts of the house of the Lord. And he made his sons pass through the fire, and observed times, and used enchantments, and dealt with familiar spirits and wizards : he wrought much wickedness in the sight of the Lord to provoke Him to anger. And he set a graven image of the Asherah that he had made in the house, of which the Lord said to David, and to Solomon his son, In this house, and in Jerusalem, which I have chosen out of all the tribes of Israel, will I put My name for ever : neither will I make the feet of Israel move out of the land which I gave to their fathers ; only if they will observe to do according to all that I have commanded them, and according to all the law that My servant Moses commanded them. But they hearkened not : and Manasseh seduced them to do more evil than did the nations whom the Lord destroyed before the children of Israel. . . . Moreover, Manasseh shed innocent blood very much, till he had filled Jerusalem from one end to the other ; beside his sin wherewith he made Judah to sin, in doing that which was evil in the sight of the Lord."

If the chapter which we are expounding was not written in these days, it is certainly an accurate prophecy of them. As soon as righteous Hezekiah had been gathered to his fathers in peace, that he might not behold the final ruin of his kingdom, a torrent of wickedness broke loose in Judah : adulterers, harlots, and their apostate brood derided the God of Israel and His prophets, worshipped idols under every green tree, sacrificed their children in the valleys to the cruel gods that they had chosen, courted the alliance of heathen kingdoms, and filled their own land with the innocent blood of Jehovah's faithful worshippers.

We have dwelt upon these details because they form in themselves a sufficient commentary on the chapter which we must now try to paraphrase.

"The righteous man dieth, but none giveth heed to his departure : the godly are gathered to their fathers, but none considereth that they are gathered home before the evil days come. They enter into peace : each one that hath walked uprightly resteth in his grave as a man resteth in his bed."

These words may or may not refer directly to Hezekiah's death : it would be unwise to speak with certainty. Calvin has left us some remarks on the passage which are deeply interesting, not only for the illustration which they give of the prophet's meaning, but for the light which they throw on the real relationship that existed between himself and Luther, two servants of God who on certain points were at variance :

"It frequently happens that God takes good men out of this world when He intends to punish severely the iniquities of the ungodly. . . . In our own times a remarkable instance of this was given in the death of Luther, who was snatched from the world a short time before that terrible calamity fell upon Germany which he had foretold many years before, when he exclaimed loudly against that contempt of the Gospel and that wickedness and licentiousness which everywhere prevailed. Frequently had he entreated the Lord to call him out of this life before he beheld that dreadful punishment, the anticipation of which filled him with trembling and horror. And he obtained it from the Lord. Soon after his death, lo, a sudden and unforeseen war sprang up, by which Germany was terribly afflicted, when nothing was farther from her thoughts than the

dread of such a calamity. Instances of this kind occur
every day ; and if men observed them, they would not
so heedlessly flatter themselves and their vices. But I
thought it right to take special notice of this event,
both because it happened lately, and because in so
distinguished a preacher of the gospel and prophet of
God it must be more clearly seen." Thus far Calvin :
we return to Isaiah.

"But come ye hither to Me, [and I will reprove you,
ye men of Judah,] ye children of witchcraft and wickedness. Will ye make sport of God ? Will ye deride
with laughter and grimace the prophets of the Holy
One ? Are ye not rebellious children, a lying brood,
inflaming your idolatrous passions under every green
tree, and slaying your own babes as sacrifices to your
gods in the depths of the valleys and the caverns of the
rocks ? [The portion of Jacob is the living God. (Jer.
li. 19.)] But thou, O Judah, hast found thy portion
among the smooth stones of the valley : they, they are
the lot of thy chosen inheritance, [the gods which thou
worshippest.] Even unto them hast thou poured out
thy drink-offerings and offered thy meal-offerings.
Shall I restrain My anger when I see such things ?
[Shall not My soul be avenged on such a nation as this ?
Jer. v. 9, 29 ; ix. 9.] Upon a lofty and high mountain
hast thou reared thine idolatrous altar, like a shameless
harlot who should bring forth her bed into the street :
and thither thou hast gone to offer sacrifice. Moreover,
thou hast set up the memorials of thy false gods within
thy doors and on thy door-posts, where I had bidden
thee record My law (Deut. vi. 9). For thou hast forsaken Me thine Husband for another, and art gone
aside to thy paramour : yea, thou hast multiplied thy
paramours, and hast entered into covenant with them ;
[thou hast relied upon Egypt, Assyria, and Babylon :]
whensoever thou sawest their bed, thou didst delight

to debase thyself. Thou didst court their kings with thy spices and thy treasures, as a scented harlot courts her lovers, and didst degrade thyself to the lowest depths of sin. The way to their distant courts was long and wearisome : yet thou saidst not, It is a hopeless journey. Thou didst find a little strength in thine hand, and therefore didst not slack thy pursuit of these thy lovers. Of whom hast thou been afraid, and whose power hast thou feared, that thou shouldest break thy faith with thy God, that thou shouldest forget Me, and be heedless of Mine anger ? Is it not because of My long forbearance that thou fearest Me not ? I will show thee what thy righteousness is worth, and thy works shall not profit thee. (See Isa. lxiv. 6.) When thou criest to Me for help, O Judah, let thy heathen allies, and the idols that thou hast gathered around thee, help thee : but nay ; the breeze shall scatter them, a breath of wind shall carry them away. But whoso trusteth in Me shall still possess the land that I have given you, and shall still inherit the mountain where I dwell. [Such shall return from their captivity, whatever may hinder :] for it shall be said, Cast ye up, cast ye up the highway for My returning people : prepare their way, and take up all stumbling-blocks out of their path."

Here Calvin's commentary may be profitably quoted again : " He addresses Cyrus and Darius, whose minds the Lord [afterwards] inspired to open up the path and grant protection to the Jews ; as if he had said that the Lord would send servants who were yet unknown to them, by whose agency He would prepare the way and bring out the people."

Now follow words full of comfort for broken-hearted penitents, intended especially for the godly who should be carried captive to Babylon, but applicable to humble and repentant souls in every age of the church's history.

" For thus saith the high and lofty One, whose dwelling place is eternity and whose name is Holy : I dwell in the high and holy place : I dwell also with him who is of a contrite and humble spirit, to revive the spirit of the humble, and to revive the heart of the contrite. For I will not prolong My chastisements for ever, neither shall Mine anger against My people last for evermore : else would their spirit fail before Me, and the souls which I have made would faint. [I know their frame : I remember that they are dust.] For the iniquity of Judah's covetousness I was wroth and smote him ; yea, in Mine anger I hid My face from him : and he went on frowardly in the evil way that his heart had chosen. I have seen his ways of folly : I will correct and heal him : I will also lead him in right ways, and will restore comforts to him, even to all that mourn over their sins and calamities. I will create upon their lips the fruit of praise and thanksgiving : for I will say, Peace, peace to those that shall be in exile and to those that shall be left in the land ; and I will heal them, saith the Lord. But the wicked are like the troubled sea : it cannot rest ; and its waters cast up mire and dirt. [There is no peace on the troubled ocean :] and there is no peace, saith my God, to the wicked."

Words that are here applied to the far-off Jews of the captivity and the nearer Jews who had been left in the land of Judah, are applied by the same Spirit in later days (Eph. ii. 17) to the near Jew and the far-off Gentile.

Chapter LVIII.

THE introductory portion of our last Half-Hour may well serve as an introduction to the present one. Let the reader turn to it and read it again ; for a knowledge of the history of the times is essential to a right understanding of the prophet's message. The two chapters are similar ; but in the latter the trumpet tones of reproof are directed, not against those who slew their children in sacifice to idol gods, but against hypocritical worshippers of Jehovah, against men who delighted in the external observance of the ceremonial law, while their daily life was a flagrant violation of its spirit and its precepts. The substance of the message is exactly this : " Behold, thou art called a Jew, and restest in the law, and makest thy boast of God, and knowest His will, and approvest the things that are more excellent, being instructed out of the law ; and art confident that thou thyself art a guide of the blind, a light of them which are in darkness, an instructor of the foolish, a teacher of babes, which hast the form of knowledge and of the truth in the law. Thou therefore which teachest another, teachest thou not thyself ? Thou that preachest a man should not steal, dost thou steal ? Thou that sayest a man should not commit adultery, dost thou commit adultery ? Thou that makest thy boast of the law, through breaking the law dishonourest thou God ? . . . He is not a Jew which is one outwardly, neither is that circumcision which is

outward in the flesh ; but he is a Jew which is one
inwardly, and circumcision is that of the heart, in the
spirit, and not in the letter, whose praise is not of men,
but of God " (Rom. ii. 17–29).

" [The Lord hath sent me to rebuke the hypocrisy
of Judah, and hath said unto me :] Cry aloud, give thy
voice free course, lift it up as the voice of a trumpet :
tell My people of their transgressions, and charge the
house of Jacob with their sins. [For they have forsaken Me and departed from My ways :] yet they come
before Me in worship every day, and glory in their
knowledge of My law, as if they were a righteous nation,
a nation that held fast to the statutes of its God.   They
ask Me to teach them statutes of righteousness, and
they delight to draw near to Me with their mouths.
Yea, they observe a fast day, and complain that I regard
not their fasting : they observe a day of humiliation,
and wonder that I accept them not.

" Behold [this is the reason why I regard you not :]
when ye keep a fast day, ye seek your own pleasure and
oppress your servants.   Behold, your fasting is made
void by your strife, contention, and wicked violence.
Is this the fast that I have chosen ?   Is this such a day
of humiliation as pleaseth Me ?   Ye bow down your
heads to the ground, and sit in sackcloth and ashes
[while your hearts are destitute of My fear :] and will
ye call this a fast acceptable to the Lord ?

" Nay ; this is the fast that pleaseth Me, saith the
Lord : the loosing of those who are unjustly imprisoned,
the untying of the bonds of tyranny, the release of the
oppressed, the breaking off of the yoke from every
neck.   Moreover, if thou wouldst so fast as to please
Me, deal out thy bread to the hungry, open thy house
to the homeless outcast, search out the naked and
clothe them, and shut not up thy bowels of compassion
from thy poorer brother.   Then shall the light of My

favour rise upon you as surely and as gloriously as the sun riseth in the east ; thou shalt be healed of thy wounds and thy diseases, and that right early : righteousness shall lead thee on to victory (see Heb. vi. 20, and 1 Tim. v. 25), and the glory of the Lord shall defend thy rear and destroy thy pursuers (see Ex. xiv. 19, 20). The Lord shall answer thine every prayer, and when thou criest He shall appear for thine help.

" If thou cease from oppression, scorn, and evil speaking : if thine heart shall compassionate the hungry, and thine hand shall satisfy the needs of the poor : then shall the darkness of thy trouble be banished by the dawn of deliverance, and the gloom of thy captivity shall give place to the noonday of freedom. The Lord shall guide thee in all thy ways, and shall strengthen thy bones. Thou shalt be like unto a garden watered by a running spring ; yea, thou shalt be like the running spring itself, a spring whose waters fail not. Also thy children shall rebuild the cities that have long been desolate, and shall raise up the walls that have lain in ruins age after age. Thou shalt be called the re-builder of the city, the restorer of the land, that it may be inhabited.

" If thou cease from profaning My Sabbath, and from doing thine own pleasure on My holy day, if thou call the Sabbath a delight, and call the day which the Lord hath sanctified an honourable day, and honour it by ceasing from thine own ways and pleasures : then shalt thou have delight in the Lord, and I will make thee to be a triumphant possessor of the earth ; I will bless thee with plenty and safety in the land which I gave for a heritage to thy father Jacob : for the mouth of the Lord hath said it."

Various writers have referred the fulfilment of this prophecy to various epochs in the history of the Jewish nation and of the church of God. It seems to us wiser, and more consistent with the mind of the Spirit, to regard it as a message delivered by Isaiah to his contemporaries in Manasseh's reign ; a message, however, full of instruction and full of warning for all time, to which we should do well to give heed in our own day.

Chapter LIX.

WE write for simple people. If we were to discuss the difficulties which translators have to face in rendering such a chapter as this from Hebrew into English, or were to mention one-tenth of the various opinions which commentators have expressed concerning its meaning and fulfilment, our Half-Hour would be worse than useless to the great majority of our readers. We shall therefore follow our usual course, giving the sense of the chapter so far as we understand it, and shewing by a quotation or two that our interpretation is in agreement with that set forth by one of the great reformers.

It seems to us that the prophet in this chapter continues to deliver his message of rebuke to the men of his own time, adding for the comfort of penitents the assurance of their forgiveness and salvation. But we see also that his words are words of eternal truth, more or less suitable to every age of the world ; and that his promises of deliverance, though they have had minor fulfilments at various periods of Israel's history, have their truest and sublimest fulfilment in the person and work of Him who brought life and immortality to light through the Gospel, delivering the true Israel of God from the bondage of sin and death.

Now we will give a quotation or two from Calvin, with which we heartily agree, though we can say that we do not slavishly take our views from him or any other man. We greatly value his exposition of the Scriptures, and consider him far in advance of any other writer whom we have read, both for penetrating discernment and for sobriety of judgment. On the redemption promised to Zion at the close of this chapter Calvin says :

" The question now arises, What redemption does the prophet mean ? I reply, as I have already suggested in another place, that these promises ought not to be limited, as is commonly done both by Jews and Christians, to a single redemption. The former refer them exclusively to the deliverance from Babylon, while the latter refer them to Christ alone. For my part, I join both, so as to include the whole period after the return of the people from Babylon down to the days when Christ came into the world. For this prophecy was not completely fulfilled in any other than Christ ; and what is said here cannot apply to any other. Never was the glory of God revealed to the whole world, nor His enemies put to flight so as not to recover their strength, till Christ achieved a conquest and an illustrious triumph over Satan, sin, and death. . . . By the name of Zion the prophet denotes here, as in other places, captives and exiles ; for however far they had been banished from their country, still they must have carried the temple in their hearts."

We may add that this last statement is fully justified by the sad song of the exiles in Psa. cxxxvii. : " By the waters of Babylon, there we sat down ; yea, we wept, when we remembered Zion."

" [Ah, sinful Judah ! A people laden with iniquity ! (Isa. i. 4.) Ye think that the Lord cannot deliver you, or will not hear your prayer.] Behold, His hand can reach you as easily as in former days, and His ear is still quick to hear the voice of prayer : but the iniquities committed in the land have separated between you and your God ; and the sins of the nation have caused Him to hide His face and reject your prayer. For your hands are defiled with murder, and your fingers with iniquity : your lips are given to lies, and your tongue muttereth words of wickedness. Your courts of law are destitute of righteousness and truth : ye trust in vanity, and speak falsehood : ye conceive thoughts of mischief, and bring forth deeds of iniquity. The imaginations of your hearts are venomous as the eggs of adders ; the works of your hands treacherous and useless as the webs of spiders. If a man eateth of such eggs, he dieth ; and if he crusheth them, a viper issueth forth. Even as the web of the spider cannot clothe you, so your works shall not be your righteousness : for your works are works of iniquity, and your hands are filled with deeds of violence. Your feet run eagerly to evil, and ye make haste to slay the innocent : your thoughts are thoughts of iniquity, and your paths are paths of desolation and destruction. Ye have marked out for yourselves crooked paths, in which if a man walk, he shall never find peace."

Here some thoughtful reader asks : "Are not these words of the prophet quoted in the Epistle to the Romans as descriptive of the wickedness of mankind at large ? How then can you refer them to the state of Jewish society in the days of Isaiah ? " Our answer to this most reasonable question is, that the awful state of Jewish society at that time is a miniature picture of this fallen world. If the veil could be lifted from the life of our great cities, should we be able to boast of our superior goodness ? And when the veil of ignorance is lifted from our own hearts by God's convincing Spirit (John xvi. 8), are we not ready to say with Paul, " Sinners, of whom I am chief " ?

From verse 9 to verse 15 the prophet goes on to amplify and drive home the statement of verse 2 ; that the iniquity of the nation is the root of all its trouble.

"This is the reason why the God of judgment does

not deliver us; why the God of justice does not draw
nigh to help us. We look for the light of His favour;
but behold, darkness surroundeth us: we long for the
brightness of prosperity; but we walk in the obscurity
of disaster. In our perplexity we are as a blind man
that gropes his way along a wall; yea, we grope as if
we had no eyes. We stumble at noonday as if night
had fallen: we dwell in darkness like the dead.
[Another translation, which seems to be more accurate,
is: In the midst of fatness we are as dead men. That
is, even our advantages profit us not.] Our cries of
distress are loud as the roaring of bears, and sad as the
moaning of doves: we look for God's righteous help,
but it cometh not; for His delivering hand, but it is
far from us. For our multiplied transgressions have
been committed in the presence of God, and our own
sins bear witness against us; for we are conscious of
our transgressions, and acquainted with our iniquities:
transgressing Thy law and denying Thee; forsaking
the ways of our God; speaking words of oppression
and rebellion; conceiving falsehood in our hearts, and
uttering it with our mouths. Right judgment is
banished from our courts, and justice is driven far from
them: truth is trampled under foot in the gates, and
there is no place among us for equity. Yea, there is
no truth in the land; and whoso departeth from evil
maketh himself a prey to the malice of the wicked
(Prov. xxix. 27). The Lord hath seen it, and is dis-
pleased that there is no justice among us. He hath
seen that there is none to stand in the breach as Moses
did (Psa. cvi. 23); He is amazed (Mark vi. 6) that there
is none to plead for the people and to stay His hand.

" Therefore by His own power shall He save those
whom He loveth, and His own righteous faithfulness
shall uphold Him in His resolve to save. He shall go
forth as a man of war: righteousness shall be His

breastplate, salvation His helmet, just vengeance His
clothing, and holy zeal His mantle. [Let the reader
observe how exactly this sublime description fits the
Christ of God, the Saviour and Judge of mankind.]
As have been the deserts of His foes, so shall He repay
them : He shall repay wrath to His adversaries, and
recompense to His enemies, a recompense which shall
reach them in their far-off lands beyond the sea. So
shall men see the glory of the Lord and fear His name
from the farthest west to the remotest east. Whatso-
ever adversaries shall rise up against Him, His Spirit
shall lift the standard of battle and shall overcome
them. A Redeemer [Cyrus, Christ] shall come to
Zion's captives, and to the penitents of Israel, saith
the Lord. And I, even I, will make with them this
new covenant, saith the Lord : My Spirit that is upon
thee, O Jacob, and My words that I have put in thy
mouth (John xiv. 16 ; Rom. iii. 2), shall not depart out
of thy mouth, nor out of the mouth of thy children, nor
out of the mouth of thy children's children, saith the
Lord, from henceforth and for ever."

God is faithful. He has delivered Israel from Babylon : He has sent forth His Son : the work of redemption
has been accomplished, and its blessings are accessible
to all true penitents. Moreover, the word of the Gospel
and the power of the Comforter are gone forth among
the nations, and shall not stay their march until the Son
of Man come to judge the world in righteousness.

Chapter LX.

THE explanation of particular words and phrases which occur in this chapter must depend to a great extent upon our knowledge of its general scope : in other words, before we can say what is meant by the camels of Midian, the rams of Nebaioth, and the ships of Tarshish, we must first answer the questions, What is that city whose walls are salvation and whose gates are praise, and to what events in its history does the chapter as a whole refer ?

A Jew would say that the city is Jerusalem, and that the great event foretold is its deliverance from the Babylonian yoke by the edict of Cyrus. A Christian who looks forward (as many real Christians do, though we do not) to a personal reign of Christ on earth, would say, with the Jew, that the city is Jerusalem ; but, in opposition to the unbelieving Jew, that the glories foretold are those pertaining to the personal reign of Jesus on this earth during a happy period which is to precede the end of all things here below.

For our own part, we believe that both these expositions are wrong. We are convinced that the prophet's words foretell the glories of the gospel, of the life and immortality which were to be brought to light, and now have been brought to light, by the incarnation, life, death, resurrection, and doctrine of Jesus Christ the Son of God. This view seems to us to be amply justified by the use which Matthew makes of the kindred prediction of Isa. ix. 2. We read there, The people that walked in darkness have seen a great light : they that dwell in the land of the shadow of death, upon them hath the light shined ; and the Evangelist tells us that this was fulfilled when Christ went to Capernaum and preached in Galilee. We feel that we have here sure ground to go upon in our interpretation of the present chapter ; and we see its fulfilment, as we have said, in the gospel and its triumphs, in the spiritual kingdom of Him who said, I am the Light of the world. This exposition is not vitiated by the fact that the prophetic picture of gospel blessings seems to melt into the glories of heaven, so that some of its expressions are used in that sense in the Revelation of John.

Having given our own independent reasons for taking this view of the prophecy, we will add a few instructive quotations from Calvin, whose exposition of this and of many other prophecies appears to us superior to that given by Dr. Gill. We may add that this view is endorsed by the summary given in our Authorised Version : " The glory of the church in the abundant access of the Gentiles, and the great blessings after a short affliction."

On verse 2, Calvin says : " These things relate to the spiritual kingdom of Christ, when the light of the gospel shone in every part of the world, and foreign nations were enlightened by it."

On verse 3 : " So far as the doctrine of the gospel has been spread throughout the whole world, Judea has held out the light to the Gentiles, formerly blinded, in order to point out the way. By making the brightness peculiar to a single nation, the prophet shews that in no other way could the world be enlightened, or come to share in the benefit, than by seeking light from the word which proceeded from the Jews, and was heard at Jerusalem, where the lamp of the Lord was kindled, and where the Sun of Righteousness arose, that from Jerusalem He might diffuse His light to the ends of the earth. This we have previously seen in the second chapter, where it is written : Out of Zion shall go forth the law."

On verse 14. The sons also of them that afflicted thee shall come bending unto thee : " This was indeed partly fulfilled when the Jews returned from Babylon to their native country ; but that return was nothing more than a dark shadow of the deliverance which we have obtained through Christ. These things were actually accomplished under the reign of Christ ; yet so that the full accomplishment of them may be expected at His second coming."

One other sentence from Calvin's pen must be quoted, being too valuable and instructive to be omitted here. Instead of referring verses 19 and 20 to any personal reign of Christ on earth, or even in heaven, he writes : " I have no doubt that in these words, They shall inherit the land for ever, the prophet had his eye on Judea, . . . as if he had said, Though I drive out My people from their inheritance, yet after seventy years I will restore them, that they may possess it for ever. . . . This was not in every respect fulfilled in the Jews ; but a beginning was made with them when they were restored to their native country, that by their agency the possession of the whole earth might afterwards be given to them, that is, to the children of God. . . . This possession of the land must not be limited to Judea, since it is more extensive, and all men are called to it, that by faith they may be children of Abraham, and may thus become heirs of it. We must observe carefully those modes of expression which are customary among the prophets, that we may understand their meaning, and not break off detached sentences, or torture them to a meaning different from what was intended. Exceedingly unnatural and inconsistent with the style of the prophets is the interpretation of those who explain ' the land ' to mean heaven and the blessed life. . . . To dwell in the land by right of inheritance means nothing else than to remain in the family of God."

We have quoted Calvin at greater length than usual because of the increasing prevalence of " premillennial " interpretation in the present day. We believe that that scheme of exposition rests on the unsound basis of a false literalism ; and as in this conclusion we find ourselves at variance with some Christians whose zeal we admire and whose godliness we love, we are glad of the support of that great reformer who is, in our esteem, the soundest of theologians and the prince of expositors.

One word before we begin our paraphrase. The words translated " shine " and " light " in the first verse are in the original practically the same in sense and sound. It is difficult to give in a translation the effect which this produces, but we shall do our best. It is evident that the command to arise and shine is addressed by the prophet in the name of the Lord to the city mentioned in verse 14, the city of the Lord, the Zion of the Holy One of Israel : we may also call her the Church of Christ, the pillar and ground of the truth.

" City of God, arise from the dust and beam with light : for Messiah cometh to enlighten thee, and the glory of the Lord dawneth upon thee. For, behold, when the whole world shall lie in darkness, when gross darkness shall cover the nations, the Lord Himself shall be thy morning sun, and thou shalt reflect His glory, and give the dark world light. Then shall the nations come to thy light, and their kings to the brightness of thy daybreak. Look round about thee, and see : the Gentiles assemble and come to thee ; thy sons come from far, and thy daughters are carried, as in a nurse's arms, from distant lands. [Sons and daughters of Zion

are citizens of Zion, children of God. See Isa. liv. 13
and John vi. 45.] And when this shall come to pass,
thine eyes shall look upon it and be lighted up with joy,
and thine heart shall throb with awe and exultation.
For the merchandise of the sea shall flow to thy shores,
and the wealth of the nations shall be thine. [That is,
the Gentiles shall be thy converts and thy friends, and
shall join together to aid thee in the worship of thy
God.] The children of Midian and Ephah shall come
unto thee on their camels and their dromedaries, all
the sons of Sheba shall bring thee gold and frankincense,
and shall join in publishing the praises of thy God.
The sons of Kedar with their flocks shall be gathered
to thee, and the children of Nebaioth with their rams
shall minister unto thee. [Midianites, Ishmaelites and
Arabians (see Gen. xxv. 1-4, for Midian, Sheba, and
Ephah) are classed among the then future converts to
the Church of Christ. Compare Acts ii. 9-11.] Their
worship shall be accepted of Me, and I will glorify My
glorious house. [See Heb. iii. 6 : Whose house are
we.] In that day, O Zion, thou shalt say in thine heart,
Who are these that fly to me like unto a vast cloud, and
swift as doves returning to the windows of the dovecot ?
[These are the sons whom I will give unto thee from
among the Gentiles ;] for in their lands beyond the seas
they shall look unto Me and do My bidding, saith the
Lord ; and the ships of the west shall be eager to serve
Me, bringing thy converts from far with offerings of
silver and gold to do honour to the name of the Lord
thy God, the name of the Holy One of Israel ; for His
glory shall be revealed in thee. Strangers shall
strengthen thee, and their kings shall serve thee : for
though I have smitten thee in Mine anger, yet in My
grace will I shew thee mercy. Thy gates shall be ever
open to admit thy thronging converts ; day and night
shall they stand open to receive the wealth of the

nations and the submission of their kings. For the
nation that will not join thee nor aid thee in worshipping Me shall perish : yea, all such nations shall be
utterly destroyed. [No salvation outside of the faith
of the true Church. Acts iv. 12.] As a temple built
of the cedars of Lebanon, and beautified with fir and
pine and box, so will I beautify My holy city, so will I
glorify the place where I stand. Then shall the nations
that have oppressed thee come to make obeisance
before thee ; yea, all those that despised thee shall
bow down to the ground before thee, and shall acknowledge that thou art the city of the Lord, the Zion of the
Holy One of Israel. (Compare Rev. iii. 9.) Whereas
thou hast been forsaken and hated, a desolate land
through which no man passed, [this may refer to the
dark and desolate state of the church between Malachi
and Christ,] I will make thee an eternal excellency and
a joy for ever. Nations shall nourish thee and their
kings shall support thee ; and thou shalt perceive that
I, the Lord, am thy Saviour; that I, the Holy One of
Israel, am thy Redeemer. Thy wealth shall surpass
the wealth of Solomon ; thine officers shall be officers
of peace, and thine exactors shall do their work in
righteousness. No violence shall thenceforth have
place in thy land, no desolation nor destruction shall
come within thy borders : thou shalt be compassed
about with walls of salvation, and thy gates shall
resound with praise and thanksgiving. Brighter than
the sun shall be the light of thy days, brighter than the
moon the light of thy nights : for the Lord Himself
shall be unto thee an everlasting light, and thy God
shall be thy glory. Thy sun shall no longer set, nor
thy moon wane : for the Lord shall be thine everlasting
light, and the days of thy mourning shall be ended.
Thy citizens shall be all righteous (Rev. xxi. 27), and shall
possess their inheritance for ever : for I will plant them,

and My hands shall form them, for My own glory. They shall become a number that no man can number : in the fulness of time I the Lord will accomplish it speedily."

Our Half-Hour would be too long if we tried to explain all the details of this prophetic picture. We are quite convinced that they have a spiritual significance, and that the whole prophecy has an adequate and complete fulfilment in the blessings and triumphs of the gospel, beginning in apostolic days, stretching onward to the end of time, and culminating, for all the election of grace, in the glory of the heavenly Jerusalem, whose builder and maker is God.

Chapter LXI., LXII.

IN expounding these two chapters, which seem to form one continuous prophecy, we are again compelled to face the question, Unto what time does the Spirit of God here point ? (1 Pet. i. 11.) We know from the apostle Peter's words that this question presented great difficulties to the prophets themselves : we need not therefore wonder that it costs us much thought and prayer ; nor need we be surprised that uninspired men have come to very different conclusions with regard to it. Two or three quotations will serve to show the diversity of opinion that exists among commentators whose capability and integrity cannot well be questioned. Between these divergent views we have prayerfully and thoughtfully made our own choice, as will be seen in our paraphrase. Some of our readers may differ from us ; but they will, we trust, admit that we have written words of soberness and truth, even if they consider our exposition to be in some respects defective.

One learned writer says that verses 3 and 4 of chapter lxi. " admit of no consistent interpretation except on the principle that the Jews are to be restored to the land of their fathers. The ruins and desolations are those of cities that had once been inhabited, and cannot without the utmost violence be applied to the heathen world." He means that these verses must be understood to foretell the future restoration of the cities of Judah and Israel, and cannot be referred to that renovation of the ruined Gentiles which was to be brought about by the preaching of the Gospel.

In reply to this, another writer, equally learned and conscientious, says with a touch of irony : " If the prophet's words be thus expounded, the only prospect opened to the Gentiles in the whole prediction is that of becoming ploughmen, shepherds, and purveyors to the favoured nation ! "

Another, whose profound spiritual insight into the meaning of the Scriptures has often filled us with admiration, speaks thus : " As to what follows about feeding sheep and cultivating fields and vines, these are metaphorical expressions. The prophet is writing of the kingdom of Christ, which is spiritual ; but he describes its perfect happiness by means of these figures, that we may understand it better from examples that are drawn from things which are known to us. . . . The Jews, indeed, seize eagerly on such declarations, and already devour with covetousness the wealth of the nations, as if they would one day possess it, and vaunt as if the glory of the whole world would one day become their own. . . . We must not understand the enjoyment of the wealth of others to mean that they who are converted to Christ shall seize on the wealth, or glory, or rank of others, which is most inconsistent with true religion ; but that all things shall be brought under the dominion of Christ, so that He alone shall hold authority and rule. . . . But when they come under the power of Christ, they are called ours, because Christ possesses nothing separate from His church." In confirmation of this statement we may refer to 1 Cor. iii. 21–23.

If the views expressed in this last quotation, which is from Calvin, do not commend themselves to the reader's understanding, we fear it would be waste of time to try to enforce them by further argument. For our own part, we have no doubt that the prophet here predicts the gospel glories that should follow upon the death of Christ ; and this conviction will influence the whole of the paraphrase by which we shall attempt to explain his language.

Our Lord and Saviour applied to Himself the opening words of chapter lxi. by saying to the Jews of Nazareth, "This day is this scripture fulfilled in your ears" (Luke iv. 16–21). We are therefore sure of our ground when we say that they are a prophecy of the Saviour's own personal ministry, and have therein their true fulfilment. At the same time, they are remarkably true of the ministry of Isaiah himself, which stood in the power of the Spirit of God, and has been a constant source of consolation to the poor in spirit of all generations. They are equally true of the other prophets, of the apostles, and of all real ministers of Christ's gospel.

It is not so easy to say who is the immediate speaker in lxi. 10, lxii. 1, and lxii. 6. It seems to us that the first of these three passages is the predicted language of the redeemed Church of Christ, to be uttered by her when the previous promises should have been fulfilled ; that the second is the language of the Messiah, expressive also of the prophet's own feelings and determination ; and that the third is the voice of God the Father, promising to guard His people by the agency of faithful watchmen (Ezek. ii. 16–21 ; xxxiii. 1–9), and pledging His own almighty power to keep them in perfect safety.

O that this gracious God may help us to cast some light upon His Word by our feeble explanation !

" [There shall come forth a Shoot out of the stem of Jesse, and a Branch shall grow out of his roots ; and He shall say :] The Spirit of the Lord God of the holy prophets is upon Me : for He hath anointed Me with the anointing of His Spirit, that I may preach good tidings to the lowly in heart ; He hath sent Me to heal the wounds of the broken-hearted, to proclaim a release to the captives, the restoration of light to them that sit in bondage and darkness ; to proclaim the year of the jubilee of the Lord's good pleasure, the day of His righteous judgment. [Compare Matt. xxv. 46 and 2 Thess. i. 6–10. The year of jubilee for the church is the day of destruction for its enemies.] He hath sent Me to comfort all that mourn ; to appoint consolation to every afflicted subject of Zion's King ; to give unto them a wreath of joy for the ashes of humiliation, the oil of gladness for mourning, a garment of glory for the spirit of heaviness, saying unto them, Ye now have sorrow, but your sorrow shall be turned into joy : that they may be trees of righteousness, planted by My God that He may be glorified by their fruit (John xv. 8). [And this shall be their fruit :] They shall rebuild the long ruined world, and shall raise up waste places that have long lain desolate ; yea, they shall repair the ruined cities of men, the dwellings that have been desolate from age to age. [In fulfilment of this, Christianity, wherever it has reigned, has brought fresh life to the dead world of the Gentiles.] Then strangers shall assist My people to tend their flocks, and aliens from their commonwealth shall aid them to till their fields and vineyards. [Jews and Gentiles shall be united in My service.] And My people shall all be called the priests of the Lord, the servants of the God of Israel (1 Pet. ii. 9, 10). They shall live upon the wealth of the nations, and shall share their glory. (Compare Rom. xv. 26, 27.) Instead of shame, they shall have abundant honour ; and whereas they have been filled with confusion, they shall rejoice in the portion that I shall give them. They shall inherit the earth, and in their heritage they shall possess abundance, and shall have a joy which no man shall take from them (John xv. 22). For I the Lord love justice ;

I will not receive in sacrifice that which hath been
gotten by robbery. [I hate hypocrisy, and will therefore give My kingdom to a nation bringing forth the
fruits of righteousness.] I will reward My servants in
faithfulness, and will make with them an everlasting
covenant [saying unto them, I will be your God, and
ye shall be My people. (2 Cor. vi. 16–18. The covenant
of the gospel.)] Then shall the children of My servants
be known among the nations, and their offspring among
all the peoples of the earth. (See John xiii. 35.) All
that see them shall acknowledge that they are Mine, the
seed that the Lord hath blessed.

"[In those days shall the Zion of God say:] I will
greatly rejoice in the Lord: my soul shall be joyful in
my God; for He hath clothed me with righteousness
as with a robe, yea, as with the garland of a bridegroom
or the jewels of a bride. (See Rom. iv. 22–25.) For
as the earth causeth her plants to bud, as a garden
maketh its seed to grow, so will the Lord God cause
His salvation to spring forth, and the voice of His praise
to be heard among the nations of the earth."

God alone can measure the extent to which this
promise has already been fulfilled in the progress of His
gospel. (See Titus ii. 11–14.)

"[Messiah crieth, saying:] Out of love to Zion I
will not hold My peace; out of love to Jerusalem I will
not rest from My labours, until her righteousness be
made manifest as the light, until her salvation shine
forth as a burning lamp. (Compare John v. 35 and
Luke xii. 50.) The nations shall see thy righteousness,
O Zion, and all their kings thy glory; for I will give
thee a new name, with which the mouth of the Lord
shall name thee, and thou shalt be like unto a crown
of beauty held in the hand of the Lord, a diadem of
royalty held in the hand of thy God; [lifted up by
Him (Zech. ix. 16) as worthy to be admired by Himself

and all His creatures.] [I have said that I will give thee a new name,] for thy name shall no longer be ' The Forsaken City,' nor the name of thy land ' The Desolate Land '; thou shalt be called ' The Lord's Delight,' and thy land shall be called ' The Married Land,' for the Lord delighteth in thee, and thy land shall be a widow no longer (Lam. i. 1). [Of the four Hebrew words, Azubah (Forsaken), Shemamah (Desolate), Hephzibah (My delight is in her), and Beulah (Married), the first and third are known to have been used as names of women; Azubah was the wife of Asa, and Hephzibah the wife of Isaiah's royal friend Hezekiah. It is probable that the other two were also well-known names of women. This circumstance would give additional force to the prophet's address to Zion : Thou shalt be called Hephzibah instead of Azubah, and thy land shall be called Beulah instead of Shemamah.] For as a young man is united in wedlock to a virgin, so shall thy citizens be united to thee in the wedlock of filial love ; and as the bridegroom rejoiceth in the possession of his bride, so shall thy God rejoice to possess thee. (See 2 Cor. xi. 2 ; Rev. xix. 7.)

" I the Lord will set faithful watchmen upon thy walls, O City of God : all day and all night shall they keep watch over thee (Heb. xiii. 17). They shall be the Lord's remembrancers, seeking at His hand the fulfilment of His promises, taking no rest and giving their God no rest, till He exalt His Zion throughout the world (1 Cor. ix. 19–22 ; 2 Tim. ii. 10). The Lord hath sworn by His own right hand, and by His own arm of power, that He will not again allow the enemy to devour the bread of Zion's children, nor the stranger to drink the wine of the vineyards that they have planted ; they shall reap their own corn, and eat it, and praise the Lord ; they shall gather their own vintage, and drink it with gladness in His holy courts.

[An image of plenty, safety, and thanksgiving taken
from such passages as Deut. xii. 17, 18.]

"Enter ye in, O nations, enter ye in through the
gates of Zion ; let the way be made ready for the converts that shall people her. Cast up, cast up the highway [and compel them to come in that her streets may
be full]. Make straight paths for their feet (Heb. xii.
13) ; lift up an ensign to summon the nations to the
City of God. Behold, the Lord hath commanded,
saying, Go ye into all the world, and say to My dispersed, Behold, your Redeemer is come ; behold, His
reward is won, and the work that was set before Him
is accomplished. His ransomed ones shall be known
as ' The Holy People,' ' The Redeemed of the Lord,'
and Zion shall be called ' The Zion that the Lord hath
sought out,' ' The City that He hath not forsaken.' "

"The Saints," that is, "The Holy Ones," is the
name constantly given by the apostles to the children
of God, as in Rom. i. 7 ; 2 Cor. i. 1 ; and xiii. 14 ;
Eph. i. 1 ; 1 Pet. ii. 9, etc. And the Good Shepherd
has sought out His Zion, and has said unto her, " No
man shall pluck thee out of My hand."

We venture no opinion of our own for or against the
reconstitution of the Jewish nation, and its restoration
to the land of its fathers. We consider that God has
not given any predictions that can be definitely interpreted one way or the other in this matter, and that the
New Testament, even in Rom. xi., is absolutely silent
about it. But we clearly see that the eternal blessings
which flow from Christ's gospel are the highest possible
fulfilment of such a prophecy as that which we have had
before us in this Half-Hour.

Chapter LXIII. 1—6.

" [A VISION of Isaiah the son of Amoz. I saw, and lo, a Mighty One advanced to meet me: He came from Bozrah, the city of the sons of Esau. Then said I :]

" ' Who is this that cometh from the land of Edom, cometh with dyed garments from the citadel of Bozrah; this that is gloriously apparelled, that marcheth onward in the greatness of His strength ? '

" ' It is I ; I that speak in righteousness, mighty to save.'

" ' Wherefore is Thine apparel red ? Why are Thy garments stained, as the garments of one that treadeth the grapes of the vintage ? '

" ' I come from the treading of the winepress. I trod it alone ; the nations helped Me not. I trod the grapes in anger ; [for they were evil :] I trampled them in My wrath ; [for they were ripe for judgment.] Thus their blood bedewed My garments, and stained all My raiment. For it was Mine appointed day of vengeance, the year for the deliverance of My redeemed. I was as one who looketh for helpers, and findeth none ; as one who is astonied because he hath no aid. Therefore My own arm supplied Me with strength, and My holy indignation carried Me on to victory. So I trod down the nations in Mine anger, made them reel under My wrath, and shed their blood like water upon the earth.' "

Let the reader observe that the prophet at first speaks of the heavenly Warrior as at a distance : Who is this that cometh ? Then addresses to Him, as if He were nearer, a direct question : Wherefore art Thou red? This gives an additional touch of reality to the wonderful scene which his words depict.

Now comes the important question, What is the mind of the Spirit of God in the whole passage? To this question two principal answers have been given. We will bring them before our readers by actual quotations from men of undoubted learning and godliness, and then venture to state our own opinion.

1. That which we may call the orthodox interpretation is ably given by Bishop Christopher Wordsworth in his valuable edition of the Holy Bible. He says in his note on Isa. lxiii. 1: "That this is a description of Christ coming to His people as a Conqueror, from His own passion and resurrection, was the uniform judgment of the ancient expositors (Tertullian, Origen, Cyprian, Augustine, Jerome, Cyril); and this opinion has been adopted by the Church of England, appointing this chapter as the Epistle for Monday before Easter. . . . Christ at His passion and resurrection came from Edom and Bozrah, because He then overthrew His bloodthirsty, malignant, and treacherous enemies (the Chief Priests, Scribes, and Pharisees, who, though Jews in name and origin, were implacable as Edomites), and He came from Bozrah (Fortress) because He spoiled the strong man Satan in his *fortress*, and made that Bozrah to be a winepress of judgment. (See John xii. 31; xvi. 11.) He then bruised his head (Gen. iii. 15), and led captivity captive, and spoiled principalities and powers, triumphing over them by His cross; and by His death He destroyed him that had the power of death, that is, the devil, and delivered them who, through fear of death, were all their lifetime subject to bondage."

Those who take this view of the whole passage expound in accordance therewith the various details of the prophet's language.

2. But it has been strongly felt by some good men that the above view is not justified by the prophet's own language, which gives no hint of any humiliation or suffering undergone by the mighty Warrior seen in vision ; the blood upon His raiment is known by the seer to be the blood of slaughtered foes, not the blood of Him who wears the raiment. We shall make two quotations on this side of the question.

Calvin says very decidedly : " This chapter has been violently distorted by Christians, as if what is here said related to Christ, whereas the prophet speaks simply of God Himself. They have imagined that here Christ is red because He was wet with His own blood which He shed on the cross. But the prophet meant nothing of the sort. The obvious meaning is, that the Lord comes forth with red garments in the view of His people, that all may know that He is their protector and avenger. The people were weighed down by innumerable evils, and at the same time the Edomites and other enemies freely indulged in wickedness which remained unpunished. Hence the Jews were exposed to the dangerous temptation to think that these things happened by chance, or that God did not care for His people. The prophet meets this very serious temptation by representing God the avenger as returning from the slaughter of the Edomites drenched with their blood."

Dr. Alexander, who held a similar view to that of Calvin, writes : " The treading of the winepress alone is an expression often applied in sermons, and in religious books and conversations, to our Saviour's sufferings. This application is described as customary in his own time by Vitringa, who considers that it led to the forced exposition of the whole passage by the fathers and Cocceius as a description of Christ's passion. While the impossibility of such a sense in the original passage cannot be too strongly stated, there is no need of denying that the figure may be happily accommodated in the way suggested ; as many expressions of the Old Testament may be applied to different objects with good effect, provided we are careful to avoid confounding such accommodations with the strict and primary import of the passage."

For our own part we must say that we lean to Calvin's view, though we hesitate to reject the other entirely. Though the vision refers primarily to the destruction of Edom, may it not also refer to the mighty Conqueror of Rev. xix. 13 ? At the same time, we must add that though to a certain extent we agree with what Dr. Alexander says about " accommodation," we feel that there are great dangers connected with that method of treating the language of Scripture. In what God says there is always a definite meaning, which we may justly call the mind of the Spirit ; and though His words often have a deep spiritual sense which lies beneath the literal surface, the spiritual and the literal are always in strict harmony. God does not by the self-same word mean opposites such as salvation and destruction, mercy and vengeance. We therefore venture to express our own opinion as follows : this is a prophecy of God's vengeance on Edom in particular, and the enemies of His people generally. So far as Edom was concerned, the vengeance was wrought by the armies of Chaldea (see Jer. xxvii. 2, 3, 6 ; xlix. 7–22 ; Ezek. xxxv. ; Obadiah) ; but they were merely the axe in the hand of God (Isa. x. 14), who claims for Himself the honour of executing righteous judgment by their instrumentality : " I have trodden the winepress alone, and of the peoples [not people, but nations] there was none with Me."

So shall all Thine enemies perish, O Lord : but they that love Thee shall be as the sun when he goeth forth in his might.

Chapters LXIII. 7—LXIV. 12.

IT will be seen by the following table of comparison, which might be made longer, that Isaiah's words in this portion of his prophecies are remarkably similar to the words of Jeremiah in the Lamentations :—

ISAIAH.	JEREMIAH.
But they rebelled, and vexed His holy Spirit ; therefore He was turned to be their enemy, and fought against them (lxiii. 10).	We have transgressed and have rebelled : Thou hast not pardoned. The Lord was as an enemy : He hath swallowed up Israel (Lam. iii. 42 ; ii. 5).
Our adversaries have trodden down Thy sanctuary (lxiii. 18).	The heathen entered into her sanctuary (Lam. i. 10).
Oh that Thou wouldest rend the heavens, that Thou wouldest come down (lxiv. 1).	Mine eye trickleth down, and ceaseth not, . . . till the Lord look down and behold from heaven (Lam. iii. 49, 50).
Be not wroth very sore, O Lord, neither remember iniquity for ever (lxiv. 9).	Thou art very wroth against us. Wherefore dost Thou forget us for ever ? (Lam. v. 22, 20).
Our holy and our beautiful house, where our fathers praised Thee, is burned up with fire : and all our pleasant things are laid waste (lxiv. 11).	The stones of the sanctuary are poured out in the top of every street. The adversary hath spread out his hand upon all her pleasant things (Lam. iv. 1 ; i. 10).

We know that Isaiah, with a supernatural and God-given foresight, foresaw the Babylonian captivity (Isa. xxxix. 5–7), foresaw the troubles amid which Jeremiah lived and died. Those who honestly believe this will see nothing fanciful in the exposition which we are about to give of the passage now under consideration. In few words, our view is this : that Isaiah prophetically describes the afflictions and feelings, fears and hopes, confessions and supplications, of godly Jews who should live to see the horrors of Nebuchadnezzar's invasion, and should have to endure the sorrows of the subsequent captivity.

We are led to this conclusion partly by the remarkable similarity of the language to that used by Jeremiah in the Lamentations, as shown above, and partly by the suitability of Isaiah's words to the circumstances of that time. They may be outlined thus. We have first a recapitulation of the Lord's past mercies to Israel from the time of Moses onward, mingled with confessions of the base returns made by the nation to its gracious God (lxiii. 7–14) ; then ardent entreaties that the Lord may renew His former loving-kindnesses, and again put forth His miraculous power as of old (lxiii. 15–lxiv. 9). Finally, a complaint which reminds us forcibly of the closing verses of the book of Lamentations, a book which shows clearly that the faithful in Jeremiah's day did indeed use the language long before uttered by Isaiah.

Some expositors look upon lxiv. 11 as a prophecy of the distress of the Jewish nation after the destruction of the temple by the Romans in apostolic times. One objection to this view is the consideration that the godly in those days found their all in Christ, and saw that the rejection of Messiah was an incomparably greater calamity than the destruction of any material sanctuary ; they were more likely to pray that their countrymen might believe in Him whom they had rejected than to lament the destruction of the temple.

We believe that the simplicity of our view will commend it ; we shall not, therefore, attempt to confirm it by quotations from commentators. Indeed, most of those whom we have consulted give a much more complex interpretation.

The above introductory remarks, and the paraphrase given below, will, we hope, lead to a correct understanding of the mind of the Spirit in this prophecy regarded as a whole. There are special difficulties connected with the translation and exposition of some of the verses, difficulties which we shall not attempt to discuss for fear of perplexing our readers : in the paraphrase they will find the results at which we have arrived by much prayer and thought. We will only mention here the passage : " Then (He) remembered the days of old, Moses (and) his people," etc. (lxiii. 11). Neither " He " nor " and " is expressed in the original. While it seems impossible to say with certainty what is the exact and literal rendering of the words, we think that they mean, " Then the people remembered the days of old, the times when Moses was their leader ; and they said, Where is the God who delivered us then ? " The same question is mentioned with approval, or rather the people's failure to use it is noted with disapproval, in Jer. ii. 6.

" [Judah shall say in the day of distress :] I will remind the Lord of His former loving-kindnesses ; yea, I will remind the Lord of all the glorious benefits which He hath bestowed on us, of the great goodness which the Lord hath bestowed on the house of Israel out of the fulness of His mercy and the abundance of His love. For He said of us, ' They are the people whom I have chosen to be My faithful children ' : therefore He delivered them in time of need. He made all their afflictions His own, and saved them by the Angel of His presence, [the Angel in whom was the name of the Lord (Ex. xxiii. 20, 21).] In His love and compassion He redeemed them from bondage, bare them as an eagle beareth her young (Deut. xxxii. 11, 12), and carried them as a parent carrieth a child, during all the days of old.

" But they rebelled against their God, and grieved His Holy Spirit by their evil ways, so that He turned and became their enemy, yea, fought against them with His own right hand. (See Jud. ii. 1–3 ; 11–15 ; iii. 7, 8, etc.) Then in their distress they called to remembrance the olden days, the days of Moses, and said : Where is the God whose glorious arm did wondrous things by the hand of Moses, dividing the waters of the sea before Israel to get unto Himself a name that should never be forgotten ? Where is the God who caused us to walk through the depths without stumbling, as one leadeth a horse in the field ? As cattle descend into the valley to lie down, so the Spirit of the Lord led us to our rest. Thus didst Thou lead Thy people, O Lord, to get unto Thyself a glorious name. Now, therefore, O our God, hear Thou in heaven Thy dwelling-place, and look upon us from the habitation of Thy holiness and of Thy glory. Where is the jealousy of Thine ancient love to us ? Where is the power that wrought for us of old time ? Surely the yearnings of Thine heart and the compassions of Thy soul are withdrawn from us. [And yet we look for them :] for Thou art our Father, though we are not worthy to be known as the seed of Abraham, or to be acknowledged as the sons of Jacob. Thou, O Lord, art still our Father ; Thy name for ever is Our Redeemer. Why then forsakest Thou us, making us to err from Thy ways, and hardening our hearts from Thy fear ? [Our sins are our own, but without Thy mercy we cannot forsake them.] Return, O Lord, for we are all Thy servants, the tribes of Thine inheritance, [the nation that Thou hast chosen for Thine own possession.] Thy holy people have not long possessed the land which Thou gavest them ; for our adversaries have taken it from

us, and have trodden down Thy sanctuary. We are
made like unto a people over whom Thou never barest
rule, that were never called the people of the Lord.
Oh that Thou wouldst break forth from heaven, and
come down to deliver us! Oh that the fire of Thy
presence might melt the mountains, as fire burneth
wood, as fire maketh water to boil! [Oh that Thou
wouldest again show Thy majesty as Thou didst at
Sinai!] Then should Thy name be made known to
Thine adversaries, and the heathen should tremble at
Thy presence.

" In days gone by, when Thou didst terrible things that
we looked not for, Thou didst come down to help us, and
the mountains were melted by the fire of Thy presence.
[Mount Sinai was shaken, and mountains of trouble
and difficulty were removed from before us.] For never
have men known, their ear hath not heard, nor their
eye seen, a God like unto Thee, performing all things
for them that trust in Thee. [Paul quotes this passage
with an apostle's freedom and authority in a form
which differs somewhat from the literal translation
given in our Bible and other versions, and employs it
with respect to the mysteries of the gospel, known only
by those who are taught by God's revealing Spirit
(1 Cor. ii. 9, 10)]. Thou drawest nigh unto every man
who delighteth in Thy holy service, and remembereth
to walk in Thy ways. But behold, Thou hast been
angry with us; therefore have we sinned more and
more. Yet Thy ways of mercy are everlasting, and
[because Thou changest not] we shall be saved.

" [We have deserved Thy wrath:] for we are all
become like a man that is unclean, and our best deeds
are as garments that are defiled: we are like withered
leaves, [dry, worthless, the sport of every wind:] and
our iniquities like a storm have driven us away [into
apostasy and misery.] And yet there is none among

us that fleeth unto Thee by prayer, that seeketh diligently to find Thee : for Thou hast hidden Thy face from us, and hast given us up to be consumed by the fire of our sins.

" But now, O Lord, remember that Thou art a Father unto Israel (Ex. iv. 22), and that we are in Thine hand as clay in the hand of the potter, to do with us as Thou wilt ; it is Thou that hast made us all. Be not wrath to extremity, O Lord : remember not our offences for ever! See, we beseech Thee : lo, we are all Thy people !

" The cities of Thy holy land are turned into wastes ; even Zion is a waste, and Jerusalem a desolation. Our temple, once holy and beautiful, once the place where our fathers worshipped Thee, is burned with fire, and all the things in which we once delighted are destroyed. And wilt Thou shut Thine heart against the voice of our trouble ?   Wilt Thou afflict us more and more ? "

The people's sins and the judgments of God ran their course till the cry of prophecy became the cry of history. After long silence, the Lord answered it by turning the captivity of His chosen nation, and by sending His Son to save His people from their sins.

Chapter LXV.

ALTHOUGH this chapter contains expressions which have been and are very perplexing to the best of commentators, its general meaning is not at all obscure. We know by the testimony of the Holy Spirit (Rom. x. 20, 21) that the first verse foretells the calling of the Gentiles, and the second the rejection of the Jews. Hence we conclude with certainty that this part of God's Word is included in the comprehensive statement of the apostle Peter: "Yea, and all the prophets from Samuel, and those that follow after, as many as have spoken, have likewise foretold of these days," the days of the setting up of Christ's kingdom by the ministry of the apostles.

Yet here we are met by a difficulty. The Lord says by the prophet in verse 17, "I create new heavens and a new earth"; and it seems evident that Peter looked for a literal accomplishment of this promise after the day of judgment (2 Pet. iii. 7, and 10–13). Are we not, therefore, bound to conclude that the latter part of this chapter refers exclusively to the world to come? After careful consideration of the whole chapter we think not.

Doubtlessly the complete fulfilment of God's promise to create new heavens and a new earth is yet in the future; but it had what has been well called "a germinant fulfilment" in the sending of Christ and the establishment of His gospel kingdom. The whole creation is to be delivered from the bondage of corruption into the glorious liberty of the sons of God:

and this deliverance is begun in the regeneration of the sons of God by that gospel which is the power of God unto salvation. This may be clearly seen, we think, in those remarkable words, " He shall also quicken your mortal bodies by His Spirit that dwelleth in you : " the Spirit of regeneration will be the author of the resurrection and of all the glory that shall follow it. We consider, therefore, that in this, as in other prophecies, the eye of the prophet, scanning the vista of the ages which to him were future, saw the glory of the gospel and the glory of the world to come in one far-reaching vision, and spoke of it all as the creation of new heavens and a new earth. Only by an exposition of this kind can we find room, after the mention of a new creation, for such words as " the sinner shall die accursed," and for such promises as " before they call I will answer, and while they are yet speaking I will hear " (lxv. 20, 24).

The word translated " thence " in verse 20 is by some expositors supposed to mean " thenceforward " ; but its ordinary sense is " from there," or " from that place." Again, the word translated " child " often, if not always, means more than the word child in English. For instance, in Gen. xliv. 33 it is used of a young man who is already a father. The present passage, therefore, may be literally rendered thus : " There shall be no more from that place [Jerusalem] an infant of days, nor an old man that hath not filled his days : for the young man shall die an hundred years old ; but the sinner an hundred years old shall be accursed."

We could fill several pages by quoting the various explanations which have been given of this verse ; but not one of them has seemed to us absolutely clear and certain. The prophet is here describing the blessings of gospel times under figures drawn from the promises of the old covenant : length of life, secure possession of property, and enjoyment of the fruits of one's own labour. This will be evident to the reader if he will compare Isa. lxv. 20–23 with Ex. xx. 12 ; Deut. iv. 40, xi. 21, xxviii. 3–5 ; and, by way of contrast, with Deut. xxviii. 30 and Amos v. 11. We are inclined to think, therefore, that the true sense of Isa. lxv. 20 is that the subjects of Christ shall be blessed with absolute safety, promised under the figure of length of days, but that the ungodly, though they might share for a season the temporal safety of the godly, should in the end be cut off for their impenitence. (See Rom. ii. 3–9.)

Since the prophets often speak of future events as if they had already taken place, we shall use the future tense in our paraphrase of the first verse.

" I will be inquired of by them that have not asked after Me ; I will be found of the Gentiles, who have not sought Me : unto nations that have not hitherto been known as My people I will say, Here am I, Here am I ! [Behold me, is the Hebrew way of saying, Here am I, and is so translated in Gen. xxii. 7, 11, and in other places. The reader who knows French may compare the expression *Me voici*. But what gracious condescension, for the great God to say in His gospel to us Gentile sinners, Here am I !] For My people Israel are a rebellious people. I have continually sent unto them by My prophets words of warning and entreaty : but they walk in a way that is not good ; they follow the devices of their own hearts ; they anger Me to My face continually. They sacrifice to their idols in the gardens which they have dedicated to them, and burn incense on the altars of brick which they have built for their false gods. They sit among the graves to consult the dead ; they lodge in caves to deal with familiar spirits. They eat swine's flesh, concerning which I have said that it is unclean, and their cauldrons are filled with forbidden meats. They say to their fellow-creatures, Stand off! Touch me not, for I am holier than thou. Thus are they as a smoke in My nostrils, a smoke that vexeth Me all day long.

"Behold, I have recorded in My book their iniquity and its sentence. I will no longer forbear, but will recompense their iniquity; yea, I will recompense into your bosom your own iniquity and the iniquity of your fathers also, saith the Lord: for your fathers have burned incense to their false gods upon the mountains of Israel, and have dishonoured Me by their idolatry upon the hills; and I will measure their former work into the bosom of their evil children."

A word here from Calvin: "Not that the son bears the iniquity of the father (Ezek. xviii. 20), and endures the punishment which the father deserved; but that, since they carry on the crimes of their fathers, they must be included and condemned in the same judgment, as their obstinacy shows that their diseases are incurable." (Compare Matt. xxiii. 35, 36.)

"And yet as one spareth a vine for the sake of a ripe cluster that is found thereon, saying, 'Destroy not this vine, for the wine that it shall yield will be a blessing': so for the sake of them that serve Me in Israel will I forbear to destroy the whole nation. I will preserve a remnant of the seed of Jacob, a remnant of Judah to inherit My land; Mine elect shall inherit it, and My servants shall dwell in it. They shall fold their flocks on the plains of Sharon in the west, and in the east they shall lead their herds to pasture in the valleys about Jericho: for I will give peace and plenty to Mine own people who have cleaved to the worship of their God.

"But as for you that have forsaken the Lord, and have forgotten His temple for the shrines of idols, have made feasts in honour of Fortune, [this is an ancient, and we believe correct, translation of the word here used, a word which occurs also in Gen. xxxii., and should

be similarly translated there,] and have poured out
drink-offerings to Destiny, I will destine you to the
sword of your enemies, and ye shall fall before the
slaughter weapons of your foes (see Ezek. ix. 1–11,
and 2 Kings xxv. 18–21) : because ye have refused to
answer My calls, and have shut your ears against the
voices of My prophets, doing that which was evil in
Mine eyes, and choosing that which is an abomination
unto Me."

This righteous sentence has been executed by various
agents, especially by the victorious armies of Nebuchadnezzar and Titus.

" Therefore thus saith the Lord God : [I will make a
difference between those who serve Me, and you who
serve your idols.] Behold, My servants shall drink
when ye shall perish with thirst : behold, My servants
shall rejoice, when ye shall be put to shame : behold,
My servants shall sing for joy of heart, when ye shall
cry for sorrow of heart and wail for anguish of spirit.
[This reminds us of Isaiah iii. 10, 11, and Luke xiii. 28.]
For ye shall leave behind you a name which shall serve
My chosen for a form of cursing, when the Lord God
shall have slain you. [That is, men shall say, when
they utter a curse, The Lord make thee as the idolaters
whom He slew ! See Jer. xxix. 18, 22.]

" But unto My servants will I give a new name
(Isa. lxii. 2, 4, 12). Then he that wisheth for himself a
blessing in the land, shall invoke it in the name of the
God of truth ; and he that sweareth an oath in the land
shall swear it in the name of the God of truth. [Men
shall neither love false gods nor fear them, but shall love
and fear the true God ; they shall know Him as revealed
in Messiah, and shall worship Him alone.] For former
troubles shall be forgotten by man and God."

Let us confirm our view of vv. 17–25 by two quotations.
The first is from Dr. Alexander, and refers especially

to verses 9 and 10 of this chapter. " If it should please God to call the natural descendants of the patriarch in that land, and convert them in a body to the true faith, there would be an additional coincidence between the prophecy and the event, even in minor circumstances, such as we often find in the history of Christ. But if no such national restoration of the Jews to Palestine should ever happen, the extension of the true religion over that benighted region, which both prophecy and providence encourage us to look for, would abundantly redeem the pledge which God has given to His people in this and other parts of Scripture."

The second is from Calvin, on the promise of new heavens and a new earth in verse 17. " By these metaphors He promises a remarkable change of affairs ; as if God had said that He has both the inclination and the power not only to restore His church, but to restore it in such a manner that it shall appear to gain new life, and to dwell in a new world. These are hyperbolical modes of expression ; but the greatness of such a blessing, which was to be manifested at the coming of Christ, could not be described in any other way. Nor does He mean only the first coming, but the whole reign, which must be extended as far as to the last coming, as we have already said in expounding other passages."

Let us return to the prophet himself.

" For behold, I will create new heavens and a new earth ; [Messiah cometh, and restoreth all things ; (compare John iv. 25, and Mark ix. 12 ;)] and the things which are done away shall not be remembered, nor ever come to mind. But ye, My servants, shall be glad, and rejoice for ever and ever in My new creation : for I will create Jerusalem to be a city of rejoicing, and her people to be sons of joy. Yea, I Myself will rejoice in Jerusalem, and will joy in My people ; and the voice of weeping and wailing shall be heard no more among them.

[It shall be said in Zion, Whom having not seen, ye love ; in whom, though now ye see Him not, yet believing, ye rejoice with joy unspeakable, and full of glory.] No longer shall there go forth from Jerusalem [perhaps-the sense is ' go forth to the grave '] an infant who hath lived but a few days, nor a man that hath not lived to the limit of old age : for the young men of Zion shall live to be old ; but sinners, though they reach old age, shall die accursed. My people shall pass their lives in safety under My keeping : they shall inhabit the houses that they build, and shall eat the fruit of the vineyards that they plant. They shall not build that others may inhabit, nor plant that others may eat, [as in the days when I smote them with the sword of Assyria and Chaldea.] For My people shall prolong their days as a tree, and Mine elect shall long enjoy the work of their hands. They shall not labour for vanity, nor bring forth children for the sword : for they and their offspring with them shall be counted for a seed that the Lord hath blessed. [Moreover, I will be very nigh unto them in all things for which they call upon Me (Deut. iv. 7 :)] for it shall come to pass that I will answer them before they call, and hear them while they are yet speaking. (See Heb. iv. 14–16 ; vii. 25 ; x. 19–22.) Then shall wolves become lambs, and ravening lions shall be turned into peaceful and laborious oxen. [For an instance of fulfilment see Acts ix. 26–28 ; 1 Tim. i. 13, 14.] And My curse shall be executed upon the serpent : nothing shall hurt nor destroy any that worship at My holy hill, saith the Lord." (Compare Mark xvi. 17, 18.)

The chapter which we have now tried to expound is full of the mysteries of the kingdom of God : if our prayerful labour has furnshed the reader with even an imperfect hint at its true interpretation, we would be thankful to Him without whom we can do nothing.

Chapter LXVI.

WE believe that the whole substance of this chapter
can be expressed in the language of the New
Testament. Let us try to do this.

God is a Spirit, and they that worship Him must
worship Him in spirit and in truth (verses 1, 2). But
as for those who reject the truth and have pleasure in
unrighteousness, God shall send them strong delusions,
that they should believe a lie to their own ruin (3, 4).
They that are born after the flesh only shall persecute
you that are born after the Spirit : but all your adversaries shall be put to shame (5) ; for the day of Jerusalem's visitation cometh (6). Yet the true children of
Zion shall be speedily and miraculously increased, and
multitudes, both of men and women, shall be added to
the Lord (7–9). And I the Lord will grant unto them,
according to the riches of My glory, to be strengthened
with might by My Spirit, that they, being rooted and
grounded in love, may be able to comprehend with all
saints what is the breadth, and length, and depth, and
height, and to know My love, which passeth knowledge,
that they may be filled with all My fulness (10–14).
But Mine enemies, who would not that I should reign
over them, shall be brought before My judgment-seat,
and shall be slain (15–17). And I will say unto My
servants, Go ye into all the world, and summon the
nations that they may see My glory ; and I will confirm
the word of My servants with signs and wonders, and
with divers miracles (18, 19). Then those who receive
their word shall become their brethren, and shall be

brought swiftly and surely into the assembly of My people to be presented before Me as an acceptable sacrifice, being sanctified by My Spirit (20). Yea, they shall be unto Me a chosen generation, a royal priesthood (21), whom I will never leave nor forsake; they shall become citizens of a kingdom that cannot be moved (22). For in every nation those that fear Me shall worship Me unceasingly (23). But the wicked shall go away into everlasting punishment, where their worm dieth not and their fire is not quenched (24).

We request our readers to compare this chapter carefully with the various parts of the New Testament from which our illustrative quotations have been drawn.

But we imagine that we hear one say: These Half-Hours speak of all the prophecies as fulfilled in the gospel. And why not, dear reader? Is it not written that all the prophets from Samuel, as many as have spoken, foretold of the days of the gospel? Did not Peter say at Pentecost: This is that which was spoken of the prophet Joel? Did not James say: To this agree the words of the prophets; as it is written, After this I will return, and will build again the tabernacle of David, which is fallen down?

When we see such fulfilments, we hesitate to say, "Yes, but there will be a further literal fulfilment of all that has been predicted; leopards will yet lie down with lambs, and sandy deserts will yet bloom with roses and be beautified with myrtles." Our plan is to reject such interpretations where they are positively opposed to the analogy of faith, and to treat them as dubious even where they seem to be harmless. The event alone can show whether God will grant a further fulfilment of prophecies which have been already accomplished in the gospel. We say with Calvin: "We ought to abide by the general rule of which we have often spoken already, that these promises must be extended from the return of the people [under Zerubbabel] down to the reign of Christ, and to the full perfection of that reign."

A few special words must be said about the remarkable promise given in verse 19 : " And I will send those that escape of them unto the nations, to Tarshish, Pul, and Lud, that draw the bow, to Tubal, and Javan, to the isles afar off, that have not heard My fame, neither have seen My glory ; and they shall declare My glory among the Gentiles." We have long considered that this prophecy has received a wonderful and literal fulfilment in the labours of the apostles ; and we dare not look upon that fulfilment as partial or incomplete. We prefer to say, if we may again quote the words of Dr. Alexander : " It cannot be proved, and need not be affirmed, that there will not be hereafter a similar display of divine power in the further execution of this promise : but if there never should be, it will still have had a glorious fulfilment in a series of events, compared with which the restoration of the Jewish people to the land of Canaan is of little moment."

And now may the Lord help us in our last attempt to paraphrase the words of Isaiah.

" Thus saith the Lord : [My servant Solomon built Me a house.] But heaven is My throne, and earth is My footstool : what house shall man build to contain Me, or to be the place of My rest ? For Mine hand hath made heaven and earth ; I said, Let them be : and they were. [Yet they are not the dwelling-place that I have chosen for My rest :] My chosen temple is the poor and contrite heart, the heart of the man that feareth Me.

" [To what purpose is the multitude of your sacrifices unto Me, O Israel, while your heart goeth after your idols, and the evil of your doings is before Mine eyes ? (See Isa. i. 10–24.)] When ye kill an ox in My courts, I loathe it as if ye slew a man there : when ye sacrifice a lamb, it is as if ye had broken a dog's neck ; when ye offer an offering of fine flour, it is as unacceptable to Me as the blood of swine ; when ye burn incense for a memorial upon Mine altar, it is as if ye were worshipping an idol. Yea, ye have forsaken My ways, and chosen your own, and your heart delighteth in your abominations : and I will choose your calamities, and will bring upon you that which ye fear ; because when I called unto you by My prophets, ye did not answer ; when I spake by their word, ye did not hear ; but did that which was evil in Mine eyes, and chose the paths that I hated.

" But this is the word of the Lord unto you that fear Him : Ye shall be hated of your ungodly brethren, and they will cast you out for My name's sake (compare John xvi. 2, 3) ; and they will deride you, saying, Let the Lord shew His glory in delivering you, and let us see your joy ! But ye shall be delivered, and they shall be put to shame. For Jerusalem shall be filled with the voice of tumult, and the temple with the voice of destroyers : it will be the voice of the Lord, rewarding them that hate Him. (See Luke xxiii. 28–31.) But Zion shall bring forth children without travail ; she shall be delivered of sons without pain. [Suddenly and unexpectedly will I increase her offspring. (Acts ii. 41, 47 ; iv. 4 ; v. 28 ; vi. 7, etc.)] When hath such a wonder been heard or seen, a people born in a day, a nation brought into being in a moment ! For as soon as the time of her delivery cometh, Zion shall bring forth her children. Shall I bring thee to that time, O Zion, and deny thee strength to bring forth ? saith the Lord : shall I bring thee to that time, and shut thy womb ? saith thy God. [I will surely give thee increase at the appointed season.]

" Rejoice ye with Jerusalem, and be glad for the gladness of the City of God, all ye that love her : rejoice

in her joy, all ye that have mourned over her desolations : for ye shall suck the breasts of consolation with
her, and shall be satisfied ; ye shall be nourished with
her milk (1 Pet. ii. 2, 3), and shall delight yourselves in
the abundance of her glory (Eph. iii. 16–21). For thus
saith the Lord : Behold, I will give her prosperity as a
river, and glory from the Gentiles in an overflowing
stream of converts : then ye that have loved her and
mourned for her shall suck breasts of consolation ; ye
shall be as infants borne in their mother's arms, or
nursed upon their mother's knees. With comfort like
unto a mother's love will I comfort you ; and ye shall
be comforted in My holy city (John xiv. 16–18 ;
xvi. 7 and 33). And when ye shall see this, your heart
shall rejoice (John xvi. 20–22), and your strength shall
be renewed by My favour as the tender grass is revived
by rain. Thus shall be seen the good hand of God upon
His servants : but His indignation shall go forth against
His enemies (Rom. ii. 6–11 ; 2 Thess. i. 6–10).

" For behold the Lord will come in the fire of war,
and the chariots of His armies shall rush like a whirlwind. [Fulfilled more than once in the destruction of
Jerusalem ; compare Matt. xxii. 7.] He will reveal
His wrath in fury, and His judgment in flames of fire.
For the Lord will avenge Himself upon all His enemies
by fire and sword, and they that are slain by Him shall
be many. Then all they that worship idols, and everyone that defileth himself with wickedness, that worketh
abomination, that loveth or maketh a lie, shall be
consumed together, saith the Lord : for I know their
works and the imaginations of their hearts.

" The time cometh when I will gather together men
of all nations and tongues, that they may come and see
My glory (Matt. xxii. 9). I will bear witness to My
summons by mighty signs and wonders (Heb. ii. 4 ;
Rom. xv. 18–21). And certain of Israel shall be saved,

whom I will send to the remotest peoples, and to lands
beyond the sea, even to those that have never heard
My fame nor seen My glory ; and My messengers shall
declare My glory among the nations (Rom. xv. 20, 21).
Thus shall they assemble unto you all your brethren
out of all nations for an offering unto Me (Rom. xv. 16 ;
xii. 1). I the Lord will make their way plain before
them, and will bring them swiftly to My Holy City, as
when the children of Israel came up to worship at
Jerusalem, bringing their offering in a clean vessel to
My temple.   For of the Gentiles also will I take priests
and Levites, saith the Lord (1 Pet. ii. 4, 5).   For as the
new creation which I will make shall abide before Me,
so shall the generation of My children, and their name,
abide for ever and ever. It shall come to pass that I
will be worshipped continually by all nations, saith the
Lord. And My people, in the day of My judgment,
shall look forth from their place of safety upon the
carcases of Mine enemies : their worm shall not die,
nor their fire be quenched : they shall be exposed to
shame and everlasting contempt.''

Reader, heaven is real, and hell is real : to which
art thou going ?   In Christ, thou art safe : out of Christ,
thou must be lost for ever.

MORGAN & SCOTT LD., 12, PATERNOSTER BUILDINGS, LONDON, E.C.